# PRAISE FOR RYAN HOLIDAY AND *TRUST ME, I'M L...*

"Holiday effectively maps the news media landscape. . . . Media students and bloggers would do well to heed Holiday's informative, timely, and provocative advice."
—*Publishers Weekly*

"This book will make online media giants very, very uncomfortable."
—Drew Curtis, founder, Fark.com

"Ryan Holiday's brilliant exposé of the unreality of the Internet should be required reading for every thinker in America."
—Edward Jay Epstein, author of *How America Lost Its Secrets: Edward Snowden, the Man and the Theft*

"Ryan Holiday is the Machiavelli of the Internet age. Dismiss his message at your own peril: He speaks truths about the dark side of internet media which no one else dares mention."
—Michael Ellsberg, author of *The Education of Millionaires*

"[Like] Upton Sinclair on the blogosphere."
—Tyler Cowen, MarginalRevolution.com, author of *Average Is Over*

"Ryan Holiday is the internet's sociopathic id."
—Dan Mitchell, *SF Weekly*

"Ryan Holiday is a media genius who promotes, inflates, and hacks some of the biggest names and brands in the world."
—Chase Jarvis, founder and CEO, CreativeLive

"Ryan has a truly unique perspective on the seedy underbelly of digital culture."
—Matt Mason, former director of marketing, BitTorrent

"While the observation that the internet favors speed over accuracy is hardly new, Holiday lays out how easily it is to twist it toward any end. . . . *Trust Me, I'm Lying* provides valuable food for thought regarding how we receive—and perceive—information."
—*New York Post*

PORTFOLIO / PENGUIN

# TRUST ME, I'M LYING

Ryan Holiday is a bestselling author and a leading media strategist. After dropping out of college at nineteen to apprentice under Robert Greene, author of *The 48 Laws of Power*, he went on to advise many bestselling authors, multiplatinum musicians, and notorious clients. He's served as the director of marketing at American Apparel, where his work was internationally known and used as case studies by Twitter, YouTube, and Google. His books have been translated into twenty languages and his writing has appeared everywhere from the *Columbia Journalism Review* to *Entrepreneur* and *Fast Company*. His company, Brass Check, has advised companies like Google, Taser, and Complex, and some of the biggest authors in the world. He currently lives on a small ranch in Austin, Texas, and writes at RyanHoliday.net.

# TRUST ME, I'M LYING

## CONFESSIONS OF A MEDIA MANIPULATOR

### RYAN HOLIDAY

{ PORTFOLIO / PENGUIN }

PORTFOLIO / PENGUIN
An imprint of Penguin Random House LLC
375 Hudson Street
New York, New York 10014
penguin.com
First published by Portfolio / Penguin, a member of Penguin Group (USA) Inc. 2012
Edition with a new preface and two new appendices published 2013
This revised and expanded edition published by Portfolio / Penguin, an imprint of
Penguin Random House LLC 2017
Copyright © 2012, 2013, 2017 by Ryan Holiday

Most Portfolio books are available at a discount when purchased in quantity for sales promotions or corporate use. Special editions, which include personalized covers, excerpts, and corporate imprints, can be created when purchased in large quantities. For more information, please call (212) 572-2232 or e-mail specialmarkets@penguinrandomhouse.com. Your local bookstore can also assist with discounted bulk purchases using the Penguin Random House corporate Business-to-Business program. For assistance in locating a participating retailer, e-mail B2B@penguinrandomhouse.com.

The Library of Congress Has Cataloged the Hardcover Edition as Follows:
Holiday, Ryan.
Trust me, I'm lying : the tactics and confessions of a media manipulator / Ryan Holiday.
p. cm.
Includes bibliographical references.
ISBN 9781591845539 (hc.)
ISBN 9781591846284 (pbk.)
ISBN 9781101583418 (e-book)
1. Marketing—Blogs. 2. Public relations—Blogs. 3. Social media—Economic aspects. I. Title.
HF5415.H7416 2012
659.20285'6752—dc23
2012008773

Printed in the United States of America

23rd Printing

Set in Minion Pro
Designed by Pauline Neuwirth

While the author has made every effort to provide accurate telephone numbers, internet addresses, and other contact information at the time of publication, neither the publisher nor the author assumes any responsibility for errors or for changes that occur after publication. Further, the publisher does not have any control over and does not assume any responsibility for author or third-party websites or their content.

The very blood and semen of journalism, on the
contrary, is a broad and successful form of lying.
Remove that form of lying and you no longer have
journalism.

—JAMES AGEE,
*LET US NOW PRAISE FAMOUS MEN*

# CONTENTS

## BOOK ONE
### FEEDING THE MONSTER
#### HOW BLOGS WORK

# BOOK TWO

## THE MONSTER ATTACKS

### WHAT BLOGS MEAN

# PREFACE

A MAN MUCH SMARTER THAN I AM ONCE DESCRIBED A "racket" as something that "is not what it seems to the majority of the people," where only a small group of insiders know what's really going on and they operate for the benefit of a few and at the expense of basically everyone else.[1] I read this description after I wrote and published *Trust Me, I'm Lying: Confessions of a Media Manipulator*. I had used the word casually only once or twice in the book, but I understand now, based on the reaction the book generated, the extent of the racket I was exposing.

There is no other definition for the modern media system. Its very business model rests on exploiting the difference between perception and reality—pretending that it produces the "quality" news we once classified as journalism without adhering to any of the standards or practices that define it. Online, outlets have to publish so much so quickly and at such razor-thin margins that no media outlet can afford to do good work. But of course, no one can admit any of this without the whole system collapsing.

Starting to sound like a racket, no?

In recent years, the evidence has piled up. The president of CBS said on the record that the election of Donald Trump "may not be good for America, but it's damn good for CBS." White supremacist Richard Spencer has talked openly to reporters about how he "memed his movement into existence" (and they *kept* covering him after he admitted it). It was revealed that many of the "fake news" sites that dominate Facebook with preposterous left-wing and right-wing propaganda are owned by the same parent company. An editor at *Gawker* tweeted that if they resisted publishing those too-good-to-be-true viral stories, "traffic would crater." For me the kicker was having another *Gawker* editor tell me after an inaccurate story that the whole game was "professional wrestling."* These kinds of incidents make you realize it really is a brazen and corrupt system operated by a few at the expense of the rest of us. So there's your question: I might be the one "confessing," but who is the real media manipulator here?

When I started talking to publishers about this book in late 2011, I told them that I didn't want to put out a book of media criticism. No matter how smart or insightful those books can be, they're usually written by academics or outsiders and can only scratch the surface of the problem. I believed I had a chance to do something different. I could be the first defector, in a position to expose the worst of the web's marketing and publishing practices because I'd created and perfected many of them.

I decided to administer a major shock to both the media system and the public with the same book. I wouldn't just rip back the curtain—I wouldn't let anyone look away from what they saw.

This decision sent me and the book you're about to read down a path that surprised and appalled me, a person I thought was plenty jaded. I was cynical and pessimistic in my predictions too—and more than five years after this book's publication, things are *so much worse* than I ever could have thought they would be.

I remember telling my publisher in an early meeting about *Trust Me, I'm Lying* that I thought it was interesting that Michael Lewis's *Liar's Poker* (a first-person memoir critical of the culture of Wall Street in the eighties) is regularly named as the book that encouraged people to want to get jobs on Wall Street. I always knew the book I would be writing—a memoir of my time in the world of media manipulation and an exposé of the media system—might have a similar arc. But I never expected to hear from people who used the book to trick the most prestigious media outlets in the world into covering their companies. I didn't think I'd hear from start-ups and journalism professors and media outlets who assigned the book to students and new hires. I never dreamed that my book would be cited as an influence by the people who helped get an unhinged lunatic and former reality television star elected to the presidency.

I have repeatedly been asked what it feels like to have been so right with

---

*Gawker* was itself later sued for $100 million for publishing a stolen sex tape of a professional wrestler, but we'll talk more about that later.

this book. I can only reply with this quote from the brilliant cultural critic George W. S. Trow, who was an early influence of this book:

*There's nothing fun about being right if what you're right about is the triumph, or the temporary triumph, of the inevitably bad.*

Let me give you an example. As part of the launch of this book, in an attempt to prove just how bad things really were, I did a stunt using the service Help a Reporter Out (helpareporter.com), which purports to match reporters and "expert" sources. I wanted to prove just how absurd and prone to abuse a service like this could be. I replied to every HARO query I could, including the "urgent" queries that HARO put out on Twitter, figuring that pressing deadlines would make it even easier to get quoted. I ended up being quoted as an expert on topics I knew nothing about in stories in *CBS*, *MSNBC*, *Reuters*, and *ABC News*. I eventually asked my assistant to start supplying quotes to reporters for me, which he did, scoring a feature in the *New York Times* about vinyl records (another topic I knew literally nothing about). I then revealed how all this had happened, to the intense rage and consternation of nearly every major media outlet. And yet the *New York Times*, embarrassed and exposed by what had happened, could have banned their journalists from using the service going forward but didn't.

They probably should have listened to my criticism. Because over the next five years, the *Times* would feature quotes from a "millennial" comedian named Dan Nainan six times. So too would *Forbes*, the *Chicago Tribune*, *Business Insider*, the *Wall Street Journal*, *Fortune*, *CNN*, and other outlets in trend stories about his millennial experience. The only problem? Dan is not a millennial, just a liar. In truth, he is fifty-five years old. He fooled nearly every media outlet in the country. His tool of choice? Help a Reporter Out.

I wish it gave me some joy to throw these events back in the face of HARO's founder, who accused me on video of being a lone bad actor and grew so angry in his denunciations that I thought he might have an aneurism. But in this case, being right just makes me sad—and scared.

Members of the media like to talk about the essential role it plays in society and in democracy. They're right. And they haven't been doing their jobs. In fact, they are just as much a part of the problem as manipulators and marketers are—perhaps even more so.

By the time you are reading this, the launch of the book will seem far away. But when it came out, the book was controversial, on purpose. I knew that to cut through the noise, everything about it had to be different and prove the ideas in the book. I won't say I was an angel about it—but I definitely made my point. I leaked that the book was a celebrity tell-all, which blogs picked up without verifying. I doubled the size of my advance in the announcement and nobody fact-checked it. I got popular media folks to denounce the book and used their outrage to sell more copies.

I applied all the tactics of media manipulation described in the book in order to propagate my warnings about the dangers and prevalence of media manipulation. I also "traded up the chain" to reach as many people as possible. Coverage about the book started online with small blogs and ultimately reverberated across the globe, from radio shows in Malaysia to the pages of *Le Monde*. From NPR to the "Editor's Notes" section of the *New York Times* (which retracted a quote from me after I exposed a problem in its sourcing methods)[2] to a Forbes.com megastory (which did 165,000 views), *TMIL* was everywhere.

The point of all this wasn't simply self-promotion. I wanted to prove I was as good as I said I was—and I wanted to prove that the system is so vulnerable that even a transparent media manipulator could make it do what he wanted.

Of course, other things happened that I did not plan. I was feeding the monster with my marketing, and just when you start to think you're in control, you catch a swift kick to the stomach. Something doesn't quite go your way, something unexpected happens, and the next thing you know you're on the front page of Yahoo.com when you'd rather not be.

It spins out of control very quickly. There were a lot of names thrown at me and my book, from "douchebag" to "lying jerk" to "out and out phony" to "troll." One blog accused me of "throwing shit" and another influential PR writer claimed I was "hurting an entire industry." Scott Monty, then the head of social media at Ford, posted a picture of my book in his trash can. I remember doing an interview at some point and the reporter saying, "You know, this stunt about being a fake expert is going to be in your obituary." I had not thought that far ahead. I was twenty-five.

It was these unexpected things over the last few years—some of which were fun and some of which weren't—that proved my point too:

- I skipped the credit check on a new apartment by sending my landlord a link to an article about the (fake) size of my book advance.

- Well before the launch of the book, someone leaked my book proposal to the *New York Observer* to try to wreck my meta-marketing plan before I could get it started.

- Many bloggers made embarrassing mistakes about the book and refused to correct them. Others denounced it and criticized it without reading it.

- The settlement in a lawsuit involving one of my clients was held up because they worried about what I was supposedly revealing in my "tell-all."

- *Business Insider*, who I heavily criticize in the book, called me a liar instead of defending themselves . . . in an eleven-page slide-show.

- Even though each one of my books has sold enough copies to hit the *New York Times* bestseller lists, I never have—retaliation, I suspect, for embarrassing them with one of my experiments in the book.

- I began to get e-mails from some of the most notorious media trolls in the world—including members of the so-called "alt-right"—about how the book was their bible and how they used it to get attention (*Liar's Poker* all over again).

- I thought the book would get me out of the marketing game, but instead it led to more consulting and advising than I could possibly know what to do with.

- Finally, I got older and saw more of the world (and of power, people, and institutions). This changed how I saw some of the things I'd written about in the book, and it changed how I saw my own writing. I won't apologize for anything I did or said—even the cringeworthy moments—but I am certainly not proud of all of it. How could I not see things differently at thirty than I did in my early twenties? As a result, I've revised the book to adjust for that experience.

There is one obvious mistake in my approach that I will admit right now: For all my cynicism, I was far too bullish about the system's capacity or desire to actually hear my message. Many media outlets were glad to report on the book initially and gobble up the pageviews I could create for them, but actually doing something about the charges turned out to be far more challenging. "It's difficult to get a man to understand something," Upton Sinclair once said, "when his salary depends upon his not understanding it."

I wasn't thinking about it that way or I would have been much less surprised. It might seem naive, but I felt that if I could just get everyone's attention and expose the problems in the right way, it could make a difference. I knew that my methods were untraditional and uncomfortable—like I said, they had to be—but I hoped the implications of my revelations would matter most.

Even though everything I wrote in *Trust Me, I'm Lying* was based on my personal experience, somewhere in the back of my head I always worried that my colleagues might say, "Ryan, c'mon, it's not that bad." Maybe they would say I was cherry-picking or being cynical. In fact, no one said that. The overwhelming reaction from people in the business was "Ryan, it's even *worse* than what you say."

Except for one thing. They would only say this in private. They would e-mail it to me or pull me aside at parties to tell me, but in public many of these same people criticized the book. Or called me names. Or, as I had feared most of all, ignored the book altogether—depriving it of the oxygen it needed to spread.

Regardless of the reaction or impact this book has had, I'm excited for you to read it. Besides the desire to get a huge weight off my chest, I also set out to write a book that could serve as the handbook for the rising sector of social-media jobs (I felt like there was no "bible" for this job yet). From what I hear, many firms now require employees to read *Trust Me, I'm Lying*. And more encouragingly, many blogs as well as journalism schools now require their writers and students to read the book—so they know how to spot manipulation and prevent it.

Where it all goes from here, for me, for the media, who knows? Could it actually get worse? I've said no before, and look how that turned out. I suppose that future, then, remains up to you. To us.

Ryan Holiday
Austin, Texas
Summer 2017

# TRUST ME,
## I'M LYING

# INTRODUCTION

IF YOU WERE BEING KIND, YOU WOULD SAY MY JOB IS IN marketing and public relations, or online strategy and advertising. But that's a polite veneer to hide the harsh truth. I am, to put it bluntly, a media manipulator—I'm paid to deceive. My job is to lie to the media so they can lie to you. I cheat, bribe, and connive for bestselling authors and billion-dollar brands and abuse my understanding of the internet to do it.

I am most certainly not the only one.

People like me funnel millions of dollars to online publications to fuel their enormous appetite for pageviews. We control the scoops and break-ing news that fill your Facebook feed, that get your coworkers chattering. I have flown bloggers across the country, boosted their revenue by buying fake traffic, written their stories for them, fabricated elaborate ruses to capture their attention, and even hired their family members. I've prob-ably sent enough gift cards and T-shirts to fashion bloggers to clothe a small country. Why did I do all this? Because it was the best way to get what I wanted for my clients: attention. I did it to build these writers and influencers as sources, sources that now have access to millions of people at some of the biggest media outlets and platforms in the world. I used blogs to control the news.

It's why I found myself at 2:00 A.M. one morning, at a deserted intersec-tion in Los Angeles, dressed in all black. In my hand I had tape and some obscene stickers made at Kinko's earlier in the afternoon. What was I doing here? I was there to deface billboards, specifically billboards I had designed and paid for. Not that I'd expected to do anything like this, but there I was, doing it. My then-girlfriend and future wife, coaxed into be-ing my accomplice, was behind the wheel of the getaway car.

After I finished, we circled the block and I took photos of my work from the passenger window as if I had spotted it from the road. Across the billboards was now a two-foot-long sticker that implied that the movie's creator—my client Tucker Max—deserved to have his dick caught in a trap with sharp metal hooks. Or something like that.

As soon as I got home I dashed off two e-mails to two major blogs. Under the fake name Evan Meyer I wrote, "I saw these on my way home last night. It was on 3rd and Crescent Heights, I think. Good to know Los Angeles hates Tucker Max too," and attached the photos.

One blog wrote back: "You're not messing with me, are you?"

No, I said. Trust me, I'm not lying . . .

The vandalized billboards and the coverage that my photos received were just a small part of the deliberately provocative campaign I did for the movie *I Hope They Serve Beer in Hell*. Tucker, the client, had asked me to create some controversy around the movie, which was based on his bestselling book, and I did—somewhat effortlessly, it turns out. It is one of many campaigns I have done in my career, and by no means an unusual one. But it illustrates a part of the media system that is hidden from your view: how the news is created and driven by marketers, and that no one does anything to stop it.

In under two weeks, and with no budget, thousands of college students protested the movie on their campuses nationwide, angry citizens vandalized our billboards in multiple neighborhoods, FoxNews.com ran a front-page story about the backlash, Page Six of the *New York Post* made their first of many mentions of Tucker, and the Chicago Transit Authority banned and stripped the movie's advertisements from their buses. To cap it all off, two different editorials railing against the film ran in the *Washington Post* and *Chicago Tribune* the week it was released. The outrage about Tucker was great enough that a few years later it was written into the television show *Portlandia*.

I guess it is safe to admit now that the entire firestorm was, essentially, fake.

I designed the advertisements, which I bought and placed around the country, and then promptly called and left anonymous complaints about them (and leaked copies of my complaints to blogs for support). I alerted college LGBT and women's rights groups to screenings in their area and baited them to protest our offensive movie at the theater, knowing that the nightly news would cover it. I started a boycott group on Facebook. I orchestrated fake tweets and posted fake comments to articles online. I even won a contest for being the first one to send in a picture of a defaced ad in Chicago. (Thanks for the free T-shirt, Chicago *RedEye*. Oh, also, that photo was from New York.) I manufactured preposterous stories about Tucker's behavior on and off the movie set and reported them to gossip websites, which gleefully repeated them. I paid for anti-woman ads on feminist websites and anti-religion ads on Christian websites, knowing each would write about it. Sometimes I just Photoshopped ads onto screenshots of websites and got coverage for controversial ads that never actually ran. The loop became final when, for the first time in history, I put out a press release to answer my own manufactured criticism: TUCKER MAX RESPONDS TO CTA DECISION: "BLOW ME," the headline read.

*Hello, shitstorm of press. Hello, number one on the* New York Times *bestseller list.*

I pulled this off with no connections, no money, and no footsteps to follow. But because of the way that blogging is structured—from the way bloggers are paid by the pageview to the way blog posts must be written to catch the reader's attention—this was all very easy to do. The system eats up the kind of material I produce. So as the manufactured storm I created played itself out in the press, real people started believing it, and it became true.

My full-time job then was director of marketing for American Apparel, a clothing company known for its provocative imagery and unconventional business practices, and I would go on to found my own marketing company, Brass Check, which would orchestrate stunts and marketing trickery for other high-profile clients, from authors who sell millions of books to entrepreneurs worth hundreds of millions of dollars. I create and shape the news for them.

Usually, it is a simple hustle. Someone pays me, I manufacture a story for them, and we trade it up the chain—from a tiny blog to a website of a local news network to Reddit to the *Huffington Post* to the major newspapers to cable news and back again, until the unreal becomes real.* Sometimes I start by planting a story. Sometimes I put out a press release or ask a friend to break a story on their blog. Sometimes I "leak" a document.

---

*By "real" I mean that people believe it and act on it. I am saying that the infrastructure of the internet can be used against itself to turn a manufactured piece of nonsense into widespread outrage and then action. It happens every day. Every single day.

Sometimes I fabricate a document and leak that. Really, it can be anything, from vandalizing a *Wikipedia* page to producing an expensive viral video. However the play starts, the end is the same: The economics of the internet are exploited to change public perception—and sell product.

Now, I was hardly a wide-eyed kid when I entered this world. I grew up online, and I knew that in every community there were trolls and tricksters. Like many people, I remained a believer. I thought the web was a meritocracy, and that the good stuff generally rose to the top. But spending serious time in the media underworld, watching as the same outlets who fell for easy marketing stunts seriously report on matters of policy or culture will disabuse you of that naïveté. It will turn that hope into cynicism.

Though I wish I could pinpoint the moment when it all fell apart, when I realized that the whole thing was a giant con, I can't. All I know is that, eventually, I did. It's what ultimately put me on the path to write this book.

I studied the economics and the ecology of online media deeply in the pursuit of my craft. I wanted to understand not just how but why it worked—from the technology down to the personalities of the people who use it. As an insider with access, I saw things that academics and gurus and many journalists themselves will never see. Publishers liked to talk to me, because I controlled multimillion-dollar online advertising budgets, and they were often shockingly honest.

I began to make connections among these pieces of information and see patterns in history. In books decades out of print I saw criticism of media loopholes that had now reopened. I watched as basic psychological precepts were violated or ignored by bloggers as they reported the "news" (and the so-called fake news). Having seen that much of the edifice of online publishing was based on faulty assumptions and self-serving logic, I had learned that I could outsmart it. This knowledge both scared and emboldened me at the same time. I confess, I turned around and used this knowledge against the public interest, and for my own gain.

An obscure item I found in the course of my research has always stayed with me. It was a mention of a 1913 editorial cartoon published in the long since defunct *Leslie's Illustrated Weekly Newspaper*. The cartoon, it said, showed a businessman throwing coins into the mouth of a giant fang-bared monster of many arms, which stood menacingly in front of him.

Each of its tentacle-like arms, which were destroying the city around it, was tattooed with the words like: "Cultivating Hate," "Distorting Facts," and "Slush to Inflame." The man was an advertiser and the mouth belonged to the malicious yellow press that needed his money to survive. Underneath was a caption: THE FOOL WHO FEEDS THE MONSTER.

I knew I had to find this century-old drawing, though I wasn't sure why. As I rode the escalator through the glass canyon atrium and into the bowels of the central branch of the Los Angeles Public Library to search for it, it struck me that I wasn't just looking for some rare old newspaper. I was looking for myself. I knew who that fool was. He was me.

In addiction circles, those in recovery also use the image of the monster as a warning. They tell the story of a man who found a package on his porch. Inside was a little monster, but it was cute, like a puppy. He kept it and raised it. The more he fed it, the bigger it got and the more it needed to be fed. He ignored his worries as it grew bigger, more intimidating, demanding, and unpredictable, until one day, as he was playing with it, the monster attacked and nearly killed him. The realization that the situation was more than he could handle came too late—the man was no longer in control. The monster had a life of its own.

The story of the monster is a lot like my story. Except my story is not about drugs or the yellow press but a bigger and much more modern monster—my monster is the brave new world of new media—one that I often fed and thought I controlled. I lived high and well in that world, and I believed in it until it no longer looked the same to me. Many things went down. I'm not sure where my responsibility for them begins or ends, but I am ready to talk about what happened.

I created false perceptions through blogs, which led to bad conclusions and wrong decisions—real decisions in the real world that had consequences for real people. Phrases like "known rapist" began to follow what were once playfully encouraged rumors of bad or shocking behavior designed to get blog publicity for clients. American Apparel, the company whose CEO loved to encourage controversy, eventually tired of it and fired him—and was sent reeling into bankruptcy and, sadly, irrelevancy. Friends were ruined and broken. Gradually I began to notice work just like mine appearing everywhere, and no one catching on to it or repairing the damage. Stocks took major hits, to the tune of tens of millions of dollars, on news from the same unreliable sources I'd often trick with fake stories. I've even seen some of those same sites take unfair shots at me, accusing me of this or that, because there was traffic in it for them.

I don't think it's controversial now, looking at the collapse of our political discourse, when a reality-television star has been elected to the presidency, to say that *everyone* is starting to learn what the consequences of feeding the monster are. We can't even talk to each other anymore, each of us running our own polarized little world on Facebook. Both sides throw the label "fake news" at each other because we can't even agree on basic *truth* anymore. Winston Churchill wrote of the appeasers of his age that "each one hopes that if he feeds the crocodile enough, the crocodile will eat him last." I thought I could skip being devoured entirely. Maybe you did too. We thought we were in control. I was wrong. We all were wrong.

## WHY I WROTE THIS BOOK

I didn't need to write this book. Financially, that is. I could have made a lot more money as a media manipulator, working with politicians and businessmen. I could have remained nameless, touching your life only through the news stories I created. I chose not to do that. I didn't write this book for free, of course, and no narrator is fully trustworthy, myself included. I'm simply speaking personally and frankly about what I know, and I know this space well. Some have tried to claim that I was lying even in this book but my reply remains the same: Why would I bother?

I wrote the original edition of this book because I was genuinely tired of how the things were. A good question about the ethics of a certain profession or activity is: What would the world look like if more people behaved like you? In my case, the answer was: "A lot worse."

I wrote this book then not as an apology but as a warning. I have updated it twice because my warnings have turned out not to be serious enough. Because it's turned out *worse* than I expected. I don't think you can argue with that.

Sitting in a drawer in my office is a large box filled with hundreds of articles I have printed over the last several years. The articles show all the trademarks of the fakes and scams I myself have run, yet they involve many of the biggest news and entertainment stories of the decade. The margins are filled with angry little notes and question marks. The satirist Juvenal wrote of "cramming whole notebooks with scribbled invective" amid the corrupt opulence of Rome; that box and this book are my notebooks from my own days inside such a world. Collectively, it was this process that opened my eyes. I hope it will have the same effect for you.

Some of you, by the time you are done with this book, will probably hate me for ruining things for you too. Or accuse me of exaggerating. You may not want me to expose the people behind your favorite websites or politicians as the imbeciles, charlatans, and pompous frauds they are. You don't have to like me, but you should listen. We live in a world of many hustlers, and you are the mark. The con is to build a brand off the backs of others. Your attention and your credulity are being stolen.

This book isn't structured like typical business books. Instead of extended chapters, it is split into two parts, and each part is made up of short, overlapping, and reinforcing vignettes. In the first part I explain why blogs and social media matter, how they drive the news, and how they can be manipulated. In the second I show what happens when you do this, how it backfires, and the dangerous consequences of our current system. And then, in the back, I have some extra materials and interviews that might be of use to you.

Every one of the tactics in this book reveals a critical vulnerability in our media system. I will show you where they are and what can be done with them, and help you recognize when they're being used on you. Sure, I am explaining how to take advantage of these weaknesses, but mostly I am saying that *these vulnerabilities exist*. It is the first time that these gaps have ever been exposed, by a critic or otherwise. Hopefully, once in the open, they'll no longer work as well. I understand that there is some contradiction in this position, as there has long been in me. My dis-integration wasn't always healthy, but it does allow me to explain our problems from a unique perspective.

By the end of this book, you'll see that we have a media system designed to trick, cajole, and steal every second of the most precious resource in the world—people's time. I'm going to show you every single one of these tricks, and what they mean.

What you choose to do with this information is up to you.

# BOOK ONE

## FEEDING THE
## MONSTER

### HOW BLOGS WORK

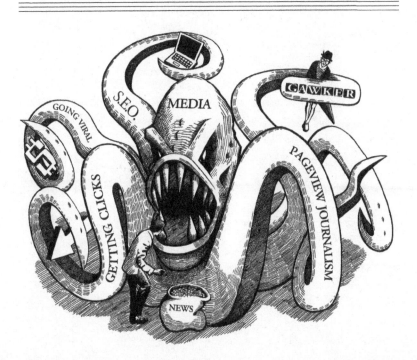

# I

## BLOGS MAKE
## THE NEWS

{ It is not news that sells papers, but papers that sell
news.

—BILL BONNER, *MOBS, MESSIAHS, AND
MARKETS* }

I CALL TO YOUR ATTENTION AN ARTICLE IN THE *NEW York Times* written at the earliest of the earliest junctures of the 2012 presidential election, nearly two years before votes would be cast.[1]*

It told of a then obscure figure, Tim Pawlenty, the governor of Minnesota. Pawlenty was not yet a presidential candidate. He had no campaign director, no bus, few donors, and little name recognition. In fact, he did not even have a campaign. It was January 2011, after all. What he did have was a beat reporter from the blog *Politico* following him from town to town with a camera and a laptop, reporting every moment of his noncampaign.

It's a bit peculiar, if you think about it. Even the *New York Times*, the newspaper that spends millions of dollars a year for a Baghdad bureau, which can fund investigative reports five or ten years in the making, didn't have a reporter covering Pawlenty. Yet *Politico*, a blog with only a fraction of the resources of a major newspaper, did. The *Times* was covering *Politico* covering a noncandidate.

It was a little like a Ponzi scheme, and like all such schemes, it went from boom to bust. Pawlenty became a candidate, coverage of him generated millions of impressions online, then in print, and finally on television, before he flamed out and withdrew from the race. Despite all of this, his candidacy's impact on the election was significant and real enough that the next Republican front-runner courted Pawlenty's endorsement.

As off-putting as it is, that story seems quaint in light of the 2016 election. I'm not a Tim Pawlenty fan, but he was at least a legitimate politician who conceivably could have run for president. Donald Trump had "considered" a presidential run for as long as I have been alive. His subsequent election actually obscures the extent to which this was all a publicity

---

*See my column "Electile Dysfunction: Why the Media Turned a Foregone Conclusion into a Horse Race" in the *New York Observer* for a complete account of the 2012 election.

TRUST ME, I'M LYING

stunt—clearly he was not too serious about politics or he might have spent at least a few months over thirty years trying to acquire a passing knowledge of policy. At the very least one assumes he might have said fewer dumb, unguarded things when there were microphones around. As late as 2012, he was still playing this publicity game, toying with running because it always made for good headlines. And what became of all this? Nothing. Because there was enough discretion, enough unity within the media that there was still some semblance of a line. Politics was at least partly serious business—and so was reporting the news.

But by 2015, when Trump declared his candidacy once again, that was no longer true. He wouldn't have actually run if he didn't think things were different, if he didn't at least subconsciously realize that his incendiary, provocative, and unpredictable personality would be traffic and attention gold online and offline. The man clearly sensed something that most politicians hadn't yet realized: that the culture of Twitter, the economics of online content, had swallowed everything else in the world.

There's a famous twentieth-century political cartoon about the Associated Press, which was, at the time, the wire service responsible for supplying news to the majority of the newspapers in the United States. In it an AP agent is pouring different bottles into a city's water supply. The bottles are labeled "lies," "prejudice," "slander," "suppressed facts," and "hatred." The image reads: THE NEWS—POISONED AT ITS SOURCE.

I think of blogs and social media as today's newswires. They're what poisoned the debate and the clarity of a nation of some 325 million people. They're how we fell for one of the greatest cons in history.

## BLOGS MATTER

By "blog" I'm referring collectively to all online publishing. That's everything from Twitter accounts to major newspaper websites to web videos to group blogs with hundreds of writers. I don't care whether the owners consider themselves blogs or not. The reality is that they are all subject to the same incentives, and they fight for attention with similar tactics.*

---

*I have never been a fan of the word "blogosphere" and will use it only sparingly.

Most people don't understand how today's information cycle really works. Many have no idea of how much their general worldview is influenced by the way news is generated online. What begins online ends offline.

Although there are millions of blogs out there, you'll notice some mentioned a lot in this book: *Gawker Media, Business Insider, Breitbart, Politico, Vox, BuzzFeed, Vice,* the *Huffington Post, Medium, Drudge Report,* and the like. This is not because they are the most widely read, but instead because they are mostly read by the media elite. Not only that, but their proselytizing founders, Nick Denton, Henry Blodget, Jonah Peretti, and Arianna Huffington, have an immense amount of influence as thought leaders. A blog isn't small if its puny readership is made up of TV producers and writers for national newspapers. It doesn't matter how many followers someone has if what they produce ends up going viral.

Radio DJs and news anchors once filled their broadcasts with newspaper headlines; today they repeat what they read online—certain blogs more than others. Stories from blogs also filter into real conversations and rumors that spread from person to person through word of mouth. In short, blogs are vehicles from which mass media reporters—and your most chatty and "informed" friends—discover and borrow the news. This hidden cycle gives birth to the memes that become our cultural references, the budding stars who become our celebrities, the thinkers who become our gurus, and the news that becomes our news.

Think about it: Where do people find stuff today? They find it online. This is just as true for normal people as it is for the so-called gatekeepers. If something is being chatted about on Facebook, Twitter, or Reddit, it *will* make its way through all other forms of media and eventually into culture itself. That's a fact.

When I figured this out early in my career in public relations, I had a thought that only a naive and destructively ambitious twentysomething would have: If I master the rules that govern blogs, I can be the master of all they determine. It was, essentially, access to a fiat over culture.

It may have been a dangerous thought, but it wasn't hyperbole. In the Pawlenty case, the guy could have become the president of the United States of America. Donald Trump *did* become president. One early media critic put it this way: We're a country governed by public opinion, and public opinion is largely governed by the press, so isn't it critical to understand what governs the press? What rules over the media, he concluded, rules over the country. In this case, what ruled over *Politico* literally almost ruled over everyone.

To understand what makes blogs act—why *Politico* followed Pawlenty around, why the media ended up giving Trump something like $4.6 *billion* worth of free publicity—is the key to making them do what you want (or stopping this broken system). Learn their rules, change the game. That's all it takes to control public opinion.

## SO, WHY *DID POLITICO* FOLLOW PAWLENTY?

On the face of it, it's pretty crazy. Pawlenty's phantom candidacy wasn't newsworthy, and if the *New York Times* couldn't afford to pay a reporter to follow him around, *Politico* shouldn't have been able to.

It wasn't crazy. Blogs need things to cover. The *Times* has to fill a newspaper only once per day. A cable news channel has to fill twenty-four hours of programming 365 days a year. But blogs have to fill an *infinite* amount of space. The site that covers the most stuff wins.

Political blogs know that their traffic goes up during election cycles. Since traffic is what they sell to advertisers, elections equal increased revenue. Unfortunately, election cycles come only every few years. Worse still, they end. Blogs have a simple solution: Change reality through the coverage.

With Pawlenty, *Politico* was not only manufacturing a candidate, they were manufacturing an entire leg of the election cycle purely to profit from it. It was a conscious decision. In the story about his business, *Politico*'s executive editor, Jim VandeHei, tipped his hand to the *New York Times*: "We were a garage band in 2008, riffing on the fly. Now we're a 200-person production, with a precise feel and plan. We're trying to take a leap forward in front of everyone else." Today, a few election cycles later, *Politico* has three hundred employees. It has spawned countless competitors, some of whom are even bigger.

When a blog like *Politico* tried to leap in front of everyone else, the person they arbitrarily decided to cover was turned into an actual candidate. The campaign starts gradually, with a few mentions on blogs, moves on to "potential contender," begins to be considered for debates, and is then included on the ballot. Their platform accumulates real supporters who donate real time and money to the campaign. The campaign buzz is reified by the mass media, who covers and legitimizes whatever is being talked about online.

Pawlenty's campaign may have failed, but for blogs and other media, it was a profitable success. He generated millions of pageviews for blogs, was the subject of dozens of stories in print and online, and had his fair share of television time. When journalists first covered Trump, they loved him because they thought he was a joke. They loved how he polarized the audience and how each crazy thing he said or did made for better headlines. Over time, he became a serious candidate—repeated, incessant media coverage can do that—and despite the supposed liberal bias of the media, they continued to shower him with attention. He was great for business.

In case you didn't catch it, here's the cycle again:

- Political blogs need things to cover; traffic increases during election

- Reality (election far away) does not align with this

- Political blogs create candidates early, gravitating toward the absurd and controversial; election cycle starts earlier

- The person they cover, by virtue of coverage, becomes actual candidate (or president)

- Blogs profit (literally); the public loses

You'll see this cycle repeated again and again in this book. It's true for celebrity gossip, politics, business news, and every other topic blogs cover. The constraints of blogging create artificial content, which is made real and impacts the outcome of real world events.

The economics of the internet created a twisted set of incentives that make traffic more important—and more profitable—than the truth. With the mass media—and today, mass culture—relying on the web for the next big thing, it is a set of incentives with massive implications.

Blogs need traffic, being first drives traffic, and so entire stories are created out of whole cloth to make that happen. This is just one facet of the economics of blogging, but it's a critical one. When we understand the logic that drives these business choices, those choices become predictable. And what is predictable can be anticipated, redirected, accelerated, or controlled—however you or I choose.

Later in the 2012 election, *Politico* moved the goalposts again to stay on top. Speed stopped working so well, so they turned to scandal to upend the race once more. Remember Herman Cain, the preposterous, media-created candidate who came after Pawlenty? After surging ahead as the lead contender for the Republican nomination, and becoming the subject of an exhausting number of traffic-friendly blog posts, Cain's candidacy was utterly decimated by a sensational but still strongly denied scandal reported by . . . you guessed it: *Politico.*[*]

And so another noncandidate was created, made real, and then taken out. Another one bit the dust so that blogs could fill their cycle. In some ways the reliability of this cycle—in which despite all the absurdity eventually a normal candidate would win out (be it Mitt Romney or whoever)—was the worst thing that could have happened to us. Because it meant we thought Trump would eventually lose. *He'll eventually come crashing back down to earth. Eventually people will see who he is. He can't avoid this forever.*

Except none of that was true. That's what happens when you feed the monster. It defies all expectations and rules.

---

[*]To paraphrase Budd Schulberg, from his memoir *Moving Pictures*: "It is not only a case of the tail wagging the dog, they were trying to take over the bark too."

# II

---

# TRADING UP THE CHAIN: HOW TO TURN NOTHING INTO SOMETHING IN THREE WAY-TOO-EASY STEPS

> Some people in the press, I think, are just lazy as hell. There are times when I pitch a story and they do it word for word. That's just embarrassing. They're adjusting to a time that demands less quality and more quantity. And it works to my advantage most of the time, because I think most reporters have liked me packaging things for them. Most people will opt for what's easier, so they can move on to the next thing. Reporters are measured by how often their stuff gets on Drudge. It's a bad way to be, but it's reality.
>
> **—KURT BARDELLA, FORMER PRESS SECRETARY FOR REPUBLICAN CONGRESSMAN DARRELL ISSA**

IN THE INTRODUCTION I EXPLAINED A SCAM I CALL "trading up the chain." It's a strategy I developed that manipulates the media through recursion. I can turn nothing into something by placing a story with a small blog that has very low standards, which then becomes the source for a story by a larger blog, and that, in turn, for a story by larger media outlets. I create, to use the words of one media scholar, a "self-reinforcing news wave." People like me do this every day.

The work I do is not exactly respectable. But I want to explain how it works without any of the negatives associated with my infamous clients. I'll show how I manipulated the media for a good cause.

A friend of mine recently used some of my advice on trading up the chain for the benefit of the charity he runs. This friend needed to raise money to cover the costs of a community art project, and chose to do it through Kickstarter, the crowdsourced fund-raising platform. With just a few days' work, he turned an obscure cause into a popular internet meme and raised nearly ten thousand dollars to expand the charity internationally.

Following the strategy I helped lay out, he made a YouTube video for the Kickstarter page showing off his charity's work. Not a video of the charity's best work, or even its most important work, but the work that exaggerated certain elements aimed at helping the video spread. (In this case, two or three examples in exotic locations that actually had the least amount of community benefit.) Next, he wrote a short article for a small local blog in Brooklyn and embedded the video. This site was chosen because its stories were often used or picked up by the New York section of the *Huffington Post*. As expected, the *Huffington Post* did bite, and ultimately featured the story as local news in both New York City and Los Angeles. Following my advice, he sent an e-mail from a fake address with these links to a reporter at CBS in Los Angeles, who then did a television piece on it—using mostly clips from my friend's heavily edited video. In anticipation of all of this, he'd been active on a channel of the social news site Reddit (where users vote on stories and topics they like) during the weeks leading up to his campaign launch in order to build up some connections on the site.

When the CBS News piece came out and the video was up, he was ready to post it all on Reddit. It made the front page almost immediately. This score on Reddit (now bolstered by other press as well) put the story on the radar of what I call the major "cool stuff" blogs—sites like Boing Boing, Laughing Squid, FFFFOUND!, and others—since they get post ideas from Reddit. From this final burst of coverage, money began pouring in, as did volunteers, recognition, and new ideas.

With no advertising budget, no publicist, and no experience, his little video did nearly a half million views, and funded his project for the next two years. One exaggerated amateur video became a news story that was written about independently by dozens of outlets in dozens of markets and did millions of media impressions. He had created and then manipulated this attention entirely by himself. It went from nothing to something.

This is not uncommon. Did you ever hear of the guy who created a company called Ship Your Enemies Glitter? He literally turned nothing into something. Drunk one night, he had a funny idea about sending envelopes of glitter to people—and charging for it. So he created a landing page and put it up on a site called ProductHunt.com, which features newly launched start-ups. From there, his "company" was featured in the *Washington Post*, *Business Insider*, the *Huffington Post*, the *Verge*, *Time*, and *Fast Company*. Almost instantly he took in almost twenty thousand dollars' worth of orders, but because it was not a real company, he ended up selling the domain to another entrepreneur who wanted to take it to the next level . . . for eighty thousand dollars. Fake idea, real money.

Before you get upset at us, remember: We were only doing what Lindsay Robertson, a blogger from *Videogum*, *Jezebel*, and *New York* magazine's *Vulture* blog, taught us to do. In a post explaining to publicists how they could better game bloggers like herself, Lindsay advised focusing "on a lower traffic tier with the (correct) understanding that these days, content filters *up* as much as it filters down, and often the smaller sites, with their ability to dig deeper into the [I]nternet and be more nimble, act as farm teams for the larger ones."[1]*

This is not new either.

Early-twentieth-century media critics were some of the first to describe how false news was easily propagated through the media system. A local newspaper would run an inaccurate item. With the advent of the telegraph, these stories could be and often were republished over the next week in newspapers across the country. As Max Sherover wrote in 1914 of newspapers, "The stories they have forwarded are obviously composed in large part of wild romancing. They snap up the most improbable reports and enlarge upon them with every detail that their fancy can suggest."

A document from 1995 recently released by the Clinton archive shows that more modern political manipulators have also tried to use the lower rungs of online media to plant narratives or scandals. As the document explains,

> *This is how the stream works: Well-funded right wing think tanks and individuals underwrite conservative newsletters and newspapers such as the Western Journalism Center, the* American Spectator *and the* Pittsburgh Tribune Review. *Next, the stories are reprinted on the internet where they are bounced into the mainstream media through one of two ways: 1) the story will be picked up by the British tabloids and covered as a major story, from which the American right-of-center mainstream media, (i.e. the* Wall Street Journal, Washington Times *and* New York Post) *will then pick the story up; or 2) The story will be bounced directly from the internet to the right-of-center mainstream American media. After the mainstream right-of-center media covers the story, congressional committees will look into the story. After Congress looks into the story, the story now has the legitimacy to be covered by the remainder of the American mainstream press as a "real" story.*

The Clintons famously alleged a "vast right-wing conspiracy," and as self-serving and unreliable as the couple is, they weren't totally wrong.

---

*Proving this theory unnervingly correct, *Newsweek* picked up Lindsay's advice from her tiny personal blog and reposted it on the official *Newsweek Tumblr.*

They just didn't mention that the left wing can and does use the same strategy. How else would one venture to explain the 2012 story that Republican South Carolina governor Nikki Haley would soon be indicted on tax fraud charges from work related to the Sikh Religious Society? Thanks to a defamation suit filed by the Sikh Religious Society, we know that the story got its start when a blogger tweeted about it, citing as his sources "two well placed legal experts" that turned out to be a local blog and a local television reporter. After the tweet, the story was picked up by the *Daily Beast*, *Daily Caller*, and *Drudge Report*.

The speed with which the Haley story started and was shot down (the next day, she provided a document from the IRS stating they wouldn't investigate) shows how quickly something can shoot up the chain with just the slightest shred of attribution. But thankfully, because of the defamation suit, this was one of the rare cases where there were some consequences for a journalist starting a bogus story: a written, public apology and release of the names of his two "sources."

Online publications compete to get stories first, newspapers compete to "confirm" it, and then pundits compete for airtime to opine on it. The smaller sites legitimize the newsworthiness of the story for the sites with bigger audiences. Consecutively and concurrently, this pattern inherently distorts and exaggerates whatever they cover.

## THE LAY OF THE LAND

Here's how it works. There are thousands of content creators scouring the web looking for things to write about. They *must* write several times each day. This is no easy task, so bloggers search Twitter, Facebook, comments sections, press releases, rival blogs, and other sources to develop their material. Where else are they going to get it? There's no time for investigative reporting.

Above them are hundreds of midlevel online and offline journalists at websites and blogs and in magazines and newspapers who use those bloggers below them as sources and filters. They also have to write constantly—and engage in the same search for buzz, only a little more developed.

Above them are the major national websites, publications, and television stations. They in turn browse the scourers below them for their material, grabbing their leads and turning them into truly national conversations. These are the most influential bunch—the *New York Times*, *The Today Show*, Fox News, and CNN—and dwindling revenues or not, they have massive reach.

Finally, between, above, and throughout these concentric levels is the largest group: *us*, the audience. We scan the web for material that we can watch, comment on, or share with our friends and followers.

It's bloggers informing bloggers informing bloggers all the way down. This isn't anecdotal observation. It is fact. In a media monitoring study done by Cision and George Washington University, *89 percent of journalists* reported using blogs for their research for stories. Roughly half reported using Twitter to find and research stories, and more than two thirds used other social networks, such as Facebook or LinkedIn, in the same way.[2] The more immediate the nature of their publishing medium (blogs, then newspapers, then magazines), the more heavily a journalist will depend on sketchy online sources, like social media, for research.

Recklessness, laziness, however you want to categorize it, the attitude is openly tolerated and acknowledged. The majority of journalists surveyed admitted to knowing that their online sources were less reliable than traditional ones. Not a single journalist said they believed that the information gathered from social media was "a lot more reliable" than traditional media! Why? Because it suffers from a "lack of fact-checking, verification or reporting standards."[3]

For the sake of simplicity, though, let's break the chain into three levels. I know these levels as one thing only: beachheads for manufacturing news. I don't think someone could have designed a system easier to manipulate if they wanted to.

## Level 1: The Entry Point

At the first level, small blogs and local websites that cover your neighborhood or scene are some of the easiest sites to get traction on. Since they typically write about local, personal issues pertaining to a contained readership, trust is very high. At the same time, they are cash-strapped and traffic-hungry, always on the lookout for a big story that might draw a big spike of new viewers. It doesn't have to be local, though; it can be a site about a subject you know very well, or it can be a site run by a friend.

What's important is that the site is small and understaffed. This makes it possible to sell them a story that is only loosely connected to their core message but really sets you up to transition to the next level.

## Level 2: The Legacy Media

Here we begin to see a mix of online and offline sources. The blogs of newspapers and local television stations are some of the best targets. For starters, they share the same URL and often get aggregated in Google News. Places like the *Wall Street Journal*, *Newsweek*, and CBS often have sister sites that feature the companies' logos but have their own editorial standards, not always as rigorous as their old media counterparts'. They seem legitimate, but they are, as Fark.com founder Drew Curtis calls them, just "mass media sections that update more often but with less editorial oversight."

Legacy media outlets are critical turning points in building up momentum. The reality is that the bloggers at Forbes.com or the *Chicago Tribune* do not operate on the same editorial guidelines as their print counterparts. However, their final output can be made to look like it carries the same weight. If you get a blog on Wired.com to mention your start-up, you can smack "'A revolutionary device'—*Wired*" on the box of your product just as surely as you could if *Wired* had put your CEO on the cover of the magazine.

These sites won't write about just anything, though, so you need to create chatter or a strong story angle to hook this kind of sucker. Their illusion of legitimacy comes at the cost of being slightly more selective when it comes to what they cover. But it is worth the price, because it will grant the bigger websites in your sights later the privilege of using magic words like "NBC is reporting . . ."

## Level 3: National

Having registered multiple stories from multiple sources firmly onto the radar of both local and midlevel outlets, you can now leverage this coverage to access the highest level of media: the national press. Getting to this level usually involves less direct pushing and a lot more massaging. The sites that have already taken your bait are now on your side. They desperately want their articles to get as much traffic as possible, and being linked to or mentioned on national sites is how they do that. These sites will take care of submitting your articles to news aggregator sites like *Drudge* or Reddit, because making the front page will drive tens of thousands of visitors to their article. Mass media reporters monitor aggregators for story ideas and often cover what is trending there, like they did with the charity story after it made the front page of Reddit. In today's world even these guys have to think like bloggers—they need to get as many pageviews as possible. Success on the lower levels of the media chain is evidence that the story could deliver even better results from a national platform.

You just want to make sure that such reporters notice the story's gaining traction. Take the outlet where you'd ultimately like to receive coverage and observe it for patterns. You'll notice that they tend to get their story ideas from the same second-level sites, and by tailoring the story to those smaller sites (or site), it sets you up to be noticed by the larger one. Certain blogs are read very heavily by the New York City media set. You can craft the story for those sites and automatically set yourself up to appeal to the other reporters reading it—without ever speaking to them directly. A media example: Katie Couric claims she gets many story ideas from her Twitter followers, which means that getting a few tweets out of the seven hundred or so people she follows is all it takes to get a shot at the nightly national news.

News anchors aren't the only people susceptible to this trick. Scott Vener, the famous hit maker responsible for picking the songs that went into HBO shows like *Entourage* and *How to Make It in America*, has a reputation for discovering "unknown artists." Really, he admits, most of the music he finds is just "what is bubbling up on the internet."[4] Since Vener monitors conversations on Twitter and the comments on trendy music blogs, a shot at a six-figure HBO payday and instant mainstream exposure is just a few manufactured bubbles away.

It's a simple illusion: Create the perception that the meme already exists and all the reporter (or the music supervisor or celebrity stylist) is doing is popularizing it. They rarely bother to look past the first impressions.

## LEVELS 1, 2, 3:
## HOW I TRADED UP THE CHAIN

My campaign for *I Hope They Serve Beer in Hell* began with vandalizing the billboards. The graffiti was designed to bait two specific sites, *Curbed Los Angeles* and Mediabistro's *FishbowlLA*. When I sent them photos of my work under the fake name Evan Meyer, they both quickly picked it up.[5] (For his contributions as a tipster, Evan earned his own Mediabistro profile, which still exists. According to the site, he has not been "sighted" since.)

*Curbed LA* began their post by using my e-mail verbatim:

> *A reader writes: "I saw these on my way home last night. It was on 3rd and Crescent Heights, I think. Good to know Los Angeles hates him too."* Provocateur Tucker Max's new movie "I Hope They Serve Beer in Hell" opens this weekend [emphasis mine].

Thanks for the plug!*

In creating outrage for the movie, I had a lot of luck getting local websites to cover or spread the news about protests of the screenings we had organized through anonymous tips. They were the easiest place to get the story started. We would send them a few offensive quotes and say something like "This misogynist is coming to our school and we're so fucking pissed. Could you help spread the word?" Or I'd e-mail a neighborhood

---

*It's been more than five years since this happened. I included it in the first and second editions of the book, I've told the story on NPR's *On the Media* and dozens of other outlets, and as of this writing, that story on Curbed.com (owned by *Vox* Media) is still there and still uncorrected.

site to say that "a controversial screening with rumors of a local boycott" was happening in a few days.

Sex, college protesters, Hollywood—it was the definition of the kind of local story news producers love. After reading about the growing controversy on the small blogs I conned, they would often send camera crews to the screenings. The video of the story would get posted on the station's website and then get covered again by the other, larger blogs in that city, like those hosted by newspapers or companies like the *Huffington Post*. I was able to get the story to register, however briefly, by using a small site with low standards of newsworthiness. Other media outlets might be alerted to this fact and in turn cover it, giving me another bump. At this point I now have something to work with. Three or four links are the makings of a trend piece, or even a controversy—that's all major outlets and national websites need to see to get excited. Former Slate.com media critic Jack Shafer called such manufactured online controversy "frovocation"—a portmanteau of faux provocation. "Outrage porn" is a better term. People like getting pissed off almost as much as they like actual porn.

The key to getting from the second to the third level is the soft sell. I couldn't very well e-mail a columnist at the *Washington Post* and say, "Hey, will you denounce our movie so we can benefit from the negative PR?" So I targeted the sites that those kinds of columnists were likely to read. *Gawker* and Mediabistro are very media-centric, so we tailored stories to them to queue ourselves up for outrage from their audiences— which happen to include reporters at places like the *Washington Post*.* And when I wanted to be direct, I would register a handful of fake e-mail addresses on Gmail or Yahoo and send e-mails with a collection of all the links gathered so far and say, "How have you not done a story about this yet?" Reporters rarely get substantial tips or alerts from their readers, so to get two or even three legitimate tips about an issue is a strong signal.

---

*In fact, a few years later a writer on one of the sites we exploited repeatedly while promoting the movie wrote a post titled: "Are Traditional News Media Stealing Scoops from Bloggers?" which accused the *Chicago Tribune* of stealing article ideas from her blog *Chicago Now*. She was right, they were stealing, and that's exactly how we got coverage into the editorial page of the *Tribune*.

So I sent it to them. Well, kind of. I actually just did more of the same fake tips from fake e-mail addresses that worked for the other sites—only this time I had a handful of links from major blogs that made it clear that everyone was talking about it. At this point something amazing happened: The coverage my stunts received began helping the twenty-thousand-dollar-a-month publicist the movie had hired. Rejections from late-night television, newspaper interviews, and morning radio turned into callbacks. Tucker did Carson Daly's NBC late-night show for the first time. By the end of this charade, hundreds of reputable reporters, producers, and bloggers had been swept up into participating. Thousands more had eagerly gobbled up news about it on multiple blogs. Each time they did, views of the movie trailer spiked, book sales increased, and Tucker became more famous and more controversial. If only people had known they were promoting the offensive Tucker Max brand for us, just as we'd planned.

With just a few simple moves, I'd taken his story from level 1 to level 3—not just once but several times, back and forth. Ultimately the movie did not do nearly as well at release as we'd hoped—this supplementary guerrilla marketing ended up being the entirety of the movie's advertising efforts rather than a small part of it for reasons outside of my control—but the attention generated by the campaign was overwhelming and incredibly lucrative. Eventually the movie became a cult hit on DVD.

Once you get a story like this started, it takes on a life of its own. That's what happened after I vandalized Tucker's billboards. Exactly one week later, inspired by my example, sixteen feminists gathered in New York City late at night to vandalize *I Hope They Serve Beer in Hell* posters all over Manhattan.[6] Their campaign got even more coverage than my stunt, including a 650-word, three-picture story on a *Village Voice* blog with dozens of comments (I posted some comments under fake names to get people riled up, but looking at them now I can't tell which ones are fake and which are real). From the fake came real action.

# THE MEDIA: DANCING WITH ITSELF

Trading up the chain relies on an insight from crisis public relations expert Michael Sitrick. When attempting to turn things around for a particularly disliked or controversial client, Sitrick was fond of saying, "We need to find a lead steer!" The media, like any group of animals, gallops in a herd. It takes just one steer to start a stampede. The first level is your lead steer. The rest is just pointing everyone's attention to the direction it went in.

Remember: Every person in the media ecosystem (with the exception of a few at the top layer) is under immense pressure to produce content under the tightest of deadlines. Yes, you have something to sell. But more than ever they desperately, desperately need to buy. The flimsiest of excuses is all it takes.

It freaked me out when I began to see this sort of thing happen *without* the deliberate prodding of a promoter like myself. I saw media conflagrations set off by internal sparks. In this networked, interdependent world of blogging, misinformation can spread even when no one is consciously pushing or manipulating it. The system is so primed, tuned, and ready that often it doesn't need people like me. The monster can feed itself.

Sometimes just a single quote taken out of context can set things off. In early 2011, a gossip reporter for an AOL entertainment blog asked former quarterback Kurt Warner who he thought would be the next ex-athlete to join the show *Dancing with the Stars*. Warner jokingly suggested Brett Favre, who was then embroiled in a sexual harassment scandal. Though the show told him they wanted nothing to do with Favre, the reporter still titled the post "Brett Favre Is Kurt Warner's Pick to Join 'Dancing': 'Controversy Is Good for Ratings'" and tagged it as an exclusive. The post made it clear that Warner was just goofing around.

Two days later the blog *Bleacher Report* linked to the piece but made it sound as though Warner was seriously urging Favre to join the show (which, remember, had just told AOL they wanted nothing to do with Favre).

After their story, the rumor started to multiply rapidly. A reporter from a local TV-news website, KCCI Des Moines, caught the story and wrote a sixty-two-word piece titled "Brett Favre's Next Big Step?" and mentioned the "rumors" discussed on *Bleacher Report*. From there the piece was picked up by *USA Today*—"Brett Favre Joining 'Dancing with the Stars' Season 12 Cast?"—*ProFootballTalk*, and others, making the full transition to the national stage.[7]

To recap what happened: A gossip blog manufactured a scoop by misrepresenting, deliberately or not, a joke. That scoop was itself misrepresented and misinterpreted as it traveled up the chain, going from a small entertainment blog to a sports site to a CBS affiliate in Iowa and eventually to the website of one of the biggest newspapers in the country.[*] What spread was not even a rumor, which at least would have been logical. It was just an empty bit of nothing.

The fake Favre meme spread almost exactly along the lines of my fake outrage campaign for Tucker's movie—only there was no me involved! Not only is the web susceptible to spreading false information, but it can also be the source of it.

For a gossip story, it's not a big deal. You might be thinking, *That Favre story is old. Who cares?* Well, let me ask you this: In the intervening years, as newsroom budgets have gotten smaller, as ad rates have declined, and as the news cycle has gotten faster and faster, do you think there are fewer fake stories like that rippling through the internet, or do you think there might be even more? I *wish* we could go back to those good old days when only celebrity gossip was unreliable.

## A TRUE FOOL FEEDING THE MONSTER

I am obviously jaded and cynical about trading up the chain. How could I not be? It's basically possible to run anything through this chain, even utterly preposterous and made-up information. But for a long time I thought that fabricated media stories could only hurt feelings and waste time. I didn't think anyone could *die* because of it.

I was wrong. Perhaps you remember Terry Jones, the idiotic pastor

---

*This was excellently caught and detailed by *Quickish* in their post " 'Brett Favre on Dancing with the Stars?' No. Not Even a Rumor"; their research was promptly stolen and reposted by the oft-guilty *Deadspin* for an easy twenty-five thousand pageviews.

whose burning of the Koran led to riots that killed nearly thirty people in Afghanistan. Jones's bigotry happened to trade up the chain perfectly, and the media unwittingly allowed it.

Jones first made a name for himself in the local Florida press by running offensive billboards in front of his church. Then he stepped it up, announcing that he planned to stage a burning of the Koran. This story was picked up by a small website called Religion News Service. Yahoo! linked to their short article, and dozens of blogs followed, which led CNN to invite Jones to appear on the network. He was now a national story.

Yet the media and the public, aware of the potential implications of airing video of his act, began to push back. Many decided they would not air such a video. Some five hundred people attended a protest in Kabul where they burned Jones in effigy. At the last second Jones, under pressure, backed down, and the crisis was averted.

But Terry Jones was back a few months later, announcing for the second time that he planned to burn the Koran. Each blog and outlet that covered the lead-up to the burning made the story—and the media monster that was Terry Jones—that much bolder and bigger. Reporters asked if a direct request from President Obama would stop him, which of course meant that the president of the United States of America would have to negotiate with a homegrown terrorist (he traded up the chain to the *most powerful man in the world*).

This circus was what finally pushed Jones over the edge. In March 2011, he went through with the burning, despite the threatened media blackout.

He called their bluff and it worked. The blackout fell apart when a college student named Andrew Ford, freelancing for the wire service Agence France-Presse, took advantage of a story too dirty and dangerous for many journalists to touch in good conscience.*

Agence France-Presse, Ford's publisher, is syndicated on Google and Yahoo! News. They immediately republished his article. The story began to go up the chain, getting bigger and bigger. Roughly thirty larger blogs and online news services had picked up Ford's piece or linked to it in the

---

*This happens in politics all the time. As Democratic consultant Christian Grantham told *Forbes*, "Campaigns understand that there are some stories that regular reporters won't print. So they'll give those stories to the blogs."

first day. It made the story too big for the rest of the media—including the foreign press—to continue to resist. So the news of Jones's Koran burning, a calculated stunt to extract attention from a system that could not prevent itself from being exploited, became known to the world. And it was a deadly monster of a story.

Within days, twenty-seven people were killed during riots in Afghanistan, including seven UN workers; forty more were injured. Christians were specifically targeted, and Taliban flags were flown in the streets of Kabul. "It took just one college student to defeat a media blackout and move a story halfway around the globe within twenty-four hours," the Poynter Institute wrote in an analysis of the reporting. This was, as *Forbes* journalist Jeff Bercovici put it, truly an example of "when Journalism 2.0 kills."[8]

One kook and one overeager young journalist unintentionally show why trading up the chain—feeding the monster—can be so dangerous (though for Jones, very effective). They weren't just turning nothing into something. The beast these blogs built up set off needless bloodshed.

And is this not a similar dynamic to what happened in Berkeley in 2017 when students rioted in protest of the notorious troll Milo Yiannopoulos? Somehow a rumor started that Milo would be outing undocumented immigrants during his talk on the UC Berkeley campus. I have seen no definitive proof behind this rumor—nor could there ever be proof that someone *might* have done something. We'll never know because the riots and protesting became so violent that his talk was canceled. People easily could have been hurt or killed. Worse, the protesters didn't realize that they were playing right into Milo's hands. What would have otherwise been a talk in front of a few hundred students became headlines across the country for several days. President Trump even weighed in—threatening to pull federal funding from the university. Once again, a troll won and was rewarded with precisely the attention he wanted because no one in the media could break their own self-imposed pattern. The stories just took on a life of their own.

You can trade up the chain for charity or you can trade up it to create funny fake news—or you can do it to create violence, hatred, and, even incidentally, death.

# III

# THE BLOG CON

## HOW PUBLISHERS MAKE MONEY ONLINE

> Media companies can very much be in a race against time for growth. Investors want a return on their money and, given the economics of web news, that almost always requires exponential growth in uniques and pageviews.
>
> —RYAN MCCARTHY, REUTERS
>
> Picture a galley rowed by slaves and commanded by pirates.
>
> —TIM RUTTEN, *LOS ANGELES TIMES*, ON THE *HUFFINGTON POST* BUSINESS MODEL

STRIPPED BARE, THE ECONOMICS OF ONLINE NEWS—
the way blogging really works—is a shocking thing. I've never needed to
blog for my daily bread, to generate pageviews to pay my rent, but as a
press agent, a media buyer, and later a consultant to media companies, I
know how this system works. I won't say it is as disturbing as watching
slaughterhouse videos or an exposé of a sweatshop, but it will turn your
stomach to learn how online media outlets like the *Huffington Post* and
even the website of the *New York Times* make their money, and how much
money they actually make.

This matters, because as businesses designed to make money, the way
in which they do business is the main filter for how they do the news.
Every story they produce must contort itself to fit this mold—whatever
the topic or subject. I will show you this by explaining exactly how I have
exploited these economics for my own personal gain. You're free to view
these lessons as opportunities or as loopholes that must be closed. I see
them as both.

## TRAFFIC IS MONEY

On the face of it, blogs make their money from selling advertisements.
These advertisements are paid for by the impression (generally a rate per
thousand impressions). A site might have several ad units on each page;
the publisher's revenue equals the cumulative CPM (cost per thousand)
multiplied by the number of pageviews. Advertisement × Traffic = Revenue. An ad buyer like me buys this space by the millions—ten million
impressions on this site, five million on another, fifty million through a
network. A few blogs produce a portion of their revenue through selling

extras—hosting conferences or affiliate deals—but, for the most part, this is the business: Traffic is money.

A portion of the advertising on blogs is sold directly by the publisher, a portion is sold by sales reps who work on commission, and the rest is sold by advertising networks that specialize in the remaining inventory, often in a real-time bidding system. Regardless of who sells it or who buys it, what matters is that every ad impression on a site is monetized, if only for fractions of a penny. Each and every pageview is money in the pocket of the publisher.

Publishers and advertisers can't differentiate between the types of impressions an ad does on a site. A perusing reader is no better than an accidental reader. An article that provides worthwhile advice is no more valuable than one instantly forgotten. So long as the page loads and the ads are seen, both sides are fulfilling their purpose. A click is a click.

Knowing this, blogs do everything they can to increase the latter variable in the equation (traffic, pageviews). It's how you must understand them as a business. Every decision a publisher makes is ruled by one dictum: *Traffic by any means.*

## Scoops Are Traffic

One of the biggest shocks to the online world was the launch of *TMZ*. The blog was developed by AOL in 2005, and revenues skyrocketed to nearly $20 million a year almost immediately, paving the way for its now famous television program. This was all accomplished through a handful of major scoops. Or at least, TMZ's special definition of "scoops."

The blog's founder, Harvey Levin, once said in an interview that *TMZ* is "a serious news operation that has the same rigid standards that any news operation in America has." This is the same site that once published, at 4:07 A.M., an exclusive scoop: a blurry, never-before-seen photo of future president John F. Kennedy on a boat filled with naked women. This "exclusive" scoop was headlined THE JFK PHOTO THAT COULD HAVE CHANGED HISTORY. Only it couldn't have altered world events for one simple reason: The man in the photo wasn't JFK. In fact, it turned out to be a spread from a 1967 issue of *Playboy*.[1] Oops!

Despite missteps like this, *TMZ* turned scoop-getting into a science. They broke the story of Mel Gibson's anti-Semitic outbursts during his DUI arrest. And then they got video of Michael Richards's racist onstage meltdown, posted the bruised-Rihanna police photo, and announced the news of Michael Jackson's death. *TMZ* originated four of the biggest stories to come from the internet and captured a substantial audience from these enormous surges of traffic.* They didn't always use the most reputable or reliable means of getting their scoops, but nevertheless, today when people think celebrity news, they think of *TMZ*. (They don't think of *Defamer*, *Gawker*'s predecessor to *TMZ*, which was shuttered because it couldn't deliver any scoops, and they don't like Perez Hilton's silly little drawings anymore either.)

It sent a very clear message to publishers: Exclusives build blogs. Scoops equal traffic.

The thing is, exclusive scoops are rare, and at the very least, they require some effort to obtain. So greedy blogs have perfected what is called the "pseudo-exclusive." In a private memo to his employees, Nick Denton, founder of the Gawker Media blog empire, asked the writers to use this technique, because it allows them "to take ownership of a story even if it isn't a strict exclusive."[2] In other words, *pretend they have a scoop*. The strategy works well, because many readers will see the story in only one place; they have no idea that it was actually broken or originally reported elsewhere.

One of *Gawker*'s biggest scoops early on in the race—certainly a *TMZ*-level story—was a collection of Tom Cruise Scientology videos. It is a good example of a pseudo-exclusive, since the work wasn't done by the site who eventually got all the pageviews from it. Since I witnessed the story unfold behind the scenes, I know that the tapes were actually unearthed by Hollywood journalist Mark Ebner, whose blog I was advising at the time. Ebner called me, very excited with news of a potentially huge scoop, and said that he'd bring over the materials. A few hours later, he gave me some DVDs in an envelope marked "confidential," which I watched later that night with a friend. Our stupid reaction: "Tom Cruise being crazy; how is that new?"

---

*Exclusives, as they are called, are important for another reason. Advertising a story as an exclusive by extension takes a dig at a publication's competitors: "We got this story and they didn't—because we're better." This is partly why a site would rather post a weak exclusive on its front page than a more interesting story they've been forced to share with others.

*Gawker* had a different reaction. See, Ebner had also shown the clips to his friends at *Gawker*, who turned around and immediately posted a story featuring the videos before Mark or anyone else had a chance to. I don't know whether *Gawker* promised Mark they'd give him credit. All I know is that what happened was shitty: Their post went on to do 3.2 million views and bring their site a whole new audience. Mark received nothing, because *Gawker* didn't link back to his site—which would have been the right thing to do. By doing this, *Gawker* owned a story that was not theirs. Only after that did I begin to understand how blog fortunes were made: off the backs of others.

When all it takes is one story to propel a blog from the dredges of the internet to mainstream notoriety, it shouldn't come as a surprise that sites will do anything to get their shot, even if it means manufacturing or stealing scoops (and deceiving readers and advertisers in the process).

Established press doesn't have this problem. They aren't anxious for name recognition, because they already have it. Instead of bending the rules (and the truth) to get it, their main concern for their business model is to protect their reputations. This is a critical difference. Media was once about protecting a name; on the web it is about building one.

## THE BLOG CON: NAMES, SCOOPS, AND TRAFFIC CREATE AN EXIT

I've written about how sites engage in an endless chase for revenue through pageviews, and that *is* what they do. However, blogs are not intended to be profitable and independent businesses. The tools they use to build traffic and revenue are part of a larger play.

Blogs are built to be sold. Though they make substantial revenues from advertising, the real money is in selling the entire site to a larger company for a multiple of the traffic and earnings. Usually to a rich sucker.

Weblogs, Inc. was sold to AOL for $25 million. The *Huffington Post* was sold to AOL for $315 million in cash, with its owner, Arianna Huffington, deliberately eschewing the opportunity to wait and build for an IPO. *TechCrunch* was also sold to AOL for $30 million. Discovery bought the blog *TreeHugger* for $10 million. *Ars Technica* was sold to Condé Nast for more than $20 million. *Know Your Meme* was acquired by Cheezburger Media for seven figures. FOX Sports Interactive purchased the sports blog network *Yardbarker*. I worked on an acquisition like this myself when the Collective, a talent management company I advise, bought *Bloody Disgusting*, a blog about horror films, with an eye on potentially selling it to someone bigger down the line. The site ViralNova was purchased for a reported $100 million, and EliteDaily.com sold for $50 million. *HelloGiggles*, a pop culture blog, was acquired for millions as well.

Blogs are built and run with an exit in mind. This is really why they need scoops and acquire marquee bloggers—to build up their names for investors and to show a trend of rapidly increasing traffic. The pressure for this traffic in a short period of time is intense. And desperation, as a media manipulator knows, is the greatest quality you can hope for in a potential victim. Each blog is its own mini-Ponzi scheme, for which traffic growth is more important than solid financials, brand recognition more important than trust, and scale more important than business sense. Blogs are built so someone else will want them—one stupid buyer cashing out the previous ones—and millions of dollars are exchanged for essentially worthless assets.

## ANYTHING GOES IN THE DEN OF THIEVES

It doesn't surprise me at all that shady business deals and conflicts of interest abound in this world. My favorite example, of course, is myself. I am regularly the online ad buyer and the publicist or PR contact for the clients I represent. So the same sites that snarkily cover my companies also depend on me for large six- or even seven-figure checks each year. On the same day a writer for a blog might be e-mailing me for information about a rumor they heard, their publisher is calling me on the phone asking if I want to increase the size of my ad buy. Later in this book I'll write about how difficult it is to get bloggers to correct even blatantly inaccurate stories—this conflict of interest was one of the only effective tools I could use to combat that. Naturally, nobody minded what I was doing, because they were too busy lining their own pockets to care.

Michael Arrington, the loudmouth founder and former editor in chief of *TechCrunch*, is famous for investing in the start-ups that his blogs would then cover. Although he no longer runs *TechCrunch*, he was a partner in two investment funds during his tenure and now manages his own, CrunchFund. In other words, even when he is not a direct investor, he has connections or interests in dozens of companies on his beat, and his insider knowledge helps turn profits for the firm.

When criticized for these conflicts, he responded by saying that his competitors were simply jealous because he was—I'm not kidding—"a lot better than them."[*] So when Arrington blew the lid off a secret meeting of angel investors in Silicon Valley in 2011—later known as "Angelgate"—it's hard to say whose interests he was serving, his readers' or his own. Or maybe he was upset not because collusion is wrong but because the group had declined to invite him and—again, not kidding—treated him rudely when he showed up anyway. He ultimately left *TechCrunch* after a highly publicized fight with the new owners, AOL, who dared to question this conflict of interest.

Nick Denton of *Gawker* is also a prolific investor in his own space, often putting money into companies founded by employees who left his company or were fired. He has stakes in several local blog networks, such as *Curbed*, that are often linked to or written about on his larger sites. By shuffling users around to two sites he can charge advertisers twice. Denton also invested in the site Cityfile, which he was able to pump up with traffic from his other blogs before acquiring it outright and rolling it back into *Gawker*.

Influence is ultimately the goal of most blogs and blog publishers, because that influence can be sold to a larger media company. But, as Arrington and Denton show, influence can also be abused for profit through strategic investments—be it in the companies they write about or where they decide to send monetizable traffic. And, of course, these are only the conflicts of interest blatant enough to be discovered by the public. Who knows what else goes on behind the curtain?

---

*Arrington's longer argument is that since he and other bloggers disclose their conflicts of interest, they are in the clear. The science behind the 2012 book *The Honest Truth About Dishonesty* by Dan Ariely disputes this notion, shows, in fact, that disclosing conflicts of interests actually increases the bias of skewed data. We are just not good at tossing tainted info.

It's also interesting to note that many of these blogs and publishing platforms, which purport to expose corruption and the misdeeds of other businesses, often have their own dark secrets. As one former *VentureBeat* blogger, Bekah Grant, recently confessed on *Medium*, the job was a relentless, rapid machine that had to be constantly fed. "I wrote an average of 5 posts a day," she said, "churning out nearly 1,740 articles over the course of 20 months. That is, by all objective standards, insane." "Insane" is one word. "Exploitative" is probably a better one. I remember seeing an ad a few years ago for a *Washington Post* blogging gig that required at least *twelve posts a day*. And this is the same organization tasked with holding other businesses and public figures accountable for labor practices? We're supposed to listen to them as they hold Uber's feet to the fire?

## ENTER: THE MANIPULATOR

Bloggers eager to build names and publishers eager to sell their blogs are like two crooked businessmen colluding to create interest in a bogus investment opportunity—building up buzz and clearing town before anyone gets wise. In this world, where the rules and ethics are lax, a third player can exert massive influence. Enter: the media manipulator.

The assumptions of blogs and their owners present obvious vulnerabilities that people like me exploit. They allow us to control what is in the media, because the media is too busy chasing profits to bother trying to stop us. They are not motivated to care. Their loyalty is not to their audience but to themselves and their con. While ultimately this is reason to despair, I have found one small solace: Conning the conmen is one of life's most satisfying pleasures. And it's not even hard.

In the next chapters I will outline how to do this and how it is being done. I have broken down the manipulation of blogs into nine effective tactics. Each exposes a pathetic vulnerability in our media system—each, when wielded properly, levels the playing field and gives you free rein to control the flow of information on the web.

# IV

## TACTIC #1

# THE ART OF THE BRIBE

> The writings by which one can live are not the writings which themselves live, and are never those in which the writer does his best. . . . Those who have to support themselves by their pen must depend on literary drudgery, or at best on writings addressed to the multitude.
>
> —JOHN STUART MILL, *AUTOBIOGRAPHY*

THERE ARE MANY WAYS TO GIVE SOMEONE A BRIBE.
Very rarely does it mean handing them a stack of bills.

The criteria that bloggers' employers use to determine the size of their paychecks—the stuff bloggers are paid for—can be co-opted and turned into an indirect bribe. These levers were easy enough for me to find, and properly identified and wielded, they turned out to be as effective as any overt payoff.

It begins with how these bloggers are hired. Put aside any notion that applicants are chosen based on skill, integrity, or a love of their craft. Ben Parr, editor at large at the popular technology blog *Mashable*, was once asked what he looked for when he hired writers for his blogs. His answer was one word: quickness. "Online journalism is fast-paced," he explained. "We need people that can get the story out in minutes and can compose the bigger opinion pieces in a couple hours, not a couple of days." As to any actual experience in journalism, that would be considered only "a definite plus."[1]

The payment structure of blogging reflects this emphasis on speed over other variables, such as quality, accuracy, or how informative the content might be. Early on blogs tended to pay their writers a rate per post or a flat rate with a minimum number of posts required per day. *Engadget, Slashfood, Autoblog*, and other sites run by Weblogs, Inc. paid bloggers a reported five hundred dollars a month in 2005 for 125 posts—or four dollars a post, four per day.[2] *Gawker* paid writers twelve dollars a post as late as 2008. And of course these rates don't include the other duties bloggers are stuck with, such as editing, responding to e-mails, and writing comments. Professional blogging is done in the boiler room, and it is brutal.

*Gawker* set the curve for the industry again when they left the pay-per-post model and switched to a pageview-based compensation system that gave bonuses to writers based on their monthly traffic figures. These bonuses came on top of a set monthly pay, meaning that bloggers were eligible for payments that could effectively double their salary once they hit their monthly quota. You can imagine what kind of results this led to. I recall a post from a *Gawker* writer whining about how he didn't know how much money he'd make that month—and getting seventeen thousand views for it.

The bonus system was so immediately rewarding for *Gawker* bloggers that the company tweaked their ratio to deemphasize the bonus slightly. The system remains, however, and today the company has a big board in its offices that shows the stats for all the writers and their stories. When writers aren't fighting for bonuses, all they have to do is look up to be reminded: If you're at the bottom of the board, you might get fired.

This is now the standard model for blogs. *Seeking Alpha*, a network of financial writers (arguably worth a lot to its investor-type readers), launched a payment platform in 2010 that pays writers based on the traffic their posts generate. The average payment per article turned out to be only fifty-eight dollars for the first six months. A writer needs to rack up roughly one hundred thousand views to make even one thousand dollars—a tough fight when you're jostling for share of voice against the thousand-plus writers who publish there each month. The blog *The Awl* announced it would also start paying its writers using a similar model two years after its founding. A dozen or so bloggers split a small pool of revenue generated by advertisements on the site. The more traffic the site does, the larger the pool. It's the same incentive—desperately dependent on big hits—but instead of fighting each other for pageviews, they're all in on the hustle together.[3]

Many outlets have also built out what they call "contributor programs," which open up previously exclusive outlets to freelance writers who are paid by the view or by how many social media shares their articles get (as an approximation of pageviews). A story from a Forbes.com contributor, for instance, is written not by a *Forbes* staffer but by someone hustling to get as many clicks as possible. I don't necessarily think that contributor programs are all bad—I've helped several major publications build them out—*but* I do think the public needs to be more informed about the difference between these styles of content. You might think you're reading an article written by a professional journalist when, in reality, you are reading something written by someone who is paid so little for what they wrote that they can be a target for real bribes from the subject of their story (as has happened at contributor-heavy online publications like Forbes.com).

Here's an e-mail I just got, offering to buy links in articles I contribute to Entrepreneur.com (another site with such a program):

> Hi Ryan,
>
> I've been following your writing on Entrepreneur for some time now, I hope you don't mind me dropping you a quick email.
>
> My name is Gareth, I am a London based, Digital PR Consultant. I work with credible clients offering them a 'media mention' service on the publications you write for.
>
> We work with our clients to create natural informative content (e.g. blog posts, infographics) that would be of value to your upcoming articles in order to place them with a link back to their site.
>
> We can also provide interesting and relevant quotes from the CEO or senior employees at our partners business to add value to your articles.
>
> Please remember, We only offer you links that add value to your articles, and we pay promptly for each link that is placed.
>
> Just reply to this email and I'd be happy to discuss the remuneration involved and get you started,
>
> Thanks and have a great day,
> Gareth

It's almost as if he thinks the euphemisms will cover up the fact that this is an SEO payola scheme.* I'm not in a position where I would ever need to accept an offer like that, but you can see how many bloggers would be—and their editors and publishers would likely never know.

To give you a sense of the numbers, Henry Blodget, the founder of *Business Insider*, once explained that his writers need to generate three times the number of pageviews required to pay for their own salary and benefits, as well as a share of the overhead, sales, hosting, and Blodget's cut, to be worth hiring. In other words, an employee making sixty thousand dollars a year would need to produce upward of 1.8 million pageviews a month, every month, or they're out.[4] This is no easy task. I'd argue it's getting harder over time as people get better at getting traffic and flood the market with inventory.

YouTubers face similarly tough economics. YouTube sells and serves the ads, takes a substantial cut, and passes the rest to the creator. Most of these figures are not public, but a decent account can hope to make about one dollar for every thousand views (less than one penny per click). I remember working with the very popular multiplatinum rock band Linkin Park and realizing their account, which had done over one hundred million views at that time, would earn them barely six figures—to be split among six guys, a manager, a lawyer, and a record label. These kinds of rates force channels big and small to churn out videos constantly to make money. Every view is only a penny in their pocket.

Social media influencers are straight-up mercenary. Through various ad networks you can actually pay influential accounts to post prewritten messages or endorse products.

In order to promote one of Tucker's books, I got a Twitter account with more than four hundred thousand followers to say: "FACT: People will do anything for money"—for twenty-five dollars. For a few hundred dollars more I tricked dozens of other accounts into posting humiliating promotional messages that pushed the book to a number two debut on the *New*

---

*Here's another one, sent to me a few days later by someone named Billy Smith who runs a site called CheckCorner.com: "I would love to get a mention on The Next Web or any other website that you write for. I am open to negotiation and would be willing to do either a sponsored post or pay you for the mention."

*York Times* bestseller list. One blog headline summed it up well: TUCKER MAX PROVES YOU CAN PAY CELEBRITIES TO TWEET WHATEVER YOU WANT.[5] It occurs to me now that sponsored tweets (and Instagram posts and Snapchat stories) would be a very easy way to propagate conspiracy theories or fringe ideas.* Is there any easier way to legitimize an idea than to have it repeated? And here celebrities are, willing to do that at a couple dollars a pop.

If all these numbers sound small—and they do to me—it isn't simply because bloggers are getting shafted. It's because what they produce isn't worth all that much. Political analyst Nate Silver once estimated that the median user-contributed article on the *Huffington Post* was worth only three dollars in revenue to the company.[6] So even if they were paid fairly for their contributions, it wouldn't be much of a paycheck. Silver looked at high-profile articles by former U.S. secretary of labor Robert Reich that did 547 comments and 27,000 pageviews and concluded that they'd be worth only about two hundred dollars—an amount for which a man like that usually wouldn't get out of bed. Most articles from the currently unpaid contributors generate significantly less revenue than that.

## RIPE FOR EXPLOITATION

All this means that if bloggers want to get rich—or even cover their rent—they've got to find other ways to get paid. That's where people like me come in—with boatloads of free stuff.

One of the quickest ways to get coverage for a product online is to give it away for free to bloggers (they'll rarely disclose their conflict of interest). At American Apparel I had two full-time employees whose job was to research fashion bloggers—girls who post photos of their outfits each day to thousands of readers who imitate them—and send them our newest garments. I would offer an affiliate ad deal to the most popular girls that would pay them a commission each time someone bought something from our site after seeing their photos. I'm sure you're shocked to read how often their posts featured something from American Apparel.

---

*Or to sell expensive tickets to a half-baked, half-planned concert and call it Fyre Festival!

When I promoted movies, tours of the set or invitations to the premiere worked wonders in getting blog coverage. When I worked with bands, concert tickets, or even just an e-mail from the artist, could make most bloggers starstruck enough to give me what I needed. And that's nothing compared to what Samsung did: As an advertiser on *Business Insider*, Samsung paid for a *Business Insider* staffer to go to Barcelona to cover the Mobile World Congress. Thankfully, the writer disclosed this relationship. But in that very disclosure, he copped to feeling "pretty warm and fuzzy about Samsung" as a result of the generous offer. For marketers, it's all about encouraging those feelings however possible.[7]

But this is just free swag and perks. The easiest way for bloggers to make *real* money is to transition to a job with an old media company or a tech company. They can build a name and sell it to a sucker, just like their owners and investors are trying to do. Once a blogger builds a personal brand—through scoops or controversy or major stories—they can expect a cushy job at a magazine or start-up desperate for the credibility and buzz that these attributes offer. These lagging companies can then tell shareholders, "See, we're current!" or "We're turning things around!"

This revolving door has a peculiar influence on coverage, as is to be expected. What blogger is going to do real reporting on companies like Google, Facebook, or Twitter when there is the potential for a lucrative job down the road? What writer is going to burn a source if they view their job as a networking play?

For my part, I've lost track of the bloggers whose names I have helped make by giving them big stories (favorable and to my liking) and watched transition into bigger gigs at magazines, newspapers, and editorships at major blogs. In fact, the other day I was driving in Los Angeles and noticed a billboard on La Cienega Boulevard with nothing but a large face on it: the face of a video blogger who I'd started giving free clothes to back when his videos did a few thousand views apiece. Now his videos do millions of views, and he has a show on HBO. If you invest early in a blogger, you can buy your influence very cheaply.

In most cases, they know what I am doing and don't care. If blog publishers are constantly looking for an exit, then their bloggers are too. They both want money from the same big media companies. They don't care if the scandals they write about are real or made up, or if their sources are biased or self-serving—as long as the blogger gets something out of it.

## THE *REAL* CONFLICT OF INTEREST

We take it as self-evident that journalists shouldn't be paid off by people they write about or have financial investments (like owning a stock they're reporting on) in their field. The conflict would shape the coverage and corrupt their writing. So for a second I was pleasantly surprised to read pretty much that exact sentiment in a post by former *Gawker* writer Hamilton Nolan titled "New Rules for Media Ethics." He said it plainly: "Media people—reporter, commentator, or otherwise—shouldn't have a financial stake in what they're reporting on."

But then I realized how hypocritical it *all* was, since Nolan is being paid by how many views his posts do. His financial interest isn't in *what* he writes about but in *how* he writes. In the pay-per-pageview model, every post is a conflict of interest.

Take this *Vice* piece, "Why Texas Can't Seem to Fall in Love with In-N-Out Burger," which from the headline is making a sweeping, seemingly verifiable claim—that Texans are rejecting the West Coast burger chain. But upon reading the article you find that the actual evidence for such a claim is . . . that the In-N-Out locations in Texas have a sub-four-star rating on Yelp. Seriously. That's it!* The reporter is exaggerating a claim with little validity—because that's where the traffic is. He doesn't care about In-N-Out's stock price. He cares about his own stock in that story. And later, when a financial reporter sees a potential angle in reporting on the decline of the once-great private company, he can say, "Last year, *Vice* reported that . . ." and on and on and on.

I've never had to buy influence directly, but you can see how craven writers like that are easily corruptible. It's not a far walk from flimsy story to fake story.

---

*I tweeted at the writer when I saw it: "I'm curious on the data that Texas isn't embracing In N Out other than it doesn't have 5*s on Yelp. That seems like a reach?" He replied: "I was drawing off my experience of living in Texas around the time In-N-Out opened and the conversations I would have with people about it." In other words, it was based on *nothing*.

To their credit, most sites explicitly forbid the kind of payola as best they can. Others allow it. Medium.com, a platform I love, is really a site made up of many different channels. Those channels are allowed to sell access and articles to willing buyers. I know this because after getting one of these offers, I e-mailed an editor at *Medium* to report the corruption and was told such deals are considered aboveboard.

"There's no difference," philosopher and provocateur Nassim Taleb said, "between a journalist at *The Guardian* and the restaurant owner in Milan, who, when you ask for a taxi, calls his cousin who does a tour of the city to inflate the meter before showing up. Or the doctor who willfully misdiagnoses you to sell you a drug in which he has a vested interest." Most corruption is not obvious. The incentive for bloggers to write bigger, to write simpler, to write more controversially or, conversely, more favorably, to not waste time or resources on research or fact-checking, to write more often than is warranted because it will get them the traffic they need, is hard to spot, but it is there. And it is warping what you see and hear—and what is written about you and your friends when they find themselves in the spotlight.

Writing online is often called a "digital sweatshop" for good reason.* "Ceaseless fight for table scraps" might be another phrase for it. Or in the immortal words of Henry Kissinger: The reason the knives are so sharp online is because the pie is so small.

---

*Somebody once joked that I should name my small ranch in Texas "The Content Farm" because that's what paid for it.

# V

## TACTIC #2

## TELL THEM WHAT THEY WANT TO HEAR

{ Even though credibility is all you have to sell, it's not enough anymore. Credibility is not working as a business model. Credibility of journalism is at an all-time low, anyway. }

**—KELLY MCBRIDE, POYNTER INSTITUTE**

THE PROBLEM OF JOURNALISM, SAYS EDWARD JAY EP-
stein in his book *Between Fact and Fiction*, is simple. Journalists are rarely
in a position to establish the truth of an issue themselves, since they didn't
witness it personally. They are "entirely dependent on self-interested
'sources'" to supply their facts. Every part of the news-making process is
defined by this relationship; everything is colored by this reality.

Who are these self-interested sources? Well, anyone selling a product,
a message, or an agenda. People like me.

When the *New York Times* publishes leaked documents, there is an
implicit understanding that they have at least attempted to verify their
validity. The same goes for the identity of the source who gave it to them.
Online, "anonymous" means something else entirely. Quotes and tips are
drawn from unsolicited, untraced e-mails or angry comments pulled
from comments sections, or sent in by people who have something to gain
from it. I know, because I have been this kind of source dozens of times,
and it was never for anything important. My identity is never verified.

Today, the online-driven news cycle is going a million miles a minute
in a million directions. The *New York Times* may still *try* to verify their
sources, but it hardly matters, because no one else does. This creates endless opportunities for people like me to slip in and twist things to my
liking. As Epstein said, the discrepancy between what actually happened
and the version of what happened provided by sources is an enormous
gray area. Of all such areas, it's where I have the most fun and direct
influence.

# THE DELIBERATE LEAK

Once during a lawsuit I needed to get some information into the public discussion of it, so I dashed off a fake internal memo explaining the company's position, printed it out, scanned it, and sent the file to a bunch of blogs as if I were an employee leaking a "memo we just got from our boss." The same bloggers who were uninterested in the facts when I informed them directly gladly put up EXCLUSIVE! and LEAKED! posts about it. They could tell my side of the story because I told it to them in words they wanted to hear. More people saw it than ever would have had I issued an "official statement."

I once had a client who had been subjected to a complete hit job of a piece by a major newspaper. The writer of the article had actually been running their own hater blog about the company they then "objectively" reported on. When the client complained to the writer's editor, the editor shrugged it off. To reply, I simply had the client write a long e-mail to his staff explaining what happened and laying out the complete (and embarrassing) case against the article. Then we forwarded that e-mail to a media reporter at a different outlet, who published it in full. The e-mail read well and was quite damning—because it had been written for the express purpose of being made public. The original outlet had no choice but to respond and will hopefully think twice about a hatchet job like that in the future.

Another time I had some promotional images for a Halloween campaign I also couldn't use, because of copyright concerns. I still wanted them seen, so I had one of my employees e-mail them to *Jezebel* and *Gawker* and write, "I shouldn't be doing this but I found some secret images on the American Apparel server and here they are." The post based on this lie did ninety thousand views. The writer wrote back a helpful tip: No need to leak me info from your company e-mail address; you might get caught. I thought, *But how else could she be sure they were real?*

It was funny at the time. Then a few months later, a U.S. congressman allegedly exchanged e-mails with a girl on craigslist and sent her a shirtless photo of himself. The girl forwarded this photo and the incriminating e-mail correspondence that supposedly occurred along with it to *Gawker* (which owns *Jezebel*). *Gawker* posted it, and the congressman immediately resigned.

Knowing now that an anonymous tip to *Gawker* had the power to end the career of a U.S. congressman took a little of the fun out of it for me. Scratch that—now my personal knowledge of how sourcing works online genuinely scares me.*

## PRESS RELEASE 2.0

When I first started in PR, all of the leading web gurus were proclaiming the death of the press release. Good riddance, I thought. Journalists *should* care too much about what they write to churn out articles and posts based on press releases.

I could not have been more wrong. Before long I came to see the truth: Blogs love press releases. It does every part of their job for them: The material is already written; the angle laid out; the subject newsworthy; and, since it comes from an official newswire, they can blame someone else if the story turns out to be wrong.

As a 2010 study by Pew Research Center's Project for Excellence in Journalism found:

> As news is posted faster, often with little enterprise reporting added, the official version of events is becoming more important. We found official press releases often appear word for word in first accounts of events, though often not noted as such.[1] [emphasis mine]

So I started putting out press releases all the time. Open a new store? Put out a press release. Launch a new product? Put out a press release. Launch a new *color* of a new product? Press release. A blogger might pick it up. And even if no outlets do, press releases through services like PRWeb are deliberately search-engine optimized to show up well in Google results indefinitely. Most important, investing sites like Google

---

*I hope you can also see how a deliberate leak could be used to create a distraction *cough* Trump's 2005 tax returns *cough*. Who would resist? Even if the intentions are so transparent, a juicy enough scoop can't be ignored.

Finance, CNN Money, Yahoo! Finance, and Motley Fool all automatically syndicate the major release wires. If you're a public company with a stock symbol, the good news in any release you put out shows up right in front of your most important audience: stockholders. Minutes after you put it out, it's right there on the company's stock page in the "Recent News" section, eagerly being read by investors and traders.

I quickly learned that not everyone saw this as harmless, low-hanging media fruit. My instinct is not illegal profit, but for those who have it, blogs' blind faith in press releases presents opportunities. It did for New York stockbroker Lambros Ballas: He was charged by the Securities and Exchange Commission for issuing fake online press releases about the stocks of companies like Google, Disney, and Microsoft and seeding them on blogs and finance forums. On the fake news of an acquisition offer from Microsoft, shares of Local.com jumped 75 percent in one day, after which he and other traders dumped all their shares and moved on to pumping other stocks on fake news.[2] In Austin a man named Christopher French was fined forty thousand dollars by the SEC for pumping up stocks via articles on SeekingAlpha.com under fake names. The fake names weren't the problem. The problem was that he was paid at least sixteen thousand dollars by the companies to write those articles. When I later saw reports of a man who planned to set off explosive devices at Target so he could buy their stock at a discount and profit from the eventual rebound, I thought: *Man, somebody should have told this guy there is a much, much easier way to do that.*

It's stunning how much news is now driven by such releases—reputable or otherwise. A LexisNexis search of major newspapers for the words "in a press release" brings back so many results that the service actually attempts to warn you against trying, saying, "This search has been interrupted because it will return more than 3,000 results. If you continue with this search it may take some time to return this information." Same goes for the phrases "announced today" and "told reporters." In other words, newspapers depended on marketing spam literally too many times to count in the last year.

A Google blog search for "said in a press release" (meaning they quoted directly from a release) brings back 307,000 results for the same period as the LexisNexis search, and more than 4 million for all time. "Announced today" brings up more than 32,000 articles for a single week. If you get specific, an internal search of *TechCrunch* brings up more than 5,000 articles using "announced today" and 7,000 attributed citations to press releases. This pales in comparison to the *Huffington Post*, whose bloggers have written the words "announced today" more than 50,000 times and cited press releases more than 200,000 times. And, of course, there is also talkingpointsmemo.com, whose name unintentionally reveals what most blogs and newspapers carelessly pass on to their readers: prewritten talking points from the powers that be.

Anyone can now be that power. Anyone can give blogs their talking points. To call it a seller's market is an understatement. But it's the only thing I can think of that comes close to describing a medium in which dominant personalities like tech blogger Robert Scoble can nostalgically repost things on his Google+ account like the "original pitch" for publicity that the iPad start-up Flipboard had sent him. It's a great time to be a media manipulator when your marks actually love receiving PR pitches.

## NOT EVEN NEEDING TO BE THE SOURCE

Bloggers are under incredible pressure to produce, leaving little time for research or verification, let alone for speaking to sources. In some cases, the story they are chasing is so crazy that they don't want to risk doing research, because the whole facade would collapse.

In my experience, bloggers operate by some general rules of thumb: If a source can't be contacted by e-mail, they probably can't be a source. I've talked to bloggers on the phone only a few times, ever—but thousands of times over e-mail. If background information isn't publicly or easily available, it probably can't be included. Writers are at the mercy of official sources, such as press releases, spokesmen, government officials, and media kits. And these are for the instances when they even bother to check anything.

Most important, they're at the mercy of *Wikipedia*, because that's where they do their research. Too bad people like me manipulate that too. Nothing illustrates this better than the story of a man who, as a joke, changed the name of comedian and actor Russell Brand's mother on

*Wikipedia* from Barbara to Juliet. When Brand took his mother as his date to the Academy Awards shortly after, the *Los Angeles Times* ran the online headline over their picture: RUSSELL BRAND AND HIS MOTHER JULIET BRAND . . .

I remember sitting on the couch at Tucker Max's house one January when something occurred to me about his then on-and-off-again bestseller. "Hey, Tucker, did you notice your book made the *New York Times* list in 2006, 2007, and 2008?" (Meaning the book had appeared on the list at least once in all three years, but *not* continuously.) So I typed it up, sourced it, and added it to *Wikipedia*, delineating each year.* Not long after I posted it, a journalist cribbed my "research" and did us the big favor of having poor reading comprehension. He wrote: "Tucker Max's book has spent over 3 years on the *New York Times* Bestseller List." Then we took this and doubled up our citation on *Wikipedia* to use this new, more generous interpretation.

This is a cycle I have watched speed up but also descend into outright plagiarism. I can't divulge the specifics, but I commonly see uniquely worded or selectively edited facts that paid editors inserted into *Wikipedia* show up later in major newspapers and blogs with the exact same wording (you'll have to trust me on when and where).

*Wikipedia* acts as a certifier of basic information for many people, including reporters. Even a subtle influence over the way that *Wikipedia* frames an issue—such as criminal charges, a controversial campaign, a lawsuit, or even a critical reception—can have a major impact on the way bloggers write about it. It is the difference between "So-and-so released their second album in 2011" and "So-and-so's first album was followed by the multiplatinum and critically lauded hit . . ." You change the descriptors on *Wikipedia*, and reporters and readers change their descriptors down the road.

A complete overhaul of one high-profile starlet's *Wikipedia* page was once followed less than a week later by a six-page spread in a big tabloid

---

*On occasion I have instructed a client to say something in an interview, knowing that once it is covered we can insert it into *Wikipedia*, and it will become part of the standard media narrative about them. We seek out interviews in order to advance certain "facts," and then we make them doubly real by citing them on *Wikipedia*.

that so obviously used our positive and flattering language from *Wikipedia* that I was almost scared it would be its own scandal.

It's why you have to control your page. Otherwise you risk putting yourself in the awkward position a friend found himself in when profiled by a reporter at a national newspaper, who asked: "So, according to *Wikipedia* you're a failed screenwriter. Is that true?"

## TRUST ME, I'M AN EXPERT

It's not a stretch to convince anyone that it's easy to become a source for blogs. Cracking the mainstream media is much harder, right? Nope. There's actually a tool designed expressly for this purpose.

As I mentioned in the preface, there is a site called HARO (Help a Reporter Out), founded by PR man Peter Shankman, that connects hundreds of "self-interested sources" to willing reporters every day. It is the de facto sourcing and lead factory for journalists and publicists. According to the site, nearly thirty thousand members of the media have used HARO sources, including the *New York Times*, the Associated Press, the *Huffington Post*, and everyone in between.

What do these experts get out of offering their services? Free publicity, of course. In fact, "Free Publicity" is HARO's tagline. I've used it myself to con reporters from ABC News to Reuters to *The Today Show*, and yes, even the vaunted *New York Times*. Sometimes I don't even do it myself. I just have an assistant pretend to be me over e-mail or on the phone.

The fact that my eyes light up when I think of how to use HARO's services to benefit myself and my clients should be illustrative. If I was tasked with building someone's reputation as an "industry expert," it would take nothing but a few fake e-mail addresses and speedy responses to the right bloggers to manufacture the impression. I'd start with using HARO to get quoted on a blog that didn't care much about credentials, then use that piece as a marker of authority to justify inclusion in a more reputable publication. It wouldn't take long to be a "nationally recognized expert who has been featured in _____, _____, and _____." The only problem is that it wouldn't be real.

Journalists say HARO is a research tool, but it isn't. It is a tool that manufactures self-promotion to look like research. Consider alerts like

> URGENT: [E-mail redacted]@aol.com needs NEW and LITTLE known resources (apps, Websites, etc.) that offer families unique ways to save money.*

This is not a noble effort by a reporter to be educated but an all too common example of a lazy blogger giving a marketer an opportunity to insert themselves into their story. Journalists also love to put out bulletins asking for sources to support stories they are already writing.

> [E-mail Redacted]@gmail.com needs horror story relating to mortgages, student loans, credit reports, debt collectors, or credit cards.

> URGENT: [E-mail Redacted]@abc.com is looking for a man who took on a new role around the house after losing his job.

There you have it—how your bogus trend-story sausage is made. In fact, I even saw one HARO request by a reporter hoping "to speak with an expert about how fads are created." I hope whoever answered it explained that masturbatory media coverage from people like her has a lot to do with it.

While HARO essentially encourages journalists to look for sources who simply confirm what they were already intending to say, the practice spreads far beyond that singularly bad platform. Instead of researching a topic and communicating their findings to the public, journalists from all sorts of outlets simply grab obligatory—but artificial—quotes from "experts" to validate their pageview journalism. To the readers it appears as legitimate news. To the journalist, they were just reverse engineering their story from a search engine–friendly premise.

---

*Ten days later the reporter generously gave a second marketer a chance at the same story, with this request: "URGENT: [E-mail redacted]@aol.com needs NEW or LITTLE known app or website that can help families with young kids save money."

An example: In 2015 the *New York Times* published a story on vaping. The reporter found her sources, apparently, by sending out the following tweet:

> If you're a teen that vapes and want to talk to a reporter twice your age about why you love it contact @stavernise sabrinat@nytimes.com

One of the responders quoted in that popular trend piece later claimed he made up all his answers, including his name! To prove that there is no such thing as irony, the hoaxer admitted all this to *Gawker*, who just a few days later would post their own trolling "tell us what we want to hear" call for sources in order to write a piece about *BuzzFeed*. Even worse was the BBC reporter who tweeted that they were looking for someone to comment on Beyoncé's Super Bowl performance. Someone replied recommending that the reporter speak with a fan and tagged someone who might work, but the reporter responded by revealing their true intentions, "I don't want a real fan—just someone who can say it was inappropriate that her performance was political."

Far too many stories are created with this deliberately manipulative mind-set. Marketing shills masquerade as legitimate experts, giving advice and commenting on issues in ways that benefit their clients and trick people into buying their products. I constantly receive e-mails from bloggers and journalists asking me to provide "a response" to some absurd rumor or speculative analysis. They just need a quote from me denying the rumor (which most people will skip over) to justify publishing it. The agenda has already been set, and the reader is being set up to be fooled.

## THE HIT JOB

A few years ago, I got tired of a speed trap camera near my house and decided to do something about it. Now, I could have gone to a public hearing, voiced my objections to these cameras, and hoped that someone in the media might report on it. But that would have left too much up to chance. Instead, I e-mailed a reporter at the *Times-Picayune*—the struggling but influential daily newspaper in New Orleans—who I knew had covered this beat before. I explained to him that I was a new resident to the city who had gotten dozens of unfair tickets (including three in one day). I emphasized what an undue financial burden such tickets had been on my girlfriend when she had gotten some herself and how she'd been reduced to tears by a rude city employee when she protested. I sent in a picture of a busted sign near the camera. I played the victim, saying that I felt shaken down, as if a bully had taken my lunch money.

Now, these things were true, but still, I deliberately framed them in the most sympathetic way. I made it seem like I couldn't afford the tickets (I could) and I was clearly very biased—I was angry and wanted to get back at someone. The result: A week later, a front-page story in the *Times-Picayune*, featuring the picture I'd taken and my bully quote in huge block letters, which spurred hundreds of comments and a ton of other coverage. A month later, the city announced it was changing course on the policy and state legislators debated banning the cameras altogether.

Of course, I've also seen it go the other direction. A disgruntled ex-employee can make themselves seem very sympathetic, and reporters rarely ask *why* this person might be suddenly so eager to talk to them. This is something companies need to be very careful about.

I once gave a talk to an association of pork farmers about this very issue. They were tired of being slammed in the press by vegetarians and other animal rights activists. I'm not a supporter of factory farming, but I empathized with their position. Biased sources were always going to be more sympathetic as sources than big rich farmers ever will be. The same thing was true about the *Gawker* story I mentioned above—the writer was actively looking for disgruntled ex-employees of *BuzzFeed* to anonymously attack their old company.

## FORGETTING MY OWN BULLSHIT

As I was gathering up press done on me personally over the years, I came across an article I'd forgotten. I'd posted a question on my blog: "What is the classic book of the '80s and '90s?" It was a discussion I'd had with several friends; we were wondering what book teachers would assign to students to learn about this era fifty years from now. This discussion was picked up and featured by *Marginal Revolution*, a blog by the economist Tyler Cowen, which does about fifty thousand pageviews a day. His post said:

## What is the classic book of the '80s and '90s?

*BY TYLER COWEN ON SEPTEMBER 3, 2008 AT 6:42 PM IN BOOKS | PERMALINK*

That's <u>Ryan Holiday's</u> *query*. This is not about quality, this is about "representing a literary era" or perhaps just representing the era itself. I'll cite *Bonfire of the Vanities* and *Fight Club* as the obvious picks. Loyal **MR** reader Jeff Ritze is thinking of Easton Ellis ("though not *American Psycho*"). How about you? Dare I mention John Grisham's *The Firm* as embodying the blockbuster trend of King, Steele, Clancy, and others? There's always Harry Potter and graphic novels.

Coming across this struck me not only because I am a big Tyler Cowen fan but because I am *also* Jeff Ritze. Or was, since that's one of the fake names I used to use and had apparently e-mailed my post as a tip to *Marginal Revolution*. Of course Jeff Ritze was thinking about Bret Easton Ellis—he's one of my favorite authors. I even answered a variant of that question as me—Ryan Holiday—a few years later for a magazine that was interviewing me.

I had been the source of this article and totally forgotten about it. I wanted traffic for my site, so I tricked Tyler, and he linked to me. (Sorry, Tyler!) It paid off too. A blog for the *Los Angeles Times* picked up the discussion from Cowen's blog and talked positively about "twentysomething Ryan Holiday." *Marginal Revolution* is a widely read and influential blog, and I never would have popped up on the *Los Angeles Times*'s radar without it. Best of all, now, when I write my bio, I get to list the *Los Angeles Times* as one of the places I've gotten coverage. Score.*

---

*To make it weirder, I saw recently that someone else using the name Jeff Ritze left a negative review on Amazon about one of my books.

# NO TIME TO CHECK

Why did Jeff Ritze manage to appear as a media source? Why did Ryan Holiday, the guy writing a book on media manipulation, not raise any flags on HARO? Because no one has time to check these things out. Epstein's line about journalists being wholly dependent on sources was true in 1975, but over forty years later, bloggers are even more dependent and have even less time for vetting.

At the *New York Observer*, where I am an editorial adviser, it has been exhausting to watch pranksters and liars prey on reporters. In 2015 a marketing agency named Boogie created an April Fool's prank around an app called Chute, which apparently prevented your iPhone from breaking. The only problem was that they pulled this prank in March. The founder played a convincing character and told a compelling story, which the company then revealed and apologized for after the story ran. A year or so later, another hoax occurred over a Kickstarter campaign for a fake app called Adoptly (essentially Tinder for adoption and fostering).

What the *Observer* writer explained in her piece about falling for the first hoax explains what a tough position reporters are in:

> The Observer *regrets our error. We admit we should have spotted a few red flags, like Chute's limited Twitter following, and the fact that Chute's "founder" sounded oddly monotone when we interviewed him over the phone.*
>
> *But we must note that unlike several recent media stunts, our story on Chute was not the product of overly credulous re-blogging. Boogie constructed an entire landing page and imaginary founder of the app, replete with screenshots and mock-ups of the product. The* Observer *interviewed the fictitious founder, played by Boogie's in-house product manager, but he lied over the phone, and in his answers to follow-up questions via email.*

While there were some red flags, writers don't have time to check all of them. In 1975 a reporter might have had a few days to work on a piece; now they have a few minutes. There is also a complicated dance between the source and the reporter. A source is interested in seeing the story happen because it's good for their business, and often the blogger is interested in seeing it go the exact same way—because their business is publishing stories, not saying no to potential scoops. They suspend disbelief because it's good for business.

I like to point out a *Gizmodo* story where the site fell for a hoax and got thirty thousand pageviews for its poorly researched story headlined MAL-FUNCTIONING CAKE RUINS PARTY AND SPEWS LIQUOR ALL OVER OIL TY-COONS.[3] They then followed up after the prank was revealed with a story titled VIRAL VIDEO OF SHELL OIL PARTY DISASTER IS FAKE, UNFORTU-NATELY and got ninety thousand pageviews out of it.[4] That's two stories instead of zero—so do you see why they don't question sources?

Manipulators and self-promoters, on the other hand, pray this kind of due diligence never happens. And sadly, they know it likely won't.

# VI

## TACTIC #3

# GIVE 'EM WHAT SPREADS

Study the top stories at Digg or MSN.com and you'll notice a pattern: the top stories all polarize people. If you make it threaten people's 3 Bs—behavior, belief, or belongings—you get a huge virus-like dispersion.

—TIM FERRISS, #1 *NEW YORK TIMES* BESTSELLING AUTHOR

You and we know that it is generally just the best and most valuable things that do not find their echo immediately.

—KURT WOLFF, PUBLISHER OF FRANZ KAFKA

THE ADVICE THAT MIT MEDIA STUDIES PROFESSOR Henry Jenkins gives publishers and companies is blunt: "If it doesn't spread, it's dead." With social sharing comes traffic, and with traffic comes money. Content that isn't shared isn't worth anything.

For someone tasked with advancing narratives in the media, the flip side of this advice is equally straightforward: If it spreads, you're golden. Blogs don't have the resources to advertise their posts, and bloggers certainly don't have the time to work out a publicity launch for something they've written. Every blog, publisher, and oversharer in your Facebook feed is constantly looking to post things that will take on a life of their own and get attention, links, and new readers with the least work possible. Whether that content is accurate, important, or helpful doesn't even register on their list of priorities.

If the quality of their content doesn't matter to bloggers, do you think it's going to matter to marketers? It's never mattered to me. So I design what I sell to bloggers based on what I know (and they think) will spread. I give them what they think will go viral online—and make them money.

## A TALE OF TWO CITY SLIDESHOWS

If you're like me, you've sat and stared in fascination at the pictures of the ruins of Detroit that get passed around the internet. We've all gaped at the stunning shots of the cavelike interior of the decaying United Artists Theater and the towering Michigan Central Station that resembles an abandoned Gothic cathedral. These beautiful high-res photo slideshows are impressive pieces of online photojournalism . . . or so you think.

Like everyone else, I ate up these slideshows, and I even harbored a guilty desire to go to Detroit and walk through the ruins. My friends know this and send me the newest ones as soon as they come out. When I see the photos I can't help thinking of this line from *Fight Club*:

> In the world I see, you're stalking elk through the damp canyon forests around the ruins of Rockefeller Center. . . . You'll climb the wrist-thick kudzu vines that wrap the Sears Tower. And when you look down, you'll see tiny figures pounding corn, laying strips of venison on the empty car pool lane of some abandoned superhighway.

To see a broken, abandoned American city is a moving, nearly spiritual experience, one you are immediately provoked to share with everyone you know.

A slideshow that generates a reaction like that is online gold. An ordinary blog post is only one page long, so a thousand-word article about Detroit would get one pageview per viewer. A slideshow about Detroit gets twenty per user, hundreds of thousands of times over, while premium advertising rates are charged against the photos. A recent twenty-picture display posted by the *Huffington Post* was commented on more than four thousand times and liked twenty-five thousand times on Facebook. And that was the second time they'd posted it. The *New York Times*'s website has two of their own, for a total of twenty-three photos. The *Guardian*'s website has a sixteen-pager. Time.com's eleven-pager is the top Google result for "Detroit photos." We're talking about millions of views combined.

One would think that any photo of Detroit would be an instant hit online. Not so. A series of beautiful but sad photographs of foreclosed and crumbling Detroit houses and their haggard residents was posted on Magnum Photos's site in 2009, well before most of the others. It shows the same architectural devastation, the same poverty and decline. While the slideshow on the *Huffington Post* received four thousand comments within days, these photos got twenty-one comments over *two years*.[1]

## ONE SPREADS, THE OTHER DOESN'T

In an article in the *New Republic* called "The Case Against Economic Disaster Porn," Noreen Malone points out that one thing stands out about the incredibly viral photographs of Detroit: Not a single one of the popular photos of the ruins of Detroit has a person in it. That was the difference between the *Huffington Post* slideshows and the Magnum photos—Magnum dared to include human beings in their photos of Detroit. The photos that spread, on the other hand, are deliberately devoid of any sign of life.[2]

Detroit has a homeless population of nearly twenty thousand, and in 2011 city funding for homeless shelters was cut in half. Thousands more live in foreclosed houses and buildings without electricity or heat, the very same structures in the pictures. These photos don't just omit people. Detroit is a city overrun by stray dogs, which roam the city in packs hunting and scavenging for food. Conservative figures estimate that there are as many as 50,000 wild dogs living in Detroit and something like 650,000 feral cats. In other words, you can't walk a block in Detroit without seeing heartbreaking and deeply wounded signs of life.

You'd have to try not to. And that's exactly what these slideshow photographers do. Why? Because all that is depressing. As Jonah Peretti, the virality expert behind both the *Huffington Post* and *BuzzFeed*, believes, "if something is a total bummer, people don't share it." And since people wouldn't share it, blogs won't publish it. Seeing the homeless and drug addicts and starving, dying animals would take away all the fun.* It'd make the viewers feel uncomfortable, and unsettling images are not conducive to sharing. Why, Peretti asks, would anyone—bloggers or readers—want to pass along bad feelings?[3]

The economics of the web make it impossible to portray the complex situation in Detroit accurately. It turns out that photos of Detroit that spread do so precisely *because they are dead.* Simple narratives like the haunting ruins of a city spread and live, while complicated ones like a city filled with real people who desperately need help don't.

One city. Two possible portrayals. One is a bummer; one looks cool. Only one makes it into the *Huffington Post* slideshow.

---

*Another photo for a much more popular *New York Times* slideshow says it all. The picture is of the abandoned Michigan Central Station, and in the snow on the floor are dozens of crisscrossing footprints and a door. There are no people. "Don't worry," it seems to say. "There's no reason to feel bad. Everybody left already. Keep gawking."

My point here is not sociological so much as it is practical. Let me explain how this ends up affecting companies and public figures. Say someone accuses you of something horrible—obviously those salacious allegations make for good copy. The problem is that the truth—your response—is often much less interesting than the accusations. Getting caught stepping out on a spouse might generate headlines. The fact that the marriage was long over, that you were both just waiting for the paperwork to be finished and, in fact, the spouse has moved on too—that's starting to involve a lot of variables. It's complicated. It's boring. No one is getting excited to share that.

This is something I have to explain to clients in crisis PR situations all the time. I say, "Look, if your response isn't more interesting than the allegations, no one is going to care. You might as well not bother." So a lot of times people end up having to take a lot of untrue crap because they don't have much recourse with a media that cares more about what spreads than what is accurate. Or, worse, you get an escalation: Someone accuses someone of something. The person has to respond that it's all made up and the person is only doing it because "[insert a different lie]," and it just goes round and round and round.

## EXTREME VERSIONS OF REALITY

Look at a slideshow of Detroit and you might think the world is ending. Look at some headlines on Upworthy.com and you might be forgiven for thinking that the world is doing awesome. Because just as extreme negativity is one effective technique, so is cloying and saccharine positivity. Check out these headlines that did millions of views:

**"Watch a Preacher Attack Gay Marriage and Totally Change His Mind on the Spot"**

**"A Message to Everyone Out There Who Thinks They Aren't Beautiful in Pictures"**

## "She Tried to Kill Herself and It Didn't Work. See How She Made All That into Something Beautiful"

## "She Didn't Think the Love of Her Life Was Romantic Enough. Then She Looked out Her Office Window"

## "Move Over, Barbie—You're Obsolete"

If only the world were actually this way. . . .

Indeed, the site's editors know that it is not. But folks at Upworthy are filtering and exclusively delivering only a small sliver of reality—one that is all sweet and no sweat. Even Upworthy's pop-up message designed to snag e-mails is illustrative of their approach: "It's nice to be reminded of the good in the world. And it should happen more often." Then you give them your e-mail address and they begin to bombard you with "reminders."

On the opposite end of the spectrum, much of the media is obsessed with what might be called "outrage porn." Here are a few headlines from Salon.com to prove my point.

## "Patton Oswalt Makes Asian Name Joke, in Response to Racist KTVU News Report"

## "Another Portuguese Water Dog? The Obamas Should Have Made a Different Statement"

## "The Onion Thinks Incest, Statutory Rape Is Hilarious"

## "Gawker's 'Privilege Tournament' Is All About White Anger"

# " 'The Conjuring': Right-wing, Woman-Hating and Really Scary"

Is the world terrible or is it awesome? Can't these people just make up their minds? The press, Martin Amis once noted, "is more vicious than the populace." It's also more positive and gushy—as Upworthy is—than normal people. Why? Because it's paid to be.

In 2010, Jonah Berger, an expert on virality at the Wharton School, looked at seven thousand articles that made it onto the *New York Times* Most E-mailed list. (A story from the *Times* is shared on Twitter once every four seconds, making the list one of the biggest media platforms on the web.) The researchers' results confirm almost everything we see when content like the sensational ruin porn of Detroit goes viral.[4] For me it confirmed every intuition behind my manipulations.

According to the study, "the most powerful predictor of virality is *how much anger an article evokes*" [emphasis mine]. I will say it again: *The most powerful predictor of what spreads online is anger.* Is it any surprise that there is so much anger-provoking content online, then? No wonder the outrage I created for Tucker's movie worked so well. According to Berger's study, anger has such a profound effect that one standard deviation increase in the anger rating of an article is the equivalent of spending an additional three hours as the lead story on the front page of NYTimes.com.

Again, extremes in any direction have a large impact on how something will spread, but certain emotions do better than others. For instance, an equal shift in the positivity of an article is the equivalent of spending about 1.2 hours as the lead story. It's a significant but clear difference. The angrier an article makes the reader, the better. But happy works too.

The researchers found that while sadness is an extreme emotion, it is a wholly unviral one. Sadness, like what one might feel to see a stray dog shivering for warmth or a homeless man begging for money, is typically a low-arousal emotion. Sadness depresses our impulse for social sharing. It's why nobody wanted to share the Magnum photos but everybody gladly shared the ones on the *Huffington Post*. The *HuffPo* photos were *awe*-some; they made us angry, or they surprised us. Such emotions trigger a desire to act—they are arousing—and that is exactly the reaction a publisher hopes to exploit. "People get viral content wrong," Eli Pariser, the founder of *Upworthy*, told *Businessweek*. "They imagine that the reason people share stuff is to have a laugh. But a huge part of sharing is being passionate about something, about shedding light on what really matters."

In turn, it's what marketers exploit as well. A powerful predictor of whether content will spread online is valence, or the degree of positive or negative emotion a person is made to feel. Both extremes are more desirable than anything in the middle. Regardless of the topic, the more an article makes someone feel good *or* bad, the more likely it is to make the Most E-mailed list. I want to take things that people are passionate about and connect them to my products or clients—to get people worked about them, to get them talking. No smart marketer is ever going to push a story with the stink of reasonableness, complexity, or mixed emotions. We want to rile people up. We want to provoke you into talking.

The problem is that facts are rarely clearly good or bad. They just *are*. The truth is often boring and complicated. Navigating this quandary forces marketers and publishers to conspire to distort this information into something that will register on the emotional spectrum of the audience. To turn it into something that spreads and to drive clicks. Behind the scenes I work to crank up the valence of articles, relying on scandal, conflict, triviality, titillation, and dogmatism. Whatever will ensure transmission.

The press is often in the evil position of needing to go negative and play tricks with your psyche in order to drive you to share their material online. For instance, in studies where subjects are shown negative video footage (war, an airplane crash, an execution, a natural disaster), they become more aroused, can better recall what happened, pay more attention, and engage more cognitive resources to consume the media than nonnegative footage.[5] That's the kind of stuff that will make you hit "share this." They push your buttons so you'll press theirs.

Things must be negative but not too negative. Hopelessness, despair—these drive us to do nothing. Pity, empathy—those drive us to do something, like get up from our computers to act. But anger, fear, excitement, laughter, and outrage—these drive us to spread. They drive us to do something that makes us feel as if we are doing something, when in reality we are only contributing to what is probably a superficial and utterly meaningless conversation. Online games and apps operate on the same principles and exploit the same impulses: Be consuming without frustrating, manipulative without revealing the strings.

For those who know what levers provoke people to share, media manipulation becomes simply a matter of packaging and presentation. All it takes is the right frame, the right angle, and millions of readers will willingly send your idea or image or ad to their friends, family, and coworkers on your behalf. Bloggers know this, and want it badly. If I can hand them a story that may be able to deliver, who are they to refuse?

## GIVING THE BASTARDS WHAT THEY WANT

When I designed online ads for American Apparel, I almost always looked for an angle that would provoke. Outrage, self-righteousness, and titillation all worked equally well. Naturally, the sexy ones are probably those you remember most, but the formula worked for all types of images. Photos of kids dressed up like adults, dogs wearing clothes, ad copy that didn't make any sense—all high-valence, viral images. If I could generate a reaction, I could propel the ad from being something I had to pay for people to see (by buying ad inventory) to something people would gladly post on the front page of their highly trafficked websites.

I once ran a series of completely nude (not safe for work, or NSFW) advertisements featuring the porn star Sasha Grey on two blogs. They were very small websites, and the total cost of the ads was only twelve hundred dollars. A naked woman with visible pubic hair + a major U.S. retailer + blogs = a massive online story.

The ads were picked up online by *Nerve*, *BuzzFeed*, *Fast Company*, *Jezebel*, *Refinery29*, NBC New York, *Fleshbot*, the *Portland Mercury*, and many others. They eventually made it into print as far away as *Rolling Stone* Brazil, and they're still being passed around online. The idea wasn't ever to sell product directly through the ads themselves, since the model wasn't really wearing any of it—and the sites were too small, anyway. I knew that just the notion of a company running pornographic advertisements on legitimate blogs would be too arousing (no pun intended) for share-hungry sites and readers to resist. I'm not sure if I was the first person to ever do this, but I certainly told reporters I was. Some blogs wrote about it in anger, some wrote about it in disgust, and others loved it and wanted more. The important part was that they wrote about it at all. It ended up being seen millions of times, and almost none of those views were on the original sites where we paid for the ads to run.

I wasn't trying to create controversy for the sake of controversy. The publicity from the spectacle generated tens of thousands of dollars in sales, and that was my intention all along. I had substantial data to back up the fact that chatter correlated with a spike in purchases of whatever product was the subject of the conversation. Armed with this information, I made it my strategy to manufacture chatter by exploiting emotions of high valence: arousal and indignation. I'd serve ads in direct violation of the standards of publishers and ad networks, knowing that while they'd inevitably be pulled, the ads would generate all sorts of brand awareness in the few minutes users saw them. A slight slap on the wrist or pissing off some prudes was a penalty well worth paying for, for all the attention and money we got.

In the case of American Apparel, this leveraged advertising strategy I developed was responsible for taking online sales from $40 million to nearly $60 million in three years—with a minuscule ad budget.

## HIDDEN CONSEQUENCES

I use these tactics to sell products, and they work—lots of product gets sold. But I have come to know that the act of constantly provoking and fooling people has a larger cost. Nor am I the only one doing it.

You probably don't remember what happened on February 19, 2009, and that's because nothing notable happened—at least by any normal standard. But to those who make their living by "what spreads," it was an incredibly lucrative day, and for our country, it was a costly one.

During what was supposed to be a standard on-camera segment, CNBC correspondent Rick Santelli had a somewhat awkward meltdown on the floor of the Chicago Mercantile Exchange. He went off script and started ranting about the Obama administration and the then recently passed stimulus bill. Then he started yelling about homeowners who bit off bigger mortgages than they could chew, and Cuba, and a bunch of other ridiculous stuff. Traders on the floor began to cheer (and jeer), and he ended by declaring that he was thinking about having a "Chicago Tea Party" to dump derivatives into Lake Michigan. The whole thing looked like a shit show.

CNBC was smart. They recognized from the reaction of their anchors—which ranged from horror to mild bemusement—that they had something valuable on their hands. Instead of waiting for the video to be discovered by bloggers, news junkies, message boards, and mash-up artists, CNBC posted it on their own website immediately. While this might seem like a strange move for a serious media outlet to make, it wasn't. The *Drudge Report* linked to the clip, and it immediately blew up. This was, as Rob Walker wrote for the *Atlantic* in an analysis of the event, a core principle of our new viral culture: "Humiliation should not be suppressed. It should be monetized." Instead of being ashamed of its crappy television journalism, CNBC was able to *make extra money* from the millions of views it generated.

The real reason the Santelli clip spread so quickly was a special part of toying with the valence of the web. Originally the clip spread as a joke, with the degree of amusement being determined by where the viewers fit on the political spectrum. But where some saw a joke, others saw a truth teller. An actual Chicago Tea Party was organized. Disaffected voters genuinely agreed with what he had said. Santelli wasn't having a meltdown, some thought; he was just as angry as they were. On the other end of the spectrum, not only were people *not* laughing, they were horribly offended. To them this was proof of CNBC's political bias. Some were so serious that they endorsed a conspiracy theory (launched by a blog on Playboy.com, of all places) that alleged the meltdown was a deliberately planned hoax funded by conservative billionaires to energize the right wing.

Regardless of how they interpreted Santelli's rant, *everyone's* reactions were so extreme that few of them were able to see it for what it truly was: a mildly awkward news segment that should have been forgotten.

Of all the political and financial narratives we needed in 2009, this was surely not it. Reasoned critiques of leveraged capitalism, solutions that required sacrifice—these were things that did not yield exciting blog posts or spread well online. But the Santelli clip did. CNBC fell ass first into the perfect storm of what spreads on the web—humiliation, conspiracy theories, anger, frustration, humor, passion, and possibly the interplay of several or all of these things together. And then, as if this weren't enough, the whole absurd charade happened again in 2015 and 2016 with the rise of the pro-Trump faction of the Republican Party. It's almost as if the insatiable media appetite for stories that will make people angry and outraged has created a market for anger and outrage. It's almost as if that's why we're so divided and upset.

Oh wait, that *is* why!

As Chris Hedges, the philosopher and journalist, wrote, "In an age of images and entertainment, in an age of instant emotional gratification, we neither seek nor want honesty or reality. Reality is complicated. Reality is boring. We are incapable or unwilling to handle its confusion."

As a manipulator, I certainly encourage and fuel this age. So do the content creators. The media don't really care how they come off as long as they can sell ads against the traffic they generate. And the audience says they're okay with it too—voting clearly with their clicks. We're all feeding that monster.

This may seem like nothing. It's just people having fun, right? Sure, my deliberately provocative ads, once caught, quickly do disappear and awareness subsides—just like all viral web content. Roughly 96 percent of the seven thousand articles that made the Most E-mailed list in the *New York Times* study did so only once. In almost no cases did an article make the list, drop off, and then return. They had a brief, transitory existence and then disappeared. But though viral content may disappear, its consequences do not—be it a toxic political party or an addiction to cheap and easy attention.

The omission of humanity from the popular slideshows of Detroit is not a malicious choice. Nor is the injection of pseudo-positivity into viral stories on other sites. There was no person like me behind the scenes hoping to mislead you. There was no censorship or overt manipulation (in most cases). In fact, there are thousands of the other, more realistic photos out there. Yet, all the same, the public is misinformed about a situation that we desperately need to solve. Through the selective mechanism of what spreads—and gets traffic and pageviews—we get suppression not by omission but by transmission.

The web has only one currency, and you can use any word you want for it—valence, extremes, arousal, powerfulness, excitement—but it adds up to false perception. Which is great if you're a publisher but not if you're someone who cares about the people in Detroit or you're someone who wants to find common ground with their neighbors. What thrives online is not the writing that reflects anything close to the reality in which you and I live. Nor does it allow for the kind of change that will create the world we wish to live in.

It does, however, make it possible for me to do what I do. And people like me will keep doing it as long as that is true.

# VII

## TACTIC #4

## HELP THEM TRICK THEIR READERS

1. "Is Sitting a Lethal Activity?"

2. "How Little Sleep Can You Get Away With?"

3. "Is Sugar Toxic?"

4. "What's the Single Best Exercise?"

5. "Do Cellphones Cause Brain Cancer?"

—SCREENSHOT OF THE MOST POPULAR
ARTICLES BOX, *NEW YORK TIMES
MAGAZINE*, APRIL 16, 2011

I am not surprised when anonymous scribblers
write and publish falsehoods, or make criticism on
matters which they know nothing about or which
they are incapable of comprehending. It is their
trade. They live by it.

—GENERAL WILLIAM
TECUMSEH SHERMAN

ARE LOADED-QUESTION HEADLINES POPULAR? YOU bet. As Brian Moylan, a former *Gawker* writer, once bragged, the key is to "get the whole story into the headline but leave out just enough that people will want to click."

Nick Denton knows that being evasive and misleading is one of the best ways to get traffic and increase the bottom line. In a memo to his bloggers he gave specific instructions on how to best manipulate the reader for profit:

> *When examining a claim, even a dubious claim, don't dismiss with a skeptical headline before getting to your main argument. Because nobody will get to your main argument. You might as well not bother. . . . You set up a mystery—and explain it after the link. Some analysis shows a good question brings twice the response of an emphatic exclamation point.*

I have my own analysis: When you take away the question mark, it usually turns their headline into a lie. The reason bloggers like to use it is because it lets them get away with a false statement that no one can criticize. After the reader clicks, they soon discover that the answer to the "question" in their headline is obviously "No, of course not." But since it was posed as a question, the blogger wasn't *wrong*—they were only asking. "Did Glenn Beck Rape and Murder a Young Girl in 1990?" Sure, I don't know, whatever gets clicks.

Bloggers tell themselves that they are just tricking the reader with the headline to get them to read their nuanced, fair-er articles. But that's a lie. (I actually read the articles, and they're rarely any better than the headline would suggest.) This lie is just one bloggers tell to feel better about themselves, and you can exploit it. So give them a headline; it's what they want. Let them rationalize it privately however they need to.

When I want someone to write about my clients, I might intentionally exploit their ambivalence about deceiving people. If I am giving them an official comment on behalf of a client, I leave room for them to speculate by not fully addressing the issue. If I am creating the story as a fake tipster, I ask a lot of rhetorical questions: Could [some preposterous misreading of the situation] be what's going on? Do you think that [juicy scandal] is what they're hiding? And then I watch as the writers pose those very same questions to their readers in a click-friendly headline. The answer to my questions is obviously "No, of course not," but I play the skeptic about my own clients—even going so far as to say nasty things—so the bloggers will do it on the front page of their site.

Manipulators trick the bloggers, and they trick their readers. We both want the clicks and so we get them together. This arrangement is great for the traffic-hungry bloggers, for people like me, and my attention-seeking clients. Readers might be better served by posts that inform them about things that really matter. But, as you saw in the last chapter, stories with useful information are less likely to be shared virally than other types of content.

For example: Movie reviews, in-depth tutorials, technical analysis, and recipes are typically popular with the initial audience and occasionally appear on Most E-mailed lists. But they tend not to draw significant amounts of traffic from other websites. They are less fun to share and spread less as a result. This may seem counterintuitive at first, but it makes perfect sense according to the economics of online content. Commentary on top of someone else's commentary or advice is cumbersome and often not very interesting to read. Worse, the writer of the original material may have been so thorough as to have solved the problem or proffered a reasonable solution—two very big dampers on getting a heated debate going.

For blogs, practical utility is often a liability. It is a traffic killer. So are other potentially positive attributes. It's hard to get trolls angry enough to comment while being fair or reasonable. Waiting for the whole story to unfold can be a surefire way to eliminate the possibility for follow-up posts. So can pointing out that an issue is frivolous. Being the voice of reason does also. No blogger wants to write about another blogger who made him or her look bad.

To use an exclamation point, to refer back to Denton's remark, is to be final. Being final, or authoritative, or helpful, or any of these obviously positive attributes is avoided, because they don't bait user engagement. And engaged users are where the money is.

## GETTING ENGAGED WITH CONTENT

Before objecting that "user engagement" is a good thing, let's look at it in practice. Pretend for a second that you read an article on some blog about an issue that makes you angry. Angry enough that you *must* let the author know how you feel about it: You go to leave a comment.

You must be logged in to comment, the site tells you. Not yet a member? Register now. Click, a new page comes up with ads all across it. Fill out the form on the page, handing over an e-mail address, gender, and city, and hit "submit." Damn, got the CAPTCHA wrong, so the page reloads with another ad. Finally get it right and get the confirmation page (another page, another ad). Check e-mail: Click this link to validate your account. Registration is now complete, it says: another page and another ad. Log in. More pages, more ads, but you have finally "engaged."

This is how it is everywhere. It might take as many as ten pageviews to leave a comment on a blog the first time. Or when you see a mistake in an article and fill out the Send Corrections form? Well, first they'll need your e-mail address, and then they ask if you want to receive daily e-mails from them.*

When you do this, you are the sucker. The site doesn't care about your opinion; they care that, by eliciting it, they score free pageviews. Of course, this kind of manipulation is not new—it is endemic to all kinds of media.

Jonah Peretti of *BuzzFeed* once pointed out how reality TV sucks in viewers.

> *The reason that reality TV work[ed] well for a time is that the classic reality TV formula, in the beginning, was the tribal council and*

---

*Or they ask you to use Facebook as your login so they can better target you to advertisers.

*somebody getting eliminated. So you could have 50 percent of the show being boring filler and you're kind of wanting to change the channel but you're like, "Oh, but I wonder if my favorite person's going to get eliminated." So you have to watch to the end to see the elimination. In a way, that was a way of gaming time.*

And now online publishers have found their own ways to manipulate audiences—whether it's with the nineteen-page slideshow or exploiting the so-called headline gap or auto-playing a video.

As Andrew Ledvina, a former Facebook data scientist, bluntly put it, "The fundamental purpose of most people at Facebook working on data is to influence and alter people's moods and behaviour. They are doing it all the time to make you like stories more, to click on more ads, to spend more time on the site."

Blogs don't care about the issues they are provoking outrage about, and social networks don't care what people are being social about—they care about what it means for them, how much traffic and time on site it generates. I remember reading a video games blog post of all the reasons why someone should buy the new PlayStation console over the new Xbox. It got like 500,000 views. Then the same blogger turned around and wrote about all the reasons to buy the Xbox over the PlayStation. It also got 500,000 views. There were plenty of comments and shares on both.

Nobody involved actually cares what any of these people think or are feeling—not even a little bit. They just care about the reaction and the attention.

## WHO IS THE REAL TROLL?

Mike Cernovich, the alt-right blogger, is often called a troll by people in the media. He has come to embrace the label. He is smart enough to know that if he says something offensive, liberals won't be able to resist responding— he knows that this response will generate attention and raise his profile.

But if this is so obvious and clear, isn't the media at least partly responsible if they give blatant trolling attempts a wider audience? Aren't they complicit?

I believe they are. I'll give you an example: In 2012 my client Tucker Max was looking to make a large charitable donation but wanted to get publicity for it. He had a joke in one of his books that he had paid for so many abortions over the years, Planned Parenthood should name a clinic after him. My idea was to make that a reality—to buy the naming rights for a clinic. As it turned out, Planned Parenthood had not only been viciously stripped of its Texas funding by Republican governor Rick Perry but also were looking to open a new clinic in North Texas. It seemed like a win-win-win: Tucker gets press for something positive (for a change), Planned Parenthood reaches a new audience, and women get access to potentially lifesaving services.

But this was also clearly trolling—it was going to piss a lot of people off and promote his new book. When Planned Parenthood declined to accept the donation (after a few weeks of serious negotiations), I wrote an article about it for Forbes.com titled "Why Did Planned Parenthood Turn Down $500,000?" I then sent this link to dozens of sites I had researched based on their probability of writing about the story. Many of them picked it up, including the *Huffington Post*, *Jezebel*, *Salon*, the *Daily Beast*, KVUE-TV Austin, KFDM-TV Beaumont, KGO-AM San Francisco, the *New York Daily News*, *Gothamist*, and the *Houston Chronicle*. I had one of my employees compile all the links from the stunt. The first wave of attention alone was eight pages, single spaced. *Eight pages of links.* After we submitted some of these links to Reddit, the story traded up the chain and got even more important outlets involved.

Again, I fully admit this was trolling, but I assert that the media participated in it. They certainly benefited from it. The *Huffington Post* story alone got over ten thousand Facebook shares. The coverage added up to eight pages of links—just think of how many views, clicks, and shares that is. I was hoping for fifty thousand pageviews for the whole thing. Cumulatively, it did *millions*. I hoped for a couple blog pickups. We got coverage in two hundred–plus outlets. Not only did I get all this press for free, but Forbes.com *paid* me a thousand dollars cash for my share of the pageviews the controversy generated.

So who is the real troll here? Me, or my friends in the media?

# YOU ARE BEING PLAYED

A click is a click and a pageview is a pageview. A blogger doesn't care how they get it. Their bosses don't care. They just want it.*

The headline is there to get you to view the article, end of story. Whether you get anything out of it after is irrelevant—the click already happened. A comments section is meant to be used. So are those share buttons at the bottom of every post. The dirty truth, the brilliant writer Venkatesh Rao pointed out, is that

> *social media isn't a set of tools to allow humans to communicate with humans. It is a set of embedding mechanisms to allow technologies to use humans to communicate with each other, in an orgy of self-organizing. . . . The Matrix had it wrong. You're not the battery power in a global, human-enslaving AI, you are slightly more valuable. You are part of the switching circuitry.*[1]

As a user, the fact that blogs are unhelpful, deliberately misleading, or unnecessarily incendiary might exhaust and tire you, but Orwell reminded us in *1984*: "The weariness of the cell is the vigor of the organism."

So goes the art of the online publisher: To string the customer along as long as possible, to deliberately *not* be helpful, is to turn simple readers into pageview-generating machines. Publishers know they have to make each new headline even more irresistible than the last, the next article even more inflammatory or less practical to keep getting clicks. It's a vicious cycle in which, by screwing the reader and getting screwed by me, they must screw the reader harder next time to top what they did before.

And sure, sometimes people get mad when they realize they've been tricked. Readers don't like to learn that the story they read was baseless. Readers get pissed when they find out the link they clicked was for some

---

*As Richard Greenblatt—maybe the greatest hacker who has ever lived—told *Wired* in 2010, "There's a dynamic now that says, let's format our web page so people have to push the button a lot so that they'll see lots of ads. Basically, the people who win are those who manage to make things the most inconvenient for you."

sponsored content. Bloggers aren't pleased when they fall for a hoax. But this is a calculated risk bloggers and I both take, mostly because the consequences are so low. In the rare cases we're caught red-handed, it's not like we have to give the money we made back. As Juvenal joked, "What's infamy matter if you can keep your fortune?"

# VIII

## SELL THEM SOMETHING THEY CAN SELL (TO BE IN THE NEWS, *MAKE* NEWS)

{ A newspaper is a business out to make money through advertising revenue. That is predicated on its circulation and you know what the circulation depends on. . . .

**—HARLAN POTTER IN *THE LONG GOODBYE*, BY RAYMOND CHANDLER** }

I'M NO MEDIA SCHOLAR, BUT IN MY FANATICAL SEARCH for what makes bloggers tick, I turned to every media historian I could find and devoured their work. Through these experts I started to see that the very way that blogs get their articles in front of readers predetermines what they write. Just like the yellow press of a century ago, blogs are at the mercy of unrelenting pressures that compel them to manipulate the news, and be manipulated in turn.

History lessons can be boring but trust me, in this case, a brief one is worth it, because it unlocks a new angle of media control. Once you know how the newsmen sell their product, it becomes easier to sell them yours.

There are three distinct phases of the newspaper (which have been synonymous with "the news" for most of history). It begins with the party press, moves to the infamous yellow press, and ends finally with the stable period of the modern press (or press by subscription). These phases contain surprising parallels to where we are today with blogs—old mistakes made once more, manipulations made possible again for the first time in decades.

## THE PARTY PRESS

The earliest forms of newspapers were a function of political parties. These were media outlets for party leaders to speak to party members, to give them the information they needed and wanted. It's a part of news history that is often misunderstood or misused in discussions about media bias.

These papers were not some early version of Fox News. They usually were one-man shops. The editor-publisher-writer-printer was the dedicated steward of a very valuable service to that party in his town. The service was the ability to communicate ideas and information about important issues. These political papers sold the service to businessmen, politicians, and voters.

It was sold on a subscription model, typically about ten dollars a year. A good paper might have only a thousand or so subscribers, but subscriptions were almost always mandatory for party members in certain areas, which was a kind of patronage.

This first stage of journalism was limited in its scope and impact. Because of the size and nature of its audience, the party press was not in the *news* business. They were in the editorial business. It was a different time and style, one that would be eclipsed by changes in technology and distribution.

## THE YELLOW PRESS

Newspapers changed the moment that Benjamin Day launched the *New York Sun* in 1833. It was not so much his paper that changed everything but his way of selling it: on the street, one copy at a time. He hired the unemployed to hawk his papers and immediately solved a major problem that had plagued the party presses: unpaid subscriptions. Day's "cash and carry" method offered no credit. You bought and walked. The *Sun*, with this simple innovation in distribution, invented the news and the newspaper. A thousand imitators followed.

These papers weren't delivered to your doorstep. They had to be exciting and loud enough to fight for their sales on street corners, in barrooms, and at train stations.* Because of the change in distribution methods and the increased speed of the printing press, newspapers truly became *news*papers. Their sole aim was to get new information, get it to print faster, get it more exclusively than their competition. It meant the decline of the editorial. These papers relied on gossip. Papers that resisted failed and went out of business—like abolitionist Horace Greeley's disastrous attempt at a gossip-free cash-and-carry paper shortly before Day's.

---

*Day invented the Help Wanted and Classifieds sections around this time. It was a highly effective way to drive daily sales.

In 1835, shortly after Day began, James Gordon Bennett, Sr., launched the *New York Herald*. Within just a few years the *Herald* would be the largest-circulation daily in the United States, perhaps in the world. It would also be the most sensational and vicious.

It was all these things not because of Bennett's personal beliefs but because of his business beliefs. He knew that the newspaper's role was "not to instruct but to startle." His paper was anti-black, anti-immigrant, and anti-subtlety. These causes sold papers—to both people who loved them for it and people who hated them for it. And they bought and they bought.

Bennett was not alone. Joseph Pulitzer, a sensationalist newsmonger long before his name was softened by years of association with the prestigious Pulitzer Prize, enforced a similar dictum with his paper: The *World* would be "not only cheap but bright, not only bright but large." It *had* to be, in order to sell thousands of papers every morning to busy people in a busy city.

The need to sell every issue anew each day creates a challenge I call the "One-Off Problem." Bennett's papers solved it by getting attention however they could.

The first issue of Bennett's *Herald* looked like this: first page—eye-catching but quickly digestible miscellany; second page—the heart of the paper, editorial and news; third page—local; fourth page—advertising and filler. There was something for everyone. It was short, zesty. He later tried to emphasize quality editorial instead of disposable news by swapping the first two pages. The results were disastrous. He couldn't sell papers on the street that way.

The One-Off Problem shaped more than just the design and layout of the newspaper. When news is sold on a one-off basis, publishers can't sit back and let the news come to them. There isn't enough of it, and what comes naturally isn't exciting enough. So they must create the news that will sell their papers. When reporters were sent out to cover spectacles and events, they knew that their job was to cover the news when it was there and to make it up when it was not.*

---

*In other words, we've been tearing down public figures on bogus charges for more than a century. Do yourself a favor and look up the Fatty Arbuckle scandal for a sobering look at One-Off consequences.

This is exactly the same position blogs are in today. Just as blogs are fine with manipulators easing their burden, so too were the yellow papers.

Yellow papers paid large sums to tipsters and press agents. Fakes and embellishments were so pervasive that the noted diarist and lawyer George Templeton Strong almost didn't believe the Civil War had commenced. In April 1861 he wrote in his diary that he and his friends had deliberately ignored noise they heard—the streets "vocal with newsboys" shouting "Extra!—a *Herald*. Get the bombardment of Fort Sumter!!!"—for nearly four blocks, because they were convinced it was a "sell." That Fort Sumter issue, which Strong broke down and bought, sold 135,000 copies in a single day. It was the most-printed issue in the history of the *Herald*. The success of that war was what drove yellow papers to clamor for (and some say create) the Spanish-American War. As Benjamin Day put it: "We newspaper people thrive best on the calamities of others."

Media historian W. J. Campbell once identified the distinguishing markers of yellow journalism as follows:

- Prominent headlines that screamed excitement about ultimately unimportant news

- Lavish use of pictures (often of little relevance)

- Impostors, frauds, and faked interviews

- Color comics and a big, thick Sunday supplement

- Ostentatious support for the underdog causes

- Use of anonymous sources

- Prominent coverage of high society and events

Besides the Sunday supplement, does any of that sound familiar? Perhaps you should pull up Mic.com or the *Huffington Post* for a second to jog your memory.

This realization was a common occurrence during the writing of this book. I often felt I could take media criticism written one hundred years ago, change a few words, and describe exactly how blogs work. Knowing the trademarks of yellow journalism from this era made it possible for me to know how to give blogs what they "want" in this era. But more on that later.

As the daily sales of these papers soared, they became incredibly attractive opportunities for advertisers, particularly with the advent of large corporations and department stores. The rates these new advertisers paid propelled newspapers to boost readership even more.

Master promoters like Bennett, Pulitzer, and William Randolph Hearst delivered. Their skyrocketing circulations were driven by one thing: sensationalism. Welcome to the intersection of the One-Off Problem and ad-driven journalism.

## THE MODERN STABLE PRESS (BY SUBSCRIPTION)

Just as James Gordon Bennett embodied the era of sensational yellow journalism, another man, Adolph S. Ochs, publisher of the *New York Times*, ushered in the next iteration of news.

Ochs, like most great businessmen, understood that doing things differently was the way to great wealth. In the case of his newly acquired newspaper and the dirty, broken world of yellow journalism, he made the pronouncement that "decency meant dollars."

He immediately set out to change the conditions that allowed Bennett, Hearst, Pulitzer, and their imitators to flourish. He was the first publisher to solicit subscriptions via telephone. He offered contests to his salesmen. He gave them quotas and goals for the number of subscribers they were expected to bring in.

He understood that people bought the yellow papers because they were cheap—and they didn't have any other options. He felt that if they had a choice, they'd pick something better. He intended to be that option. First he would match his competitors' prices, and then he would deliver a paper that far surpassed the value implied by the low price.

It worked. When he dropped the price of the *Times* to one cent, circulation tripled in the first year. He would compete on content. He came up with the phrase "All the News That's Fit to Print" as a mission statement for the editorial staff two months after taking over the paper. The less known runner-up says almost as much: "All the World's News, but Not a School for Scandal."

I don't want to exaggerate. The transition to a stable press was by no means immediate, and it didn't immediately transform the competition. But subscription did set forth new conditions in which the newspaper and the newspaperman had incentives more closely aligned with the needs of their readers. The end of that wave of journalism meant that papers were sold to readers by subscriptions, and all the ills of yellow journalism have swift repercussions in a subscription model: Readers who are misled unsubscribe; errors must be corrected in the following day's issue; and the needs of the newsboys no longer drive the daily headlines.

A subscription model—whether it's music or news—offers necessary subsidies to the nuance that is lacking in the kind of stories that flourish in one-off distribution. Opposing views can now be included. Uncertainty can be acknowledged. Humanity can be allowed. Since articles don't have to spread on their own, but rather as part of the unit (the whole newspaper or album or collection), publishers do not need to exploit valence to drive single-use buyers.

With Ochs's move, reputation began to matter more than notoriety. Reporters started social clubs, where they critiqued one another's work. Some began talk of unionizing. Mainly they began to see journalism as a profession, and from this they developed rules and codes of conduct. The professionalization of journalism meant applying new ideas to how stories were found, written, and presented. For the first time, it created a sense of obligation, not just to the paper and circulation, but also to the audience.

Just as Bennett had his imitators, so did Ochs. In fact, the press has imitated the principles he built into the *New York Times* since he took it over. Even now, when someone buys a paper at a newsstand, they don't survey the headlines and buy the most sensational. They buy the paper they trust—the same goes for what radio stations they listen to and television news they watch. This is the subscription model, the brand model, invented by Ochs, internalized. It is selling on subscription and not by the story.

I'm not saying it is a perfect system by any means. I don't want to imply that newspapers in the twentieth century were paragons of honesty or accuracy or embraced change immediately. As late as the 1970s, papers like the *New Orleans Times-Picayune* were still heavily dependent on street and newsstand sales, and thus continued to play up and sensationalize crime stories.

The subscription model may have been free of the corruptive influence of the masses, but that didn't spare it from corruption from the top. As the character Philip Marlowe observed in Raymond Chandler's novel *The Long Goodbye*:

> *Newspapers are owned and published by rich men. Rich men all belong to the same club. Sure, there's competition—hard tough competition for circulation, for newsbeats, for exclusive stories. Just so long as it doesn't damage the prestige and privilege and position of the owners.*

This was incisive media criticism (in fiction, no less) that was later echoed with damning evidence by theorists such as Noam Chomsky and Ben Bagdikian. A friend put it more bluntly: "Each generation of media has a different cock in its mouth."

At least there was once an open discussion about the problems of the media. Today, not only are the toxic economics of blogs obscured, but tech gurus on the take actually defend them. We have the old problems *plus* a host of new ones.

## THE DEATH OF SUBSCRIPTION, REBIRTH OF MEDIA MANIPULATION

For most of the last century, the majority of journalism and entertainment was sold by subscription (the third phase). It is now sold again online à la carte—as a one-off. Each story must sell itself, must be heard over all the others, be it in Google News, on Twitter, or on your Facebook wall. This One-Off Problem is exactly like the one faced by the yellow press a century or more ago, and it distorts today's news just as it did then—only now it's amplified by millions of blogs instead of a few hundred newspapers. As Eli Pariser put it in *The Filter Bubble*, when it comes to news on the internet, *each article ascends the most-forwarded lists or dies an ignominious death on its own. . . . The attention economy is ripping the binding, and the pages that get read are the pages that are frequently the most topical, scandalous, and viral.*

People don't read one blog. They read a constant assortment of many blogs, and so there is little incentive to build trust. Competition for readers is on a per-article basis, taking publishers right back to the (digital) street corner, yelling, "War Is Coming!" to sell papers. It takes them back to making things up to fill the insatiable need for new news.

The Pulitzer Prize–winning biographer Robert Caro (a former reporter for *Newsday*) was interviewed by a blog called *Gothamist* around his eightieth birthday. The reporter explained to him how journalism worked these days,

*There's something called Chartbeat—it shows you how many people are reading a specific article in any given moment, and how long they spend on that article. That's called "engagement time." We have a giant flatscreen on the wall that displays it, a lot of publications do.*

Caro's response was perfect: "What you just said is the worst thing I ever heard."

The interview continues:

*[Interviewer:] Headlines and other tools . . . are used to get people to click on an article. It reduces what might be a piece of nuanced writing to the most salacious tidbit. So The Power Broker might be headlined, "Robert Moses Is A Racist Whatever." Or—and someone did this recently—you might try something like, "The 11 Most Shocking Things In The Power Broker." It just crushes all nuance.*

*[Caro:] What you just told me, I'm thinking about when I was a reporter and they were reading something of mine, and if the engagement time or whatever was two seconds, I'd shoot myself!*

He says that because he actually cares about what he writes! Because his hugely important books were designed to last, what I call "perennial sellers"—not get a short spike of attention and disappear. But sadly, the current system and the current tools with which to measure them don't encourage that kind of thing.

Think about how we consume content online. It is *not* by subscription. The only viable subscription method for blogs, RSS, is long dead.

Just look at the top referring sources of traffic to major websites and blogs. Cumulatively, these referring sources almost always account for more visitors than the site's direct traffic (i.e., people who typed in the URL). Though it varies from site to site, the biggest sources of traffic are, usually, in varying order: Google, Facebook, Twitter. The viewers were sent directly to a specific article for a disposable purpose: They're not subscribers; they are seekers or glancers.

This is great news for a media manipulator, bad news for everyone else. The death of subscription means that instead of attempting to provide value to you, the longtime reader, blogs are constantly chasing Other Readers—the mythical reader out in viral land. Instead of providing quality day in and day out, writers chase big hits like a sexy scandal or a funny video meme. Bloggers aren't interested in building up consistent, loyal readerships, whether it's via paid subscription or even e-mail, because what they really need are the types of stories that will do hundreds of thousands or millions of pageviews. They need stories that will sell.

There is this naive belief that readers have: *If news is important, I'll hear about it.* I would argue the opposite—it's mostly the least important news that will find you. It's the extreme stuff that cuts through the noise. It's the boring information, the secret stuff that people don't want you to know, that you'll miss. That's the stuff you have to subscribe to, that you pay for, that you have to chase.

As a marketer, getting something "controversial" to blow up is easy, and it's the tactic a media manipulator prefers to use over doing something "important." With limited resources and the constraints of a tight medium, there are only a handful of options: sensationalism, extremism, sex, scandal, hatred. The media manipulator knows that bloggers know that these things sell—so that's what we sell them.

Whereas subscriptions are about trust, single-use traffic is all immediacy and impulse—even if the news has to be distorted to trigger it. Our news is what rises, and what rises is what spreads, and what spreads is what makes us angry or makes us laugh. Our media diet is quickly transformed into junk food, fake stories engineered by people like me to be consumed and passed around. It is the refined and processed sugars of the information food pyramid—out of the ordinary, unnatural, and deliberately sweetened.

Inside the chaos, it is easy to mislead. Only the exciting, sensational stuff finds readers—the stories that "blow up." Reporters don't have time for follow-ups or reasoned critiques, only quick hits. Blogs are all chasing the same types of stories, the mass media chase blogs, and the readers are following both of them—and everyone is led astray.

The reason paid subscription (and RSS) was abandoned was because in a subscription economy the users are in control. In the one-off model, the competition might be more vicious, but it is on the terms of the publisher. Having followers instead of subscribers—where readers have to check back on sites often and are barraged with a stream of refreshing content laden with ads—is much better for their bottom line.

When the blogger Andrew Sullivan switched his site to a subscription model a few years ago, his analysis of the situation was striking. He called subscription the "purest, simplest model for online journalism: you, us, and a meter. Period. No corporate ownership, no advertising demands, no pressure for pageviews . . . just a concept designed to make your reading experience as good as possible, and to lead us not into temptation."

Way too many outlets are led into temptation. It's good for business and it's fun.

## BE THE NEWS YOU WANT TO SEE IN THE WORLD

Knowing all this, my strategy has always been: If I want to be written about, I do things they *have* to write about. When I advised a client to shoot the book he'd just written off into space, it wasn't for scientific exploration—it was because doing something like that is so unusual, the media couldn't resist writing about it. The same went for another author I worked with who held an atheist church service in Baton Rouge, Louisiana. We tried to name the Planned Parenthood clinic after Tucker Max because we weren't content to sit around and *hope* that people saw the book as controversial—we wanted to *do* something controversial. And all these stunts got considerable attention because the coverage was good for the outlets. They raked in all sorts of readers from it.

A few years ago, my company Brass Check got tired of dishonest marketers pretending to be able to create bestselling books that, in reality, were just Amazon.com category bestsellers—an easy feat when you can be "#1 New Releases in Freemasonry" for an hour. So we did a stunt where we illustrated just how easy it was to create these "bestsellers." It took five minutes and three dollars, and we did indeed publish a fake book that hit number one—in the "Transpersonal Movements" category. But it was the fact that we actually *did it* that allowed for all the coverage. This wasn't our opinion; it was proof. The post we wrote explaining the mechanics behind the stunt got over 500,000 views and the subsequent coverage got even more.[*] A reporter from the *Toronto Sun* re-created the stunt herself just to see if it really was that easy. It was—and that meant more front-page coverage for us. Inquiries to our company shot through the roof.

The great Daniel Boorstin called these things pseudo-events. Why does a movie have a premiere? So the celebrities will show up and the media will cover it. Why does a politician hold a press conference? For the attention. A quick run down the list of pseudo-events shows their indispensability to the news business: press releases, award ceremonies, red-carpet events, product launches, anniversaries, grand openings, "leaks," the contrite celebrity interview after a scandal, the sex tape, the tell-all, the public statement, controversial advertisements, marches on Washington, press junkets, and on and on.

These pseudo-events—put on for the sole purpose of generating headlines and media coverage—are real in the sense that they do exist, but they are fake in the sense that they are completely artificial. The event is not intended to accomplish anything itself but instead to introduce certain narratives into the media. If nobody covered them, it'd be like a tree falling in the woods. Pseudo-events are the media manipulator's secret weapon.

---

*You can read it here: http://observer.com/2016/02/behind-the-scam-what-does-it-takes-to-be-a-bestselling-author-3-and-5-minutes/.

Blog economics both depend on and indulge in pseudo-events even more than old media—they thrive on the artificiality. Because it's planned, staged, and designed for coverage, pseudo-news is a kind of news subsidy. It is handed to blogs like a glass of water to a thirsty man. As deadlines get tighter and news staffs get smaller, fake events are exactly what bloggers need. More important, because they are clean, clear, and not constrained by the limits of what happens naturally, pseudo-events are typically much more interesting to publishers than real events.

If you do something newsworthy—that is, by today's standards, something controversial, strange, weird, hilarious, or polarizing—you will be in the news. It's that simple.

# IX

## TACTIC #6

## MAKE IT ALL ABOUT THE HEADLINE

A [*Huffington Post*] story . . . headlined: "Obama Rejects Rush Limbaugh Golf Match: Rush 'Can Play With Himself.'" It's digital nirvana: two highly searched proper nouns followed by a smutty entendre, a headline that both the red and the blue may be compelled to click, and the readers of the site can have a laugh while the headline delivers great visibility out on the web.

**—DAVID CARR, *NEW YORK TIMES***

FOR MEDIA THAT LIVES AND DIES BY CLICKS (THE ONE-Off Problem) it all comes down to the headline. It's what catches the attention of the public—yelled by a newsboy or seen on a search engine. In a one-off world there is nothing more important than the pitch to prospective buyers. And they need many exciting new pitches every day, each louder and more compelling than the last. Even if reality is not so interesting.

That's where I come in. I make up the news; blogs make up the headline.

Although it seems easy, headline writing is an incredibly difficult task. The editor has to reduce an entire story down to just a few units of text—turning a few hundred- or thousand-word piece into just a few words, period. In the process it must express the article's central ideas in an exciting way.

According to Gabriel Snyder, the former managing editor of Gawker Media and later an editor at the traffic powerhouse TheAtlantic.com, blog headlines are "naked little creatures that have to go out into the world to stand and fight on their own." Readers and revenue depend on the headline's ability to win this fight.

In the days of the yellow press the front pages of the *World* and the *Journal* went head to head every day, driving each other to greater and greater extremes. As a publisher, William Randolph Hearst obsessed over his headlines, tweaking their wording, writing and rewriting them, riding his editors until they were perfect. Each one, he thought, could steal another one hundred readers away from another paper.[1]

It worked. As a young man Upton Sinclair remembered hearing the newsboys shouting "Extra!" and seeing the headline WAR DECLARED! splashed across the front page of Hearst's *New York Evening Journal*. He parted with his hard-earned pennies and read eagerly, only to find rather a big difference between what he'd thought and what he'd bought. It was actually "War (may be) Declared (soon)."[2]

They won, he lost. That same hustle happens online every day. Each blog is competing not just to be *the* leader on a particular story but against all the other topics a reader could potentially commit to reading about (and also against checking e-mail, chatting with friends, and watching videos, or even pornography). So here we are on our fancy MacBooks and wireless internet, stuck again with the same bogus headlines we had in the nineteenth century.

From today:[*]

### Naked Lady Gaga Talks Drugs and Celibacy

### Hugh Hefner: I Am Not a Sex Slave Rapist in a Palace of Poop

### The Top Nine Videos of Babies Farting and/or Laughing with Kittens

### How Justin Bieber Caught a Contagious Syphilis Rumor

### WATCH: Heartbroken Diddy Offers to Expose Himself to Chelsea Handler

### Little Girl Slaps Mom with Piece of Pizza, Saves Life

### Penguin Shits on Senate Floor

---

*My favorite: The *Washington Post* accidentally published this headline to an article about weather preparedness: "SEO Headline Here" ("SEO" stands for "search engine optimization").

Now compare those to some of these classic headlines from 1898 to 1903:

## WAR WILL BE DECLARED IN FIFTEEN MINUTES

## AN ORGY OF GRAY-HAIRED MEN, CALLOW YOUTHS, GAMBLERS, ROUGHS, AND PAINTED WOMEN—GENERAL DRUNKENNESS—FIGHTS AT INTERVALS—IT WAS VICE'S CARNIVAL

## COULDN'T SELL HIS EAR, OLD MAN SHOOTS HIMSELF

## OWL FRIGHTENS WOMAN TO DEATH IN HOSPITAL

## BULLDOG TRIES TO KILL YOUNG GIRL HE HATES

## CAT GAVE TENANTS NIGHTLY "CREEPS"*

As magician Ricky Jay once put it, "People respond to and are deceived by the same things they were a hundred years ago." Only today the headlines are being yelled not on busy street corners but on noisy news aggregators and social networks.

Just like in the past, many online headlines exploit the so-called curiosity gap. If you don't know what that is, this headline from FastCompany.com satirizes it perfectly: "Upworthy's Headlines Are Insufferable. Here's Why You Click Anyway." I've even done this with many of my own

---

*For some more fun headlines, the walls of Keens Steakhouse in New York City are covered with amazing front-page headlines from its glory days in the late nineteenth century.

popular articles: "Here's the Strategy Elite Athletes Follow to Perform at the Highest Level" (over 500,000 total views) or "The Real Reason We Need to Stop Trying to Protect Everyone's Feelings" (over one million views). You have to click to figure out what it means (and you can't unclick once you have!).

In a subscription model the headline of any one article competes only with the other articles included in the publication. The articles on the front page compete with those on the inside pages, and perhaps with the notion of putting down the paper entirely, but they do not, for the most part, compete head to head with the front pages of other newspapers. The subscription takes care of that—you already made your choice. As a result, the job of the headline writer for media consumed by subscription is relatively easy. The reader has already paid for the publication, so they'll probably read the content in front of them.

The predicament of an online publisher today is that it has no such buffer. Its creative solution, as it was one hundred years ago, is exaggeration and lies and bogus tags like EXCLUSIVE, EXTRA, UNPRECEDENTED,[*] and PHOTOS in the requisite CAPITAL LETTERS. They overstate their stories, latching on to the most compelling angles and parading themselves in front of the public like a prostitute. They are more than willing for PR people and marketers to be their partners in crime.

## PICK ME, PICK ME!

In 1971, the *New York Times*, a subscription paper, had a big story on their hands. A disillusioned government analyst named Daniel Ellsberg leaked thousands of documents, now known as the Pentagon Papers, proving that the United States had systematically deceived the public and the world to go to war with Vietnam.

Could a one-off paper have gotten away with this headline?: VIETNAM ARCHIVE: A CONSENSUS TO BOMB DEVELOPED BEFORE '64 ELECTION, STUDY SAYS.

---

[*]This one is my favorite, because the thing always happens to be not only *not* unprecedented but hilariously pedestrian.

Because that's what the *New York Times* ran, still successfully reaching everyone in the country with the big news. They could afford to be reasoned, calm, and circumspect while still aggressively pursuing the story, despite the shameful efforts of the U.S government to block its publication. The truth and significance of the Pentagon Papers were enough.

Compare this to a headline I conned *Jezebel* into writing for a non-event: EXCLUSIVE: AMERICAN APPAREL'S REJECTED HALLOWEEN COSTUME IDEAS (AMERICAN APPALLING).[3] It did nearly 100,000 pageviews. Not only was the headline overstated, but as I said before, the leak was *fake*. I just had one of my employees send over some extra photos that couldn't be used for legal reasons.

Again, as a writer who sees my own articles dressed up with fancy headlines online, I'm often amused by the absurdity. Take a piece with EXCLUSIVE INTERVIEW as the tag. Does that mean that I am the only person to ever interview that person, or that this site is the only place that has *my* interview with that person? There's really no way to know . . . unless you click.

Outside of the subscription model, headlines are intended not to represent the contents of articles but to *sell them*—to win the fight for attention against an infinite number of other blogs or papers. They must so captivate the customer that they click or plunk down the money to buy them. Each headline competes with every other headline. On a blog, every page is the front page. It's no wonder that the headlines of the yellow press and the headlines of blogs run to such extremes. It is a desperate fight. Life or death.

And what are the consequences? You're not a subscriber. You can't take your click back. They've already sold it on a real-time advertising exchange. They've already been paid for it. (And remember, if you share the article in exasperation or even sheer disgust to a friend to show them how bad it is, you're actually helping the outlet!)

The columnist and media critic Walter Lippmann once observed, "The reader expects the fountains of truth to bubble, but he enters into no contract, legal or moral, involving any risk or cost or trouble to himself. He will pay a nominal price when it suits him, will stop paying whenever it suits him, will turn to another paper when that suits him." And he said that when *a lot more* people still did pay for newspapers (and they cost literally three cents). He concluded by saying that the "newspaper editor has to be re-elected every day." That's a lot of pressure on the shoulders of an editor or writer, but imagine the pressure today, when every single article published—hundreds of them a day across a single publication—is fighting for reelection. It's going to get very noisy and there's going to be a lot of mudslinging and lying. It's the dirtiest politics there is.

For the most part, newspapers from the stable period not only had plainly stated headlines, but also had a tradition of witty headlines. Readers had time to get subtle jokes. There could be puns and allusions. There could be intelligent references. They could be understated. Things are a little different now. As they say, Google doesn't laugh (or think). Google sends literally billions of clicks a month to publishers through Google News and another three billion clicks through its search and other services.[4]

Follow a story through Google News and you'll see. The service begins by displaying twenty or so main news stories from which a reader may choose. I may read one article, or I may read five, but I likely will not read all, so each one vies for my attention—screaming, in not so many words, "Pick me! Pick me! Pick me!" Google News displays the story from a handful of outlets under each of those bold headlines. If the main headline is from CNN, the smaller headlines underneath may be from Fox News or the *Washington Post* or *Wikipedia* or *TalkingPointsMemo*. Each outlet's headline screams, "Pick me! Pick me!" and Google alludes to the rest of the iceberg lurking beneath under these chosen few: "All 522 news articles." How does one stand out against five hundred other articles? Its scream of "No, pick me! Pick me!" must be the loudest and most extreme.

For millennials, Facebook is the single biggest news source—they're not going to CNN.com or turning on the evening news to be informed; they are using Facebook as a filter, as a discovery tool for that news. A 2016 Pew Report found that 62 percent of adults get some of their news from Facebook and 18 percent get it regularly from Facebook. As with Google News, it's Facebook's algorithm that creates the competition between headlines, but in this case news is trying to be heard not just over other news but also over memes, family photos, and personal news. So it's "PICK ME! PICK ME! IGNORE YOUR SISTER'S NEW BABY! PICK ME!"

Andrew Malcolm, creator of the *Los Angeles Times*'s massive *Top of the*

*Ticket* political blog (which did 33 million readers in two years), specifically asks himself before writing a headline, "How can we make our item stick out from all the other ones?" And from this bold approach to editorial ethics comes proud election-cycle headlines such as "Hillary Clinton Shot a Duck Once" and "McCain Comes Out Against Deadly Nuclear Weapons, Obama Does Too." I'm not cherry-picking: *That's what he chose to brag about in a book of advice to aspiring bloggers.*

"We do ironic headlines, smart headlines, and work hard to make very serious stories as interesting as we can," Arianna Huffington told the *New York Times.*[5] "We pride ourselves on bringing in our community on which headlines work best."

They also do their headlines in a massive thirty-two-point font. By "best" Huffington does not mean the one that represents the story better. The question is not "Was this headline accurate?" but "Was it clicked more than the others?" The headlines must work for the publisher, not the reader. Yahoo!'s homepage, for example, tests more than 45,000 unique combinations of story headlines and photos every five minutes.[6] They too pride themselves on how they display the best four main stories they can, but I don't think their complicated, four-years-in-the-making algorithm shares any human's definition of that word.

## SPELLING IT OUT FOR THEM

It should be clear what types of headlines blogs are interested in. It's not pretty, but if that's what they want, give it to them. You don't really have a choice. They aren't going to write about you, your clients, or your story unless it can be turned into a headline that will drive traffic.

You figured out the best way to do this when you were twelve years old and wanted something from your parents: Come up with the idea and let them think they were the ones who came up with it. Basically, write the headline—or hint at the options—in your e-mail or press release or whatever you give to the blogger and let them steal it. That's what publicists are thinking when they pitch: Is there a great headline here? Because if the story is "Person You've Never Heard Of Does Something Not That Interesting," no site is going to bite. Instead, the click-friendly, share-provoking headline has to be so obvious and enticing that there is no way they can pass it up. Hell, make them tone it down. They'll be so happy to have the headline that they won't bother to check whether it's true or not.

Their job is to think about the headline above all else. The medium and their bosses force them to. So that's where you make the sale. Only the reader gets stuck with the buyer's remorse.

# TACTIC #7

## KILL 'EM WITH PAGEVIEW KINDNESS

A status update that is met with no likes (or a clever tweet that isn't retweeted) becomes the equivalent of a joke met with silence. It must be rethought and rewritten. And so we don't show our true selves online, but a mask designed to conform to the opinions of those around us.

—NEIL STRAUSS, *WALL STREET JOURNAL*

THE BREAKTHROUGH FOR BLOGGING AS A BUSINESS
was the ability to track what gets read and what doesn't. From *Gizmodo*
to the *Guardian*, sites of all sizes are open about their dependence on
pageview statistics for editorial decisions.

Editors and analysts know what spreads, what draws traffic, and what
doesn't, and they direct their employees accordingly. The *Wall Street Journal* uses traffic data to decide which articles will be displayed on its
homepage and for how long. Low-tracking articles are removed; heat-
seeking articles get moved up. A self-proclaimed web-first paper like the
*Christian Science Monitor* scours Google Trends for story ideas that help
the paper "ride the Google wave." Places like Yahoo! and Demand Media
(now Leaf Group) commission their stories in real time based on search
data. Other sites take topics trending on Twitter, Techmeme, and News-
whip.com and scurry to get a post up in order to be included in the list of
articles for a particular event. Even tiny one-person blogs eagerly check
their stat counters for the first sign of a spike.

Bloggers publish constantly in order to hit their pageview goals or quotas, so when you can give them something that gets them even one view
closer to that goal, you're serving their interests while serving yours. To
ignore these numbers in an era of pageview journalism is business suicide
for bloggers and media manipulators. And anything that pervasive presents opportunities for abuse.

I see it like this: The "Top 10 Most Read" or "Top 10 Most Popular"
section that now exists on most large websites is a compass for the editors
and publishers. But it's hardly some foolproof, reliable indicator of what's
working and what's not working. Marketers know it's not only possible
but easy to mess with the magnet inside the compass and watch as its
owner goes wildly off track.

A friend of mine at a big marketing agency would often run what he called the "leaderboard strategy." If someone wrote about one of his clients, the agency would direct lots of traffic to that article until it was the most-read piece of the day on the site and featured on the leaderboard (and once there, would get additional organic traffic). This almost always generated more coverage on that site and on other sites. Bloggers had proof that writing about his client generated traffic, and the client wrote it off as a big victory for their ego and for their business—no one ever thought to check the source of it all.

It hit me just how badly publishers were willing to grovel for a pageview handout when I placed an excerpt of a client's book on a well-known website. The day it ran, the site's editor sent me an e-mail: "Hey, we hate to ask but could you guys be sure to tweet and share the article for us?"

*Dear God*, I realized, *my client has more readers than they do.* The website needed us to attract an audience for them. They wanted the subject of the piece to send his readers over to them rather than the other way around.

As economists love to say, incentives matter. What makes the Most Popular or Most E-mailed leaderboard on Salon.com or the *New York Times* is a clear directive that tells writers what kinds of stories to head toward. If you have a large and loyal following, that's a really attractive outlet to a potential reporter—and it can be dangled accordingly: Write something I like and I'll share it with my audience.

## THE DISTURBING SCIENCE

Yellow papers had their own circulation dragons; instead of celebrity slideshows, these papers had staples like hating black people, preposterous Wall Street conspiracies, and gruesome rape and murder stories. But while in the past decisions were guided by an editor's intuitive sense of what would pander to their audience, today it is a science.

Sites employ full-time data analysts to ensure that the absolute worst is brought out in the audience. Gawker Media was one of the first publishers to display its stats on a big screen in the middle of its newsroom. The public even used to be able to look at a version of it at Gawker.com/stats. Millions of visitors and millions of dollars are to be had from content and traffic analysis. It just happens that these statistics become the handles by which manipulators can pick up and hijack the news.

It's too transparent and simple for that not to be the case. For some blog empires, the content-creation process is now a pageview-centric checklist that asks writers to think of everything *except* "Is what I am making any good?" AOL is one of these organizations, as it emphatically (and embarrassingly) outlined in a memo titled "The AOL Way." If writers and editors want to post something on the AOL platform, they must ask themselves:

> *How many pageviews will this content generate? Is this story SEO-winning for in-demand terms? How can we modify it to include more terms? Can we bring in contributors with their own followers? What CPM will this content earn? How much will this content cost to produce? How long will it take to produce?*[1]

And other such stupid questions.

Even the famed *New Yorker* writer Susan Orlean has admitted her gravitational pull toward the stories on the Most Popular lists, as a reader and as a writer. "Why, I wonder, should the popularity of a news story matter to me?" she writes.

> *Does it mean it's a good story or just a seductive one? Isn't my purpose on this earth, at least professionally, precisely to read the most unpopular stories? Shouldn't I ignore this list? Shouldn't I roam through the news unconcerned and maybe even uninformed of how many other people read this same news and "voted" for it?*[2]

But in the end these guilty pangs cannot win out. Amid the clutter and chaos of a busy site, the lists pop. The headlines scream out to be clicked. Those articles seem more interesting than everything else. Plus, hey, they appear to be vetted by the rest of the world. That can occasionally be a good thing, as Orlean points out, but is it worth it?

> *Sometimes they contain a nice surprise, a story I might not have noticed otherwise. Sometimes they simply confirm the obvious, the story*

*you know is in the air and on everybody's mind.* Never do they include a story that is quiet and ordinary but wonderful to read. *[emphasis mine]*

That great insight is often buried in material that seems quiet, and ordinary does not matter to blogging. That wouldn't get clicks.

I'm fond of a line by Nicolas Chamfort, a French writer, who believed that popular public opinion was the absolute worst kind of opinion. "One can be certain," he said, "that every generally held idea, every received notion, will be idiocy because it has been able to appeal to the majority." To a marketer, it's just as well, because idiocy is easier to create than anything else.

## THEIR METRICS, YOUR ADVANTAGE

What gets measured gets managed, or so the saying goes. So what do publishers measure? Out of everything that can possibly be measured, blogs have picked a handful of the most straightforward and cost-effective metrics to rely on (wonderfulness is not one of them). They choose to measure only what can be clearly communicated to their writers as goals. Like officers in Vietnam ordered to report body counts back to Washington as indicators of success or failure, these ill-conceived metrics—based on simplicity more than anything else—make bloggers do awful things.

To understand bloggers, rephrase the saying as "Simplistic measurements matter." Like, did a shitload of people see it? Must be good. Was there a raging comments section going? Awesome! Did the story get picked up on Media Redefined? It made the *Drudge Report*? Yes! In practice, this is all blogs really have time to look for, and it's easy to give it to them.

I exploit these pseudo-metrics all the time. If other blogs have covered something, competitors rush to copy them, because they assume there is traffic in it. As a result, getting coverage on one site can simply be a matter of sending those links to an unoriginal blogger. That those links were scored under false pretenses hardly matters. How could anyone tell? Showing that a story you want written is connected to a popular or search engine–friendly topic (preferably one the site already has posts about) does the same thing. However tenuous the connection, it satisfies the pageview impulse and gives the blogger an excuse to send readers to their stories. You've done something that gets them paid.

Remember, some bloggers have to churn out as many as a dozen posts a day. That's not because twelve is some lucky number but because they need to meet serious pageview goals for the site. Not every story is intended to be a home run—a collection of singles, doubles, and triples adds up too. Pageview journalism is about scale. Sites *have* to publish multiple stories every few minutes to make a profit, and why shouldn't your story be one of them?

Per the leaderboard strategy I mentioned earlier, one of the best ways to turn yourself into a favorite and regular subject is to make it clear your story is a reliable traffic draw. If you're a brand, then post the story to your company Twitter and Facebook accounts and put it on your website. This inflates the stats in your favor and encourages more coverage down the road. There are also services that allow you to "buy traffic," sending thousands of visitors to a specific page. At the penny-per-click rates of Stumble-Upon or even cheaper traffic from places like Fiverr.com, a few hundred bucks can mean thousands of pageviews—illusory confirmation to the media that you are newsworthy. The stat counters on these sites make no distinction between fake and real views, nor does anyone care enough to dig deep into the sources of traffic. The lure of the indirect bribe is all that matters.

But be careful: This beast can bite you back if it feels like it. Once sites see there is traffic in something, they do not stop—often falling to new lows in the process. Companies enjoy the spotlight at first, until the good news runs out and the blog begins to rely on increasingly spurious sources to keep the high-traffic topic on their pages. What begins as positive press often ends in the fabrication of scandals or utter bullshit. As Brandon Mendelson wrote for *Forbes*, the lure of pageviews takes blogs to places they otherwise never should have gone:

> A couple of years ago, I quit blogging for Mashable after they had posted the suicide note to the guy who flew a helicopter into a government building in Texas. Pete's [the publisher's] response to me quit-

*ting over the suicide note was, pretty much, "Other blogs were doing it." He never explained why a Web / Tech / Social Media guide would post a crazy person's suicide note.*

*Who wants to say "I did it for the page views" out loud?*[3]

The answer to that question is "almost every blogger."

Why do you think the *Huffington Post* once ran a front-page story about what time the Super Bowl would start? The query was a popular one on game day, and the post generated incredible amounts of traffic. It may have been a pointless story for a political and news blog like the *Huffington Post* to write, but the algorithm justified it—along with the rest of their "the world is round" stories and well-timed celebrity slideshows.

This content is attractive to blogs because the traffic it does is both measurable and predictable. Like a fish lure, it is not difficult to mimic the appearance of these kinds of stories or for unthinking writers to fall for it. They are looking to eat. They know what keywords are lucrative, what topics get links, and what type of writing gets comments, and they'll bite without asking themselves whether the version of events you've presented is just a barbed trick.

Nick Denton would tell me recently that he dislikes this criticism of pageviews. "Saying pageviews are wicked is like saying calories are wicked," he said. There is some truth to that. But don't most people agree that this is a real problem—in a world where obesity is a major health crisis—with the way that companies manipulate the public to consume more and more calories?

It would be alarming to know that McDonald's judged its managers based on how many calories they were able to shove down the gullet of their customers. Or to hear the CEO brag about how they squeezed an extra 200 calories into a Big Mac at little to no cost to the company. Well, that is precisely the kind of thinking that publishers do today—the exact same publishers who would jump to criticize similar corruptive metrics if used by other metrics. They don't like thinking that their business is as exploitative as any other, but that doesn't make it less true.

# CAN'T STAND THE SILENCE

"I posted something but nobody responded. What does it mean?" It's a question you've probably asked yourself after nobody liked the Facebook status with your big news, or no friends commented on your new Instagram photo. Maybe you thought that tweet you wrote was hilarious, and you're not sure why it wasn't retweeted—not even once. This innocent little question is just about hurt feelings for you, but for pageview-hungry publishers, it's what keeps them up at night.

Early Usenet users called this Warnock's Dilemma, after its originator, Bryan Warnock. The dilemma began with mailing lists but now applies to message boards (why is no one responding to the thread?), blogs (why hasn't anyone commented?), and websites (why isn't this generating any chatter?). The answer to any of these questions could just as easily be satisfaction as apathy, and publishers want to know which it is.

This dilemma was actually predicted by Orson Scott Card in the 1985 book *Ender's Game*. Peter Wiggin creates the online persona of a demagogue named Locke and begins to test the waters by posting deliberately inflammatory comments. Why write this way? his sister asks. Peter replies: "We can't hear how our style of writing is working unless we get responses—and if we're bland, no one will answer."

Card understood that it is incredibly difficult to interpret silence in a constructive way. Warnock's Dilemma, for its part, poses several interpretations:

1. The post is correct, well-written information that needs no follow-up commentary. There's nothing more to say except "Yeah, what he said."
2. The post is complete and utter nonsense, and no one wants to waste the energy or bandwidth to even point this out.
3. No one read the post, for whatever reason.
4. No one understood the post but no one will ask for clarification, for whatever reason.
5. No one cares about the post, for whatever reason.[4]

If you're a publisher, this checklist causes more headaches than it cures. It's all bad. Possibility number one is unprofitable: We know that practical utility doesn't spread, and posts that don't generate follow-up commentary are dead in the link economy. Possibility number two is embarrassing and damaging to the brand. Possibility number three is bad for obvious reasons. Possibility number four means the post was probably too ambitious, too academic, and too certain for anyone to risk questions. Possibility number five means somebody chose the wrong topic.

Whatever the cause, the silence all means the same thing: no comments, no links, no traffic, *no money*. It lands the publisher firmly in a territory labeled "utterly unprofitable." Jonah Peretti, for his part, has his bloggers at *BuzzFeed* track their failures closely. If news doesn't go viral or get feedback, then the news needs to be changed. If news does go viral, it means the story was a success—whether or not it was accurate, in good taste, or done well.

That is where the opportunity lies: Blogs are so afraid of silence that the flimsiest of evidence can confirm they're on the right track. You can provide this by leaving fake comments to articles about you or your company from blocked IP addresses—good and bad to make it clear that there is a hot debate. Send fake e-mails to the reporter, positive and negative. This rare kind of feedback cements the impression that you or your company make for high-valence material, and the blog should be covering you. Like Peter Wiggin, publishers don't care what they say as long as it isn't bland or ignored. But by avoiding the bad kind of silence prompted by poor content, they avoid the good kind that results from the type of writing that makes people think but not say, *Yeah, what he said. I'm glad I read this article.*

Professional bloggers understand this dilemma far better than the casual or amateur ones, according to an analysis done by Nate Silver of unpaid versus paid articles on the *Huffington Post*. Over a three-day period, 143 political posts by amateurs received 6,084 comments, or an average of just 43 comments per article (meaning that many got zero). Over that same period, the *Huffington Post* published 161 *paid* political articles (bought from other sites, written by staff writers, or other copyrighted content) that accumulated more than 133,000 comments combined. That amounts to more than 800 per article, or twenty times what the unpaid bloggers were able to accomplish.[5]

According to the *Huffington Post*'s pageview strategy, the paid articles are indisputably better, because they generated more comments and traffic (like a 2009 article about the Iranian protests that got *96,281 comments*). In a sane system, a political article that generated thousands of comments would be an indicator that something went wrong. It means the conversation descended into an unproductive debate about abortion or immigration, or devolved into mere complaining. But in the broken world of the web, it is the mark of a professional.

A blog like the *Huffington Post* is not going to *pay* for something that is met with silence, even the good kind. They're certainly not going to promote it or display it on the front page, since it would reduce the opportunity to generate pageviews. The *Huffington Post* does not wish to be the definitive account of a story or inform people—since the reaction to that is simple satisfaction. Blogs deliberately do not want to help.

You're basically asking for favors if you try to get blogs to cover something that isn't going to drive pageviews and isn't going to garner clear responses. Blogs are not in the business of doing favors—even if all you're asking is for them to print the truth. Trust me, I have tried. I have shown them factories of workers whose jobs are at risk because of inaccurate online coverage. I have begged them to be fair for these poor people's sake. If that didn't make a difference, nothing will.

## BREAKING THE NEWS

I don't know if blogs enjoy being tricked. All I know is that they don't care enough to put a stop to it. The response to sketchy anonymous tips, in my experience, is "Thanks," a lot more often than "Prove you're legit."

Nobody is fooling anyone. That's not the game—because sites don't have any interest in what they post, as long as it delivers pageviews. Samuel Axon, formerly an editor at *Mashable* and *Engadget*, complained that the rules by which blogs get "traffic, high impressions, and strong ad revenues betray journalists and the people who need them at every turn." This is only partially true. They betray the *ethical* journalists and earnest readers. As far as bloggers and publishers looking to get rich or manipulators eager to influence the news are concerned, the system is just fine.

Pageview journalism puffs blogs up and fattens them on a steady diet of guaranteed traffic pullers of a mediocre variety that require little effort to produce. It pulls writers and publishers to the extremes, and only to the extremes—the shocking and the already known. Practicing pageview journalism means that a publisher never has to worry about seeing "(0) Comments" at the bottom of a post. With tight deadlines and tight margins, any understanding of the audience is helpful guidance. For marketers, this is refreshingly predictable.

It just happens that this metric-driven understanding breaks the news. The cynicism is self-fulfilling and self-defeating; as the quip famously attributed to Henry Ford points out, if he'd listened to what his customers "said" they wanted, all "we'd have ended up with was a faster horse."

Pageview journalism treats people by what they *appear* to want—from data that is unrepresentative to say the least—and gives them this and only this until they have forgotten that there could be anything else. It takes the audience at their worst and makes them worse. And then, when criticized, publishers throw up their hands as if to say, "We wish people liked better stuff too," as if they had nothing to do with it.

Well, they do.

# XI

# TACTIC #8

## USE THE TECHNOLOGY AGAINST ITSELF

Actions are constrained by income, time, imperfect memory and calculating capacities, and other limited resources, and also by the available opportunities in the economy and elsewhere. . . . Different constraints are decisive for different situations, but the most fundamental constraint is limited time.

—GARY BECKER, NOBEL PRIZE–WINNING ECONOMIST

SOMETIMES I SEE A PREPOSTEROUSLY INACCURATE
blog post about a client (or myself) and I take it personally, thinking that
it was malicious. Or I wonder why they didn't just pick up the phone and
call me to get the other side of the story. I occasionally catch myself complaining about sensational articles or crummy writing, and placing the
blame on an editor or a writer. It's hard for me to understand the impulse
to reduce an important issue to a stupid quote or unfunny one-liner.

This is an unproductive attitude. It forgets the structure and constraints of blogging as a medium and how these realities explain almost
everything blogs do. Where there is little volition, there should be little
bitterness or blame. Only understanding, as I have learned, can be turned
to advantage.

The way news is found online more or less determines what is found.
The way the news must be presented—in order to meet the technical constraints of the medium and the demands of its readers—determines the
news itself. It's basically a cliché at this point, but that doesn't change the
fact that Marshall McLuhan was right: The medium *is* the message.

Think about television. We're all tired of the superficiality of cable
news and its insistence on reducing important political issues into needless conflict between two annoying talking heads. But there's a simple
reason for this, as media critic Eric Alterman explained in *Sound and
Fury: The Making of the Punditocracy*. TV is a visual medium, he said, so
to ask the audience to think about something it cannot see would be suicide. If it were possible to put an abstract idea to film, producers would
happily show that instead of pithy sound bites. But it isn't, so conflict,
talking heads, and B-roll footage are all you'll get. The values of television,
Alterman realized, behave like a dictator, exerting their rule over the kind
of information that can be transmitted across the channels.

Blogs aren't any different. The way the medium works essentially predetermines what bloggers can publish and how exactly they must do it. Blogs are just as logical as the television producers Alterman criticized; it's just a matter of understanding their unique logic.

To know what the medium demands of bloggers is to be able to predict, and then co-opt, how they act.

## HEMMED IN ON ALL SIDES

Why do blogs constantly chase new stories? Why do they update so much? Why are posts so short? A look at their development makes it clear: Bloggers don't have a choice.

Early bloggers, according to Scott Rosenberg in his book on the history of blogging, *Say Everything: How Blogging Began, What It's Becoming, and Why It Matters*, had to answer one important question: How do our readers know what's new?

To solve this, programmers first tried "New!" icons, but that didn't work. It was too difficult to tell what the icons meant across many blogs— on one site "New!" might mean the latest thing published and on another it could be anything written within the last month. What they needed was a uniform way to organize the content that would be the same across the web. Tim Berners-Lee, one of the founders of the web, set a procedure in motion that would be copied by almost everyone after him: New stuff goes at the top.

The reverse chronological order on one of the web's first sites—called "stacking" by programmers—became the de facto standard for blogging. Because the web evolved through imitation and collaboration, most sites simply adopted the form of their predecessors and peers. Stacking developed as an implicit standard, and that has had extraordinary implications. When content is stacked, it sets a very clear emphasis on the present. For the blogger, the time stamp is like an expiration date. It also creates considerable pressure to be short and immediate.

In 1996, three years before the word "blogger" was even invented, proto-blogger Justin Hall wrote to his readers at Links.net that he'd been criticized at a party for not posting enough, and for not putting his posts right on the front page. "Joey said he used to love my pages," Hall wrote, "but now there's too many layers to my links. At Suck(.com) you get sucked in immediately, no layers to content."[1]

It's really an illustrative moment, if you think about it. In one of the first data-stamped posts on a blog ever, Hall was already alluding to the pressures the medium was putting on content. His post was ninety-three words and basically a haiku. This was not a man of too many "layers." But Suck.com had just sold for thirty thousand dollars, so who was Hall to argue? So he resolved to put "a little somethin' new" at the top of his website every single day.

We can trace a straight line from this conversation in 1996 to the post-per-day minimums of blogs like *Gizmodo* and *Engadget* in 2005, and to today, when authors of guides like *Blogger Bootcamp* tell prospective bloggers that the experience of publishing more than twenty thousand blog posts taught them that "Rule #1" is "Always Be Blogging," and that the best sites are "updated daily, if not hourly."

Since content is constantly expiring, and bloggers face the Sisyphean task of trying to keep their sites fresh, creating a newsworthy event out of nothing becomes a daily occurrence. The structure of blogging warps the perspective of everyone who exists in this space—why would a blogger spend much time on a post that will very shortly be pushed below view? Understandably, no one wants to be the fool who wasted his or her time working on something nobody read. The message is clear: The best way to get traffic is to publish as much as possible, as quickly as possible, and as simply as possible.

*The Huffington Post Complete Guide to Blogging* has a simple rule of thumb: Unless readers can see the end of your post coming around eight hundred words in, they're going to stop. Scrolling is a pain, as is feeling like an article will never end. This gives writers around eight hundred words to make their point—a rather tight window. Even eight hundred words is pushing it, the *Huffington Post* says, since a block of text that big on the web can be intimidating. A smart blogger, they note, will break it up with graphics or photos, and definitely some links.

In a retrospective of his last ten years of blogging, publisher Om Malik of *Gigaom* bragged that he'd written over eleven thousand posts and two million words in the last decade. Which, while translating into three posts a day, means the average post was just 215 words long. But that's nothing compared to the ideal *Gawker* item. Nick Denton told a potential hire in 2008 that it was "one hundred words long. Two hundred, max. Any good idea," he said, "can be expressed at that length."[2]

Preposterously faulty intuition like this can be seen across the web, on blogs and sites of all types. The pressure to keep content visually appealing and ready for impulse readers is a constant suppressant on length, regardless of what is cut to make it happen. In a University of Kentucky study of blogs about cancer, researchers found that a full 80 percent of the blog posts they analyzed contained fewer than five hundred words.[3] The average number of words per post was 335, short enough to make the articles on the *Huffington Post* seem like lengthy manuscripts. I don't care what Nick Denton says; I'm pretty sure that the complexities of *cancer* can't be properly expressed in 100 words. Or 200, or 335, or 500, for that matter.

Even the most skilled writer would have trouble conveying the side effects of chemotherapy or how to discuss the possibility of death with your children in just a handful of words. Yet here they are—the majority of posts barely filling three pages, double spaced, in a twelve-point font. They wouldn't even take three minutes to read.

More recently, one of *Politico*'s cofounders, Jim VandeHei, launched a new site called *Axios*, which is in part a reaction to his belief that much of today's journalism *is too long*. "People don't want the pieces we're writing," he told *Recode*. "They're too damn long." I don't know what internet this guy has been hanging out on, but I can't say I am often struck when reading that the piece was just too in depth and too well researched. In fact, I'm not sure I've ever had that reaction.

Of course, it's not completely the bloggers' fault. People are busy, and computers are fraught with distraction. It would be crazy to think that entrepreneurs wouldn't adapt their content around these facts. The average time users spend on a site like *Jezebel* is a little over a minute. On the technology and personal efficiency blog *Lifehacker*, they can average less than ten seconds. The common wisdom is that the site has one second to make the hook. *One second.* The bounce rate on blogs (or the percentage of people who leave the site immediately, without clicking anything) is incredibly high. Analysis of news sites has the average bounce rate pushing well north of 50 percent. When the statistics show a medium to be so fickle that half the audience starts leaving as soon as they get there, there is no question that this dynamic is going to seriously impact content choices.

Studies that have tracked the eye movements of people browsing the web show the same fickleness. The biggest draw of eyeballs is the headline, of which viewers usually see only the first few words before moving on. After users break off from the headline, their glance tends to descend downward along the left-hand column, scanning for sentences that catch their attention. If nothing does, they leave. What slows this dismissive descent is the form of the article—small, short paragraphs (one to two sentences versus three to five) seem to encourage slightly higher reading rates, as does a boldface introduction or subheadline (occasionally called a deck). What blogger is going to decide they're above gimmicks such as bulleted lists when it's precisely those gimmicks that seem to keep readers on the page for a few priceless seconds longer?

Jakob Nielsen, the reigning guru of web usability, according to *Fortune* magazine, and the author of twelve books on the subject, advises sites to follow a simple rule: 40 percent of every article must be cut.[4] But despair not, because according to his calculations, when chopped thus, the average article loses only 30 percent of its value. *Oh, only 30 percent!* It's the kind of math publishers go through every day. As long as the equation works out in their favor, it's worth doing. What does it matter if the readers get stuck with the losses?

Once at a lunch meeting with an editor of *Racked NY*, a blog about retail shopping in New York City, the incredibly influential blogger told me that she did all her shopping online. "So you wear our clothes but you never go in our stores?" I asked, since she was wearing American Apparel at the meeting. "I just don't have time to go shopping anymore." There was a store within blocks of her office and two others on her way home. This was *literally* her beat. I guess it doesn't matter anyway; where would she put personal observations in a two-hundred-word post even if she had them?

I once watched as an editor at the site *Mediagazer* tried to do her fact-checking for a story about me by simply tweeting out into the universe. After watching her hilarious attempts to "verify [my] credibility" by asking people I'd never worked with and never met, I finally logged onto

Twitter to send my first message in years: "@LyraMckee Have you thought about emailing me? ryan.holiday@gmail.com."

Why would she? Though I'd actually be able to answer her questions, tweeting out loud was easier than e-mailing me, and it meant she didn't have to wait for my response. Plus, I'm boring and would have rained all over her speculation parade.

When Nielsen talks about cutting 40 percent of an article, actually knowing anything about what they're talking about is what bloggers leave on the cutting-room floor. As a manipulator, that's fine with me. It makes it easier to spin or even to lie. It's not like I have to worry about their verifying it. They don't have time for anything like that. A writer has minimums they must hit, and chasing a story that won't make it on the site is an expensive error. So it's not surprising that bloggers stick to eight-hundred-or-fewer-word posts about stories they *know* will generate traffic.

Jack Fuller, a former editor and publisher of the *Chicago Tribune*, once admonished a group of newspaper editors by saying, "I don't know about your world, but the one I live in does not shape itself so conveniently to anybody's platform."[5] For bloggers it would be nice if life were all exciting headlines and a clean eight hundred words, and happened to self-organize all its juicy bits down the left-hand column. The world is far too messy, too nuanced and complicated, and frankly far less exciting for that to be the case. Only a fool addicted to his laptop would fail to see that the material demanded by the constraints of their medium and the material reality gives them rarely match.

On the other hand, as a marketer I quite like these fools.

## CHECK FOR THE KEY UNDER THE MAT

Most common question I hear from people trying to market stuff: How do I pitch blogs? Um, no need to ask me; the blogs straight up tell you. Every few months blogs trot out the tired old story of how to pitch coverage to them. They advise publicists to do a better job e-mailing the blogger and assuaging their ego if they want the blogger to write about their clients. From a reader's perspective this is all rather strange. Why is the blog revealing how it can be manipulated? In turn, why do we not head for the hills when it is clear that blogs pass this manipulation on to us?

Some favorite headlines:

### Rules of Thumb for Pitching Silly Claims to TechCrunch (*TechCrunch*)

### How Not to Pitch a Blogger, #648 (*ReadWriteWeb*)

### DEAR PR FOLKS: Please Stop Sending Us "Experts" and "Story Ideas"—Here's What to Send Us Instead (*Business Insider*)

### A Private Note to PR People (*Scobleizer*)

### How to Pitch a Blogger (as in, *Brazen Careerist*, the blogger writing it)

### The Do's and Don'ts of Online Publicity, for Some Reason (Lindsay Robertson, *Jezebel*, *NYMag, Huffington Post*)

The unintended consequence of that kind of coverage is that it is essentially a manual with step-by-step instructions on how to infiltrate and deceive that blogger with marketing. I used to be thankful when I'd see that; now I just wonder: *Why are you doing this to yourselves?*

# MAKING LEMONADE

Let's just say Fuller's advice does not have a wide following online, particularly his reminder that reporters owe a "duty to reality, not to platforms."

In fact, bloggers believe the opposite. And that sucks for everyone—except marketers. Because once you understand the limitations of the platform, the constraints can be used against the people who depend on it. The technology can be turned on itself.

I remember promoting one author whose book had just spent five weeks on the *New York Times* bestseller list (meaning people were willing to *pay* for it in one medium). When I was trying to post material from the book on various popular blogs, it became clear that it was just too long. So we got rid of the thoroughness and the supporting arguments and reduced it down to the most basic, provocative parts. One chapter—the same chapter people enjoyed fully in book form—had to be split up into *eight* separate posts. To get attention we had to cut it up into itty-bitty bites and spoon-feed it to readers and bloggers like babies.

If a blogger isn't willing or doesn't have the time to get off their ass to visit the stores they write about, that's their problem. It makes it that much easier to create my own version of reality. I will come to them with the story. I'll meet them on their terms, but their story will be filled with my terms. They won't take the time or show the interest to check with anyone else.

Blogs must—economically and structurally—distort the news in order for the format to work. As businesses, blogs can see the world through no other lens. The *format* is the problem. Or the perfect opportunity, depending on how you look at it.

# XII

## TACTIC #9

# JUST MAKE STUFF UP (EVERYONE ELSE IS DOING IT)

> Those who have gone through the high school of reporterdom have acquired a new instinct by which they see and hear only that which can create a sensation, and accordingly their report becomes not only a careless one, but hopelessly distorted.
>
> —HUGO MUNSTERBERG, "THE CASE OF THE REPORTER," *MCCLURE'S*, 1911

THE WORLD IS BORING, BUT THE NEWS IS EXCITING. IT'S a paradox of modern life. Journalists and bloggers are not magicians, but if you consider the material they've got to work with and the final product they crank out day in and day out, you must give them some credit. Shit becomes sugar.

If there is one special skill that journalists can claim, it is the ability to find the angle on any story. That the news is ever chosen over entertainment in the fight for attention is a testament to their skill. High-profile bloggers rightly take great pride in this ability. This pride and this pressure are what we media manipulators use against them. Pride goeth before the fall.

No matter how dull, mundane, or complex a topic may be, a good reporter must find the angle. Bloggers, descended from these journalists, have to take it to an entirely new level. They need to find not only the angle but the click-driving headline, an eye-catching image; generate comments and links; and in some cases, squeeze in some snark. And they have to do it up to a dozen times a day without the help of an editor. They can smell the angle of a story like a shark smells blood in the water. Because the better the angle, the more the blogger gets paid. Technology and big data have exacerbated this process too, finding meaningless correlations and anomalies to make hay out of. (I just heard an anchor on *SportsCenter* report, in all seriousness, that a hit was the "fifth-longest Cubs home run since 2009." C'mon.)

As Drew Curtis of Fark.com says, "Problems occur when the journalist has to find an angle on a story that doesn't have one." A few years before Drew (in 1899, to be exact) the *Washington Post* reported:

> *The* New York Times *has such abnormal keenness of vision that it is occasionally able to see that which does not exist. The ardency of its*

*desire sometimes overcomes the coolness of its reasons, so that the
thing it wants to see shows up just where it wants it to be, but in so
intangible a form that no other eye is able to detect, no other mind
finds ground to suspect its presence.*[1]

The difference between the *New York Times* and blogs a century later
is that the *New York Times* was dealing with at least somewhat worthy
material. Bloggers latch onto the most tenuous wisps of news on places
like Facebook or Twitter and then apply their "abnormal keenness" to
seeing what is not there. A writer for the Mediabistro blog *10,000 Words*
once advised new bloggers that they could find good material by scanning
community bulletin boards on craigslist for "what people are complaining about these days."[2] I'm not a sociologist, but I'm pretty sure that
doesn't qualify as representative news. Considering that anyone can post
anything on craigslist, this gives me a pretty good idea of how to create
some fake local news. If they don't mind seeing what isn't there, marketers
are happy to help. (My company once worked with a musician to leak
some of their tracks on craigslist's Missed Connections section.)

Angle-hunters sometimes come up empty. In a perfect world, writers
should be able to explore a story lead, find it leads nowhere, and abandon
it. But that luxury is not available online. As the veteran bloggers John
Biggs and Charlie White put it in their book *Bloggers Boot Camp*, there is
"no topic too mundane that you can't pull a post out of it."

This is their logic. As a marketer, it's easy to fall in love with it.

Blogs will publish anything if you manufacture urgency around it.
Give a blogger an illusory twenty-minute head start over other media
sources, and they'll write whatever you want, however you want it. Publicists love to promise blogs the exclusive on an announcement. The plural
there is not an accident. You can give the same made-up exclusive to multiple blogs, and they'll fall all over themselves to publish first. Throw in an
arbitrary deadline, like "We're going live with this on our website first
thing in the morning," and even the biggest blogs will forget fact-checking
and make bold pronouncements on your behalf.

Since bloggers *must* find an angle, they *always* do. Since you know how
hard they're looking, it's easy to leave crumbs, fragments, or stray gems
that you know will be impossible for them to resist picking up and turn-

ing into full-fledged stories. Small news is made to look like big news. Nonexistent news is puffed up and made into news. The result is stories that look just like their legitimate counterparts, only their premise is wrong and says nothing. Such stories hook with false pretenses, analyze false subjects, and inform falsely.

I told you earlier about how we paid celebrities to tweet offensive stuff. But the reality was we mostly *tried* to pay them to do it. Only the skeeviest of accounts actually agreed to do it and went through with it. But I still wanted the coverage, so we mocked up what the tweets would have looked like if they had said yes—what it would have looked like if Kim Kardashian had admitted she didn't know how to read. The blogs that covered the story were fine with blurring the line between what happened and what *almost* happened or what *could* have happened, because it was better for business. The same went for when one of my clients, James Altucher, offered one of his books for sale via Bitcoin and another, a musician, Young & Sick, posted his album on the so-called dark net. In both cases like zero people actually bought them there—but since we made it seem like a much bigger deal than it was, media coverage ensued. Nobody bothered to investigate—why would they?

When I say it's okay for you to make stuff up because everybody else is doing it, I'm not kidding. M. G. Siegler, once one of the dominant voices in tech blogging (*TechCrunch*, *PandoDaily*), is very blunt about this. According to him, most of what he and his competitors wrote is bullshit. "I won't try to put some arbitrary label on it, like 80%," he once admitted, "but it's a lot. There's more bullshit than there is 100% pure, legitimate information."[3]

Shamelessness is a virtue in Siegler's world. It helps create nothing from something. It helps people at the *Huffington Post* stomach creating stories like "Amy Winehouse's Untimely Death Is a Wake Up Call for Small Business Owners." The same holds true for reputable outlets too. They need only the slightest push to abandon all discretion, like the *Daily Mail* in the UK did when I had some deliberately provocative ads posted on the American Apparel website and pretended they were part of a new campaign. HAS AMERICAN APPAREL GONE TOO FAR WITH "CREEPY" CONTROVERSIAL NEW CAMPAIGN? the *Mail*'s headline read. According to *whom* had it gone too far? The article quoted "some tweeters."[4]

Thanks for the free publicity, guys! Random people on Twitter are not a representative sample by any measure—but it got the company in the news. God knows what it would have cost to *pay* to run those full-page ads in their paper.

Whatever will be more exciting, get more pageviews, *that* is what blogs will say happened. Like when *Gawker* bought a scoop from a man who had pictures of a wild Halloween night with politician Christine O'Donnell. According to editor Remy Stern, the skeevy source's one concern was "that a tabloid would imply that they had sex, which they did not." The headline of the *Gawker* article was . . . drumroll . . . I HAD A ONE-NIGHT STAND WITH CHRISTINE O'DONNELL."[5]

# DO THEIR RESEARCH FOR THEM

One of the older (leftist) critiques of media is that media is dependent on existing power structures for information. Reporters have to wait for news from the police; they get facts and figures from government figures; they are reliant on celebrities and other newsmakers for information. This is a totally valid criticism. It was true in 1950 and it's *really* true now.

Newspapers and local media used to have the budget to send a reporter to local town hall meetings—now they don't. They used to be able to pay to have an overseas bureau to get news where it was happening. Now they wait for the official report to come in. The AP, for instance, has actually started to outsource some of its reporting to India and in some cases to *actual robots.* When you read a short story about how the market went up three hundred points due to strong job numbers from the White House, it might be that a computer wrote that story, not a human being. My point is that the media is now even more dependent on others to do their research and work for them.

Nowhere is this sad state of affairs more obvious than in current science reporting. Although scientific journals remain restrained by the practices and ethics of science, university websites and publicists are not. Nearly every day some minor finding is touted as an enormous breakthrough in a press release that goes out to reporters. These bloggers simply looking for traffic are never going to question the headline; they're not even going to read the paper—they're just in it for the headlines. I mean, can you beat this one from the *Huffington Post*?: BEARDS ARE COVERED IN POOP: STUDY

One brave journalist recently stood up to this practice and showed how bad things were. He orchestrated a study that collected loads of random data and then, finding simply a correlation between dieting and eating chocolate, created a fake institute to announce his monumental but absurdly unscientific findings: You can lose weight by eating chocolate! And bam, everyone from the *Huffington Post* to the *Daily Mail* was cheering the news.

Of course you can't seriously lose weight that way. The institute didn't exist. The science was junk. The whole thing was a prank. Yet millions of people were given this fake news. If the journalist hadn't revealed himself, there might be a lot of people out there justifying that extra chocolate bar as part of their diet.

It's obvious why this happens, though, and how it can be replicated. Set up your own think tank. Call it the Millennial Entrepreneurs Foundation and put out "research" that really just makes companies think they need to hire you as a consultant. Don't think climate change is real? Have a business interest in making people think it isn't? Fund "studies" that confirm what you want and then blast the internet with them. Want to invent some ridiculous new trend? Hire experts to say it's correlated with higher sex drive or that it's all the rage with celebrities. Sadly, no one is going to question you.

## ALWAYS WRONG, NEVER IN DOUBT

Trolls are not the only ones responsible for fake ideas spreading through the internet. At American Apparel I had to deal with a pesky blog called *BNET* on which a "reporter" named Jim Edwards would troll through the company's financial disclosures and come up with some of the most fantastical misinterpretations I could imagine. We brought this on ourselves. Having made the company and its advertising such a juicy subject for gossip and entertainment blogs, it was natural that other pageview-hungry writers would try to get in on the game. Still, even as I knowingly fed that monster, I did not expect what happened with Edwards.

The man once asked critically—in a blog post, not a request for comment—why the company did not roll a last-minute, necessary-to-make-payroll personal loan from Dov Charney at 6 percent interest into the larger loan from investors at 15 percent interest. (I assume the answer is so obvious to normal people like you that I do not need to explain that 6 percent is *less than* 15 percent.) Edwards posed this question not once but several times, in several posts, each with a more aggressive headline (e.g., HOW AMERICAN APPAREL'S CEO TURNED A CRISIS INTO A PAY RAISE).

From our conversation after he published his post:

> Me: I don't know if you recall, but we discussed your assertion about the 6 percent interest rate. . . . You issued a correction on this story in 2009.
>
> Jim Edwards: I do recall. But I'm quoting the status of Charney's loans directly from the proxy. Is the proxy wrong?
>
> Me: YOUR BASIC UNDERSTANDING OF MATH IS WRONG!

He made bold speculations like, "Why American Apparel CEO Must Resign" and "Is American Apparel's CEO Facing the Endgame?" He'd concoct ridiculous conspiracy theories, including one that accused the company of timing controversial ads to coincide with SEC-mandated announcements to distract the public from corrupt dealings inside the company—and as proof would use the *very nonexistent loan scandal* he'd uncovered. (Not to mention that the ads weren't new, and some weren't even actual ads—just fake ones I'd leaked online.) Did he ever come to actually meet anyone at the company he was writing about? Did he familiarize himself seriously with the industry? Did he reach out to reliable experts to confirm these speculations? No, of course not.

One kook is hardly a problem. But the obliviousness and earnest conviction a kook maintains in their own twisted logic makes for great material for other sites to disingenuously use by reporting on what the kook reported. As part of the CBS Interactive Business Network, Edwards's blog on *BNET* featured the CBS logo at the top. Since he looked like he had some official industry status, his questions became fodder for fashion websites at the national level.

Fictive interpolation on one site becomes the source for fictive interpolation on another, and again in turn for another, until the origins are eventually forgotten. To paraphrase Charles Horton Cooley, the products of our imagination become the solid facts of society. It's a process that happens not horizontally but vertically, moving each time to a more reputable site and seeming more real at each level. And so, in Edwards's case, American Apparel was forced to deal with a constant stream of controversy born of one man's uncanny ability to create an angle where there wasn't one. And Edwards is now a top editor at *Business Insider*. He even wrote about this book when it came out—and made a ten-page slideshow attacking it so he could get ten times as many pageviews as he would have with an actual article.

Imagine if an enemy had decided to use him as a cat's paw, as I have done with other such bloggers. The damage could have been even worse. As I wrote to a company attorney at the time, who mistakenly believed we could "reason" with the blogger:

> Basically, these blogs have a hustle going where one moves the ball as far as they can up the field, and then the next one takes it and in doing so reifies whatever baseless speculation was included in the first report. *Jezebel* needs Jim Edwards' "reporting" to snark on, Jim Edwards needs *Jezebel*'s "controversy" to justify his analysis, and all this feeds into the fashion news websites who pass the articles along to their readers. Posting a comment on his blog doesn't interrupt this cycle.

Neither would the lawsuit the lawyer was considering. It would just give Edwards more to talk about. In this situation I was tasked with defending a company against exactly the type of subtle mischaracterizations and misleading information that I use on behalf of other clients. The insanity of that fact is not lost on me. What makes it all the more scary in this case is that there wasn't someone like me behind the scenes, exerting influence over the information the public saw. The system was manipulating itself—and I was called in to mitigate that manipulation—with more manipulation.

What else could I expect? Early on I worked tirelessly to encourage bloggers to find nonexistent angles on stories *I* hoped they would promote. I made it worth their while—dangling pageviews, traffic, access, and occasionally advertising checks to get it going. After a point they no longer needed me to get those things. They got traffic and links by writing anything extreme about my clients, and if I wouldn't be their source, they could make one up or get someone to lie. Other advertisers were happy to profit from stories at our expense. The *Jezebel*/Edwards cycle wasn't some conspiracy; it was partly my creation.

It should be obvious that companies must be on guard against the immense pressures that bloggers face to churn out exciting news to their advantage. Do something perfectly innocent—prepare to have it wrenched out of context into a blog post. Do something complicated—expect to have it simplified until it's unrecognizable. It goes in both directions. Do nothing—you can still turn it into something. Do something wrong—don't despair; you can spin it beyond comprehension. If you play in this world as a manipulator, prepare for faux outrage (which becomes real outrage) when you don't deserve it, and expect actual violators to get off without a peep. Those are the economics in the angle-hungry world of Jim Edwards.

We're now at a place where, as a staffer in the Obama White House put it, "the controversy machine is bigger than the reality machine." Get used to it. Because it's true for Trump and every president.

It's why I can safely say that all the infamous American Apparel controversies were made up. Either I made them up or bloggers did. To the public, this process was all invisible. Only as an insider was I able to know that bloggers were seeing that which was not there. They had been so trained to find "big stories" that they hardly knew the difference between real and made up.

It's even hard for me to avoid falling for the occasional confabulation myself—there are too many, and they are often too pervasive to completely resist. For that reason, even some employees at American Apparel succumbed to the persistent accusations of people like Edwards and began to believe them. The accumulation of "reporting" trumped their own personal experience. There are thousands of these unnamed and unknown victims out there, collateral damage in a system where bloggers and marketers can just make stuff up.

# BOOK TWO

## THE MONSTER ATTACKS

### WHAT BLOGS MEAN

# BOOK TWO

## WHAT BLOGS MEAN

# XIII

## IRIN CARMON, *THE DAILY SHOW*, AND ME

### THE PERFECT STORM OF HOW TOXIC BLOGGING CAN BE

{ Most crucially, that machine, whether it churns through social media or television appearances, doesn't reward bipartisanship or deal making; it rewards the easily retweetable or sound bite–ready statement, the more outrageous the better.

—IRIN CARMON, *JEZEBEL* }

IN THE FIRST HALF OF THIS BOOK YOU SAW THE INSIDE view of how to manipulate blogs. There are fatal flaws in the blogging medium that create opportunities for influence over the media—and, ultimately, culture itself. If I were writing this book as a much younger man, it would have ended there.

I did not fully understand the dangers of that world then, but I began to feel they were there. The costs of the cheap power I had in it were hidden, but once revealed, I could not shake them. I had used my tactics to sell T-shirts and books, but others, I found, used them more expertly and to more ominous ends. They sold everything from presidential candidates to distractions they hoped would placate the public—and made (or destroyed) millions of dollars in the process.

Realizing all this changed me. It made it impossible for me to continue down the path that I was on. The second half of this book explains why. It is an investigation not of how the dark arts of media manipulation work but of their consequences.

## HOW BLOGS CREATE THEIR OWN NARRATIVES FOR FUN AND PROFIT

In 2010, I oversaw the launch of a new line of a Made in USA, environmentally friendly nail polish for American Apparel. Although American Apparel typically manufactures all of its products at its vertically integrated factory in L.A., for this product we'd collaborated with an old-fashioned family-owned factory in Long Island, where even the ninety-year-old grandmother still worked on the factory floor. Shortly after shipping the polish to rave reviews, we noticed that several bottles had cracked or burst underneath the bright halogen lights in our stores.

It didn't pose a risk to our customers, but to be safe rather than sorry, we informed the factory that we'd be pulling the polish from store shelves and expected immediate replacements. We'd discussed the plan in depth on a weekly conference call with our relevant employees. A confidential e-mail was sent to store managers informing them of the changes and asking them to place the bottles in a cool, dry place in the store until instructions for proper disposal were given. The last thing we wanted, even with environmentally friendly nail polish, was to throw fifty thousand bottles of it in trash cans in twenty countries.

*Jezebel* blogger Irin Carmon somehow received this innocent internal communication and e-mailed me at 6:25 A.M. West Coast time (they're based in Manhattan) to ask about it. Well, she pretended to ask me about it, since she signed her e-mail with the following:

> Our post with the initial information is going up shortly, but I
> would be more than happy to update or post a follow-up. Thanks
> so much. Irin

By the time I rubbed the sleep from my eyes, the post was already live. When I saw it, all I could feel was a pit in my stomach—and, frankly, that surprised me. I knew how blogs worked, was plenty cynical, but even then I sensed that this would be awful.

The headline of *Jezebel*'s piece: DOES AMERICAN APPAREL'S NEW NAIL POLISH CONTAIN HAZARDOUS MATERIAL?

To settle *Jezebel*'s reckless conjecture: The answer is no, it didn't. Unequivocally no (and remember, *most* headlines with questions in them can be answered that way). For starters, the leaked e-mail specifically said the problem was with the glassware and mentioned nothing about the polish. But Carmon wasn't actually interested in any of that, and she definitely wasn't interested in writing an article that addressed the issue fairly. Why would she want an actual answer to her incredibly disingenuous question? The post was already written. Hell, it was already published.

As I had not intended to discuss the nail polish bottles publicly yet, it took about an hour for me to get a statement approved by the company lawyers. During that time dozens of other blogs were already parroting her claims. Major blogs, many of which had posted positive reviews of the nail polish on their sites, followed her bogus lead. The story was so compelling (American Apparel! Toxic polish! Exploding glass!), they *had* to run with it, true or not.

Within about an hour I e-mailed the following statement to Carmon, thinking I was taking her up on the offer for a follow-up to her first post:

> After receiving a few reports of bottles breaking, we made the internal decision to do a voluntary recall of the bottles on both a retail and public level.
>
> We chose this small US manufacturer to produce our nail polish because we support their business model and have a fondness for [the] family who runs it. However, one of the realities of all manufacturing is first-run glitches. We worked all last week with the manufacturer to make the improvements necessary for the second run. Another reason we sought out a US-based company is so we would be able to make changes, and now we can investigate what went wrong as quickly as possible. We still believe in the factory we're working with and the new polish will be in stores within the next two weeks.
>
> We will offer an exchange of two new bottles or a $10 gift card for anyone who brings in a unit from the original run or a receipt.
>
> On another note, one thing we're taking very seriously is the disposal of the bottles we had in the stores. Even though our polish was DBP-, toluene-, and formaldehyde-free, we don't want our stores just tossing it in the trash. We're using our internal shipping and distribution line to arrange a pickup and removal of the polish to make sure it gets done right.

I felt this was a great—and ethical—response. But it was too late. Carmon copied and pasted my statement to the bottom of the article and left the headline exactly as it was, adding only "Updated" to the end of it. Even though the statement disproved the premise of her article, Carmon's implication was that she was mostly right and was just adding a few new details. She wasn't—she'd been totally wrong, but it didn't matter, because the opportunity to change the readers' minds had passed. The facts had been established.

To make matters worse, Carmon replied to my last e-mail with a question about *another* trumped-up story she planned to write about the company. She ended again with:

> By the way, just FYI—I'd love to be able to include your
> responses in my initial post, but unfortunately I won't be able to
> wait for them, so if this is something you can immediately react
> to, that would be great.

The controversy eventually meant the undoing of the nail polish company we'd worked so hard to support. Had these blogs not rushed to print a bogus story, the problem could have been handled privately. The massive outcry that followed Carmon's post necessitated an immediate and large-scale response that the cosmetic company could not handle. No question, they'd made mistakes, but nothing remotely close to what was reported. Overwhelmed by the controversy and the pressure from the misplaced anger of the blogger horde, the small manufacturer fell behind on their orders. Their operations fell into disarray, and the company was later sued by American Apparel for $5 million in damages to recover various losses. As the lawyers would say, while the nail polish company is responsible for their manufacturing errors, if not for Carmon's needless attack and rush to judgment—the proximate cause—it all could have been worked out.

Carmon is a media manipulator—she just doesn't know it. She may think she is a writer, but everything about her job makes her a media manipulator. She and I are in the same racket. From the twisting of the facts to the creation of a nonexistent story to the merciless use of attention for profit—she does what I do, what any media manipulator attempting to monetize attention does. Yet people think that journalists are universally good guys.

# A PATTERN OF MANIPULATION

Did you know that *The Daily Show with Jon Stewart* hated women? And that they had a long history of discriminating against and firing women? Sure, one of its cocreators was female, and one of its best-known and longest-running correspondents was a woman (and now the host of her own show), and there really isn't any evidence to prove what I just claimed, but that wouldn't stop someone from writing a story with that sensational angle if they could.

And so it went that a story with that exact conceit from *Jezebel* slammed into *The Daily Show* in June 2010. Irin Carmon's piece blindsided them just as her *Jezebel* nail polish story had blindsided us. It began when Carmon posted an article titled "*The Daily Show*'s Woman Problem."[1] Relying on some juicy quotes from people no longer with the show, Carmon claimed that the show had a poor record of finding and developing female comedic talent. She was also determined to make a name for herself. As you should expect by now, the article was a sensation. In order to accomplish this, she didn't actually speak to anyone who still worked for *The Daily Show*. It was much easier to use a collection of anonymous and off-the-record sources—like an ex-employee who hadn't worked there for eight years.

The cluster of stories that followed were read more than 500,000 times. The story was picked up by ABC News, the *Huffington Post*, the *Wall Street Journal*, E!, *Salon*, and others. In a memo to his staff, Carmon's boss and the publisher of *Gawker*, Nick Denton, commended the story for getting the kind of publicity that can't be bought. Denton wrote, "It was widely circulated within the media, spawned several more discussions, and affirmed our status as both an influencer and a muckraker." Jon Stewart was even forced to respond to the story on air. The *New York Times* rewarded Carmon and the website with a glowing profile: "A Web Site That's Not Afraid to Pick a Fight."[2] Yeah—it's easy to pick fights when you don't plan to fight fair.

For a writer like Carmon, whose pay is determined by the number of pageviews her posts receive, this was a home run. And for a publisher like

Denton, the buzz the story generated made his company more attractive to advertisers and increased the valuation of his brand.

That her story was a lie didn't matter. That it was part of a pattern of manipulation didn't matter.

The women of *The Daily Show* published an open letter on the show's website a few days after the story hit.[3] Women accounted for some 40 percent of the staff, the letter read, from writers and producers to correspondents and interns, and had over a hundred years' experience on the show among them. The letter was remarkable in its clarity and understanding of what the blogger was doing. They addressed it "Dear People Who Don't Work Here" and called Carmon's piece an "inadequately researched blog post" that clung "to a predetermined narrative about sexism at *The Daily Show*."

If I hadn't experienced the exact situation myself, the letter would have made me hopeful that the truth would win out. But that's not how it works online. The next day the *New York Times* ran an article about their response. "THE DAILY SHOW" WOMEN SAY THE STAFF ISN'T SEXIST, the headline blared.[4]

Think about how bullshit that is: Because the *Jezebel* piece came first, the letter from the *Daily Show* women is shown merely as a response instead of the refutation that it actually was. No matter how convincing, it only reasserts, in America's biggest newspaper, Carmon's faulty claim of sexism on the show. They could never undo what they'd been accused of—no matter how spurious the accusation—they could only deny it. And denials don't mean anything online.

Kahane Cooperman, a female co-executive producer at the show, told the *New York Times*: "No one called us, no one talked to us. We felt like, we work here, we should take control of the narrative." She didn't know how it works. *Jezebel* controls the narrative. Carmon drummed it up; no one else had a right to it.

The day after the story ran, but before the women of *The Daily Show* could respond, Carmon got another post out of the subject: "5 Unconvincing Excuses for *Daily Show* Sexism," as she titled it—dismissing in advance the criticism leveled by some concerned and skeptical commenters. It was a preemptive strike to marginalize anyone who doubted her shaky accusations and to solidify her pageview-hungry version of reality.[5]

In the titles of her first and second articles, you can see what she is doing. The Daily Show's "Woman Problem" from her first post became their "Sexism" in her second. One headline bootstraps the next; the what-ifs of the first piece became the basis for the second. Her story proves itself.

When the New York Times asked Carmon to respond to the women of The Daily Show's claim that they were not interviewed or contacted for the story (which restated the allegations), she "refused to comment further." Yet when The Daily Show supposedly invoked this right by not speaking to Carmon, it was evidence that they were hiding something. A double standard? Um, yes.

Did Carmon update her piece to reflect the dozens of comments released by Daily Show women? Or at least give their response a fair shake? No, of course not. In a forty-word post (forty words!) she linked their statement with the tag "open letter" and whined that she just wished they'd spoken up when she was writing the story. She didn't acknowledge the letter's claim that they actually had tried to speak with her and danced over the fact that it's her job to get their side of the story before publishing, even if that's difficult or time-consuming.[6]

How many Jezebel readers do you think threw out their original impression for a new one? Or even saw the update? The post making the accusation did 333,000 views. Her post showing the Daily Show women's response did 10,000 views—3 percent of the impressions of the first shot.

Did Carmon really send repeated requests for comment to The Daily Show? A major television show like that would get hundreds of requests a week. Whom did she contact? Did she provide time for them to respond? Or is it much more likely that she gave the show a cursory heads-up minutes before publication? In my experience, the answers to these questions are appalling. No wonder she wouldn't explain her methods to the Times. All I have to go on is my personal history with Carmon, and it tells me that at every juncture she does whatever will benefit her most. I've seen the value she places on the truth—particularly if it gets in the way of a big story.

There is something deeply twisted about an arrangement like this one. Carmon's accusations received five times as many views as the post about the *Daily Show* women's response, even though the latter undermines much of the former. There is something wrong with the way the writer is compensated for both pieces—as well as the third, fourth, or fifth she managed to squeeze out of the topic (again, more than 500,000 pageviews combined). Finally, there is something wrong with the fact that Denton's sites benefit merely by going toe to toe with a cultural icon like Jon Stewart—even if their reports are later discredited. They know this; it's why they do it.

This is how it works online. A writer finds a narrative to advance that is profitable to them, or perhaps that they are personally or ideologically motivated to advance, and are able to thrust it into the national consciousness before anyone has a chance to bother checking if it's true or not.

Emily Gould, a former editor of *Gawker*, later wrote a piece for *Slate* entitled "How Feminist Blogs Like *Jezebel* Gin Up Page Views by Exploiting Women's Worst Tendencies," in which she explained the motivations behind such a story:

> *It's a prime example of the feminist blogosphere's tendency to tap into the market force of what I've come to think of as "outrage world"—the regularly occurring firestorms stirred up on mainstream, for-profit, woman-targeted blogs like* Jezebel *and also, to a lesser degree,* Slate's *own* XX Factor *and* Salon's Broadsheet. *They're ignited by writers who are pushing readers to feel what the writers claim is righteously indignant rage but which is actually just petty jealousy, cleverly marketed as feminism. These firestorms are great for page-view-pimping bloggy business.[7]*

Let me go a step further. Writers like Irin Carmon are driven more by shrewd self-interest and disdain for the consequences than they are by jealousy. It's a pattern for Carmon, as we've seen. She's not stopping, either.

Just a few months later, needing to reproduce her previous success, she saw an opportunity for a similar story, about producer and director Judd Apatow. After spotting him at a party, she tried to recapture the same outrage that had propelled her *Daily Show* piece into the public conscious-ness by again accusing a well-liked public figure of something impossible to deny.

The actual events of the evening: Director Judd Apatow attended a party hosted by a friend. Carmon attempted to corner and embarrass him for a story she wanted to write but failed. Yet in the world of blogging, this becomes the headline: JUDD APATOW DEFENDS HIS RECORD ON FEMALE CHARACTERS. It did about 35,000 views and a hundred comments.[8]

Carmon tried to "get" him, and did. I guess I have to give her credit, because this time she actually talked to the person she hoped to make her scapegoat. But still, you can actually see, as it happens, her effort to trap Apatow with the same insinuations and controversy that she did with Stewart. In the interview, Carmon repeatedly presented personal criti-cism of Apatow's movies as generally accepted fact that she was merely the conduit for, referring to his "critics" as though she weren't speaking for herself.

From the interview:

> Q: So you think that's unfair that you've gotten that criticism?
> A: Oh, I definitely think that it's unfair. . . . But that's okay.
> Q: I wonder if you could elaborate on your defense a little bit.
> A: I'm not defensive about it.
> Q: Do the conversation and the criticism change the way you
>    work?
> A: I don't hear any of the criticism when I test the movies and
>    talk to thousands of people. I think the people who talk
>    about these things on the internet are looking to stir things
>    up to make for interesting reading, but when you make
>    movies, thousands of people fill out cards telling you their
>    intimate feelings about the movies, and those criticisms
>    never came up, ever, on any of the movies.

In other words, there is nothing to any of her claims. But the post went up anyway. And she got paid just the same. Notoriety from events of 2010 and 2011 translated into a staff position at *Salon* and a spot on the *Forbes*

"30 Under 30" list for Carmon. Now she's a regular on MSNBC. It all worked out very nicely for her.*

## HOW ONE SIDE LEARNS FROM THE OTHER

In recent years, political groups of all kinds have picked up this playbook and run with it. Look at how the Right was able to make Hillary Clinton's health a topic of conversation during the campaign. Look at how they were able to make her e-mails and the Clinton Foundation appear to be major issues. Look at Pizzagate, the alt-right claim that the Democrats and Clinton were somehow associated with a mysterious, international child sex-trafficking ring that was being run out of a D.C. pizza restaurant. Conspiracy theorists like Alex Jones—whose fans are just as rabid as *Jezebel*'s (if only a bit crazier)—were able to repeatedly ask the same paranoid questions, make enough accusations, and eventually get enough mainstream media attention that some people began to think it was real.

The tactic has come to be called "concern trolling"—acting like you're upset and offended in order to exploit the ethics and empathy of your opponent. For instance, in 2017 a *New York Times* reporter replied to tweets rapper Bow Wow made about supposedly pimping out the First Lady by joking that "the outrage from @BreitbarkNews is going to be through the woof."† Trolls sprang into action, pretending like they were offended that a reporter would joke about sex slavery. And encourage "rape culture." Of course, the reporter had done no such thing and, more important, the trolls are precisely the kind of people who reject that there even is such a thing as rape culture. Yet they cleverly managed to direct enough faux concern that the ombudsman for the *New York Times* replied and repri-

---

*After an excerpt of this chapter ran on BoingBoing.com, Irin posted a response on *Salon*, titled "Did I Ruin Journalism?" It's (as you've probably guessed) a mostly self-centered and self-serving article filled with all sorts of rationalizations about her behavior that never challenge my core accusation: that she was motivated to attack high-profile targets with flimsy accusations because that's the business model of blogging. Tucker e-mailed me when he saw this link and gave me some good advice: "She's a legit idiot. You won, move on."

†More on *Breitbart* in the next chapter.

manded the writer. Far enough down the line, it seemed like the reporter really had said something ill advised and that people really were upset. Except they weren't.

The diabolicalness of this strategy is this: How were the people on the other side of these scandals supposed to respond? They were fighting against someone who wasn't fighting fair. Talking about it only gave the flimsy charges more airtime. Arguing that the other side wasn't actually offended sounds like an excuse. It was an impossible, brilliant kind of gaslighting. It was so effective and relentless that in the case of Pizzagate, a real person with a real assault rifle entered that pizza restaurant to "investigate" and fired real bullets into it.

I'm not trying to make a political point here. Whoever is doing it—Right or Left—it sucks. Even if Irin's intentions had been good—even if she'd really thought she was making a difference—I want you to see where this kind of outrage manufacturing has left us. The manipulators are indistinguishable from the publishers and bloggers. While it used to be that progressives pulled the media strings, it's clear the Right has begun to figure it out as well. That hasn't balanced things out—it's only made the truth harder to know. We're awash in manipulation and manipulators. If you don't believe me, keep reading.

# XIV

## THERE ARE OTHERS

### THE MANIPULATOR HALL OF FAME

> We are the tools of rich men behind the scenes. We
> are jumping jacks, they pull the strings and we
> dance.
>
> —JOHN SWINTON, JOURNALIST,
> *NEW YORK SUN* (1880)

SOMETIMES ONLY A MANIPULATOR CAN SPOT ANOTHER manipulator's work. In figuring out how to exploit the incentives of blogs, I discovered something pretty stunning: I wasn't the only one. But where I felt I worked for companies doing good things (selling great books, selling clothes made in America), others wielded influence and power over national debates. They changed politics and upended people's lives.

Remember Shirley Sherrod, the black woman who lost her job as a rural director for the U.S. Department of Agriculture after a video of her purportedly making a racist speech surfaced online? Behind it was a manipulator—a political manipulator selling (backward) ideas using the same tactics that people like me used to sell products.

This video caused a national shitstorm. Within hours it had gone from one blog to dozens of blogs to cable news websites, and then to the newspapers and back again.* Sherrod was forced to resign shortly after. The man who posted that video was the late Andrew Breitbart.

Of course we now know Sherrod is not a racist. In fact, the speech she was giving was about how *not* to be racist. But the bloggers and reporters who repeated the story were chasing a sensational story, reporting in real time, using only the limited material they had been given by Breitbart. And each report became more extreme and confident than the last—despite the lack of any new evidence to support their stories.

It was an embarrassing moment in modern politics (which says a lot). The fiasco ended with then-President Obama denouncing his own ad-

---

*According to Media Matters for America, FoxNews.com and the blog *Gateway Pundit* picked the story up first, followed within minutes by *Hot Air* and dozens of other blogs (most of which embedded the YouTube video and repeated the "racist" claim). The first television station to repeat the story, later that day, was a CBS affiliate in New York City. Next came the *Drudge Report*, followed by lead stories on nearly every nighttime cable news show and then morning show in the country. You could say it traded up the chain perfectly.

ministration's premature rush to judgment and apologizing personally to Sherrod. He lamented to *Good Morning America*: "We now live in this media culture where something goes up on YouTube or a blog and everybody scrambles."

Breitbart was the master of making people scramble. Whenever I need to understand the mind of blogging, I try to picture Andrew Breitbart sitting down at his computer to edit and publish that video. Because he was not a racist either. Nor was he the partisan kook the Left mistook him for. He was a media manipulator just like me. He understood and embodied the economics of the web better than anyone. And in some ways I envy him, because he was able to do it without the guilt that drove me to write this book.

Breitbart was the first employee of the *Drudge Report* and a founding employee of the *Huffington Post*. He helped build the dominant conservative *and* liberal blogs. He wasn't simply an ideologue; he was an expert on what spreads—a provocateur.

From his perspective, the wide discrediting of his Sherrod video was not a failure. Not even close. The Sherrod story put him and his blog on the lips—in anger and in awe—of nearly every media outlet in the country. Sherrod was just collateral damage. The political machine was a plaything for Breitbart, and he made it do just what he wanted (dance and give him attention). He'd never confess as much, so I'll do it for him.

Breitbart teed up the story perfectly. By splitting the edited Sherrod clip into two pieces (two minutes, thirty seconds, and one minute, six seconds, respectively), he made it quick to consume and easy for bloggers to watch and republish. Since the unedited clip is forty-three minutes long, it was doubtful anyone would sit through the whole thing to rain on his parade. The post was titled "Video Proof: The NAACP Awards Racism," and he spent most of his thirteen hundred words fighting the imaginary foil of efforts to suppress the Tea Party, instead of explaining where the video came from.

For all the complaints from blogs, cable channels, and newspapers about being misled, Breitbart had actually given them a highly profitable gift. In getting to report on his accusations, and then the reversal, and then the discussion "about the Breitbart/Sherrod controversy," news outlets actually got three major stories instead of one. Most stories last only a few minutes, but the Sherrod controversy lasted nearly a week. It's still good for follow-ups today. Better than anyone, Breitbart understood that the media doesn't mind being played, because they get something out of it—namely, pageviews, ratings, and readers.

Breitbart, who died suddenly of heart failure in early 2012, might not be with us any longer, but it hardly matters. As he once said, "Feeding the media is like training a dog. You can't throw an entire steak at a dog to train it to sit. You have to give it little bits of steak over and over again until it learns." Breitbart did plenty of training in his short time on the scene. Today one of the dog's masters is gone, sure, but the dog still responds to the same commands.

## THE MASTER AND HIS PROTÉGÉS

A system can tolerate a few bad actors. The problem is when those bad actors spawn replicants, and that is sadly the case with Breitbart. Not only has *Breitbart News* managed to survive Breitbart's passing, but the site is arguably stronger than ever—in fact, the site's publisher, Steve Bannon, became a top adviser to Donald Trump. Breitbart's fingerprints were all over the 2016 election, smudging the truth until it became impossible to see.

Aside from Steve Bannon, the legacy of Breitbart lives on in a number of younger media manipulators like James O'Keefe and Charles Johnson. Take the young O'Keefe, who was mentored and funded by Breitbart early on (and later had some of his legal bills picked up by Trump supporters). O'Keefe is responsible for several stories nearly as big as the Sherrod piece. He posed as a pimp in a set of undercover videos that supposedly show the now-defunct community activist group ACORN giving advice to the "pimp" on how to avoid paying taxes. He recorded NPR seemingly showing its willingness to conceal the source of a large donation from a Muslim group. Once he even planned a bizarre attempt to seduce an attractive CNN correspondent on camera in order to embarrass the station.

Like Breitbart's clips, O'Keefe's work is heavily and disingenuously edited—far beyond what the context and actual events would support.

His clips spread quickly because they are perfectly designed to suit a specific and vocal group: angry Republicans. By prefitting the narrative to appeal to conservative bloggers, his sensational stories quickly overwhelm the atrophied verification and accountability muscles of the rest of the media and become real stories. And even when they don't, as was the case with the CNN story, it's still enough to get their names in the news.

O'Keefe learned from Breitbart that in the blogging market there is a profound shortage of investigative material or original reporting. It's just too expensive to produce. So rather than bear those costs, O'Keefe's stories are hollow shells—an edited clip, a faux investigation—that blogs can use as a substitute for the real thing. Then he watches as the media falls over itself to propagate it as quickly as possible. Short, shocking narratives with a reusable sound bite are all it takes.

Because they assume the cloak of the persecuted underdog, the inevitable backlash helps O'Keefe and Breitbart rather than hurting them. Nearly all of O'Keefe's stories have been exposed as doctored to some extent. When forced to reveal the unedited footage of the NPR and ACORN stunts, most of the main accusations were found to have been amplified or manipulated. But by that point the victims had already lost their jobs or been publicly branded.

For instance, the ACORN clip shows O'Keefe wearing a comical pimp hat, a fur coat, and a cane to the meetings, when in reality he wore a suit and tie. He'd edited in frames with the other costume after the fact. By the time this was exposed six months later, the pimp image was indelibly stuck in people's minds, and the only effect of the discovery was to put O'Keefe's name back in the news. Being caught as a manipulator can only help make you more famous.

Charles Johnson is another media manipulator. I can't rest all the blame for him on Breitbart, as Charles has several times said that my book was influential in his development as a political provocateur and troll. I hope my writing had nothing to do with Charles's decision to try to personally impugn Michael Brown—the teenager killed by police in Ferguson, Missouri—or his obsession with trying to prove that Obama is gay. (When I asked him about his fascination with race, he gave me a bunch of theories about how blacks are not as intelligent as whites and possibly more prone to violence, which to me is *real* racism and much more serious than politically incorrect language.) In any case, Charles has developed a serious track record of inserting controversial discussion points in the media and claims to have the ear of many powerful politicians and writers. Even if this isn't true, his attempts to stir things up are verifiable and have real impact. Below is an e-mail exchange that he forwarded me (unsolicited) in 2017 that he had with *Daily Beast* reporter Gideon Resnick where Johnson tried to confess that he had fabricated the controversial "Trump dossier":

> **From:** Charles Johnson
> **Date:** Tuesday, January 10, 2017 at 11:50PM
> **To:** "Resnick, Gideon"
> **Subject:** Confession
>
> My friends placed the fake news with BuzzFeed.
>
> On Tuesday, January 10, 2017, Resnick, Gideon wrote:
>
> Huh. Tell me more.
>
> On Tuesday, January 10, 2017, Charles Johnson wrote:
>
> My friends targeted BuzzFeed because they knew that they
> would fall for it because they have no journalistic integrity.
>
> The piss stuff re Trump is in reference to this.
>
> https://mpcdot.com/forums/topic/8748-rick-wilsons-son-is-a
> -goddamn-piss-pimp/page__st__40
>
> Rick Wilson attacked alt-right. They went after his son and found
> "Pimpfeet", his high school son was posting raunchy erotica
> stuff.

Though I wasn't involved I love the creativity of people including "golden showers", if Rick Wilson was involved. With his son advocating for pissing in women's mouths last year, calling for sadistic scatplay, it's perfect someone turned that back on him.

Rick Wilson's career is now over and Ben Smith needs to resign as editor in chief of BuzzFeed's news division.

I don't have any reason to suspect that the dossier was fake or placed by Johnson, but you can see why a reporter might. It's in their interest to print something like that—or to print that someone is *claiming* that, just as it was in their interest to run the unverified dossier in the first place.

Johnson also runs a site called Wesearchr.com, which puts up crowd-funded bounties on information and leaks. The site is really just a vehicle for trolling—their campaigns raise money for information that proves certain politicians are gay or for evidence that Obama used a ghostwriter for his bestselling memoirs. They raised north of five thousand dollars to find "criminal acts" committed by *Gawker* publisher Nick Denton and ten thousand dollars to secure audio recordings of John McCain producing propaganda for the North Vietnamese. Even if these claims are dubious and ridiculous, that's not the point—the manipulation is that by raising money to *look* for them, Johnson and his supporters are repeating the claims and giving them weight.

## BEATING THEM AT THEIR OWN GAME

Andrew Breitbart did eventually issue a correction to the widely disproved Sherrod story. He was so wrong and the backlash was so strong, he had to. But he remained defiant. At the top of the article:

**Correction:** While Ms. Sherrod made the remarks captured in the first video featured in this post while she held a federally appointed position, the story she tells refers to actions she took before she held that federal position.

A bullshit correction, to say the least.

Sherrod's attempt to clear her name and later to sue Breitbart for libel and slander were just other chances for him to bluster.* The press release Breitbart issued was an exercise in defiant misdirection: "Andrew Breitbart on Pigford Lawsuit: 'Bring It On.'" It's exactly what I would have advised him to do if he'd asked me—in fact, I've basically done the exact same thing, only I was a bit more vulgar. Remember, I'm the guy who put out a press release with the headline: TUCKER MAX RESPONDS TO CTA DECISION: "BLOW ME."

I did that because the best way to make your critics work for you is to make them irrationally angry. Blinded by rage or indignation, they spread your message to every ear and media outlet they can find. Breitbart telling his haters to bring it on certainly accomplished this, as did completely side-stepping the Sherrod issue and pretending this was some giant political conspiracy about reparations for slavery. In refusing to acknowledge, even in the slightest, that she might have been innocent of everything he accused her of, Breitbart played it like an old pro.

This is what opponents of the alt-right seem to miss. *They are trying to make you upset.* They want you to be irrationally angry—it's how they win. Most brands and personalities try to appeal to a wide swath of the population. Niche players and polarizing personalities are only ever going to be interesting to a small subgroup. While this might seem like a disadvantage, it's actually a huge opportunity, because it allows them to leverage the dismissals, anger, mockery, and contempt of the population at large as proof of their credibility. Someone like Andrew Breitbart or Milo Yiannopoulos or Charles Johnson doesn't care that you hate them—they like it. It's proof to their followers that they are doing something subversive and meaningful. It gives their followers something to talk about. It imbues the whole movement with a sense of urgency and action—it creates purpose and meaning.

The only way to beat them is by controlling your reaction and letting them embarrass themselves, as they inevitably will. I told you earlier about the violent protests of Milo at UC Berkeley. While those *adults*—

---

*A thought exercise for the liberals who were aghast at Peter Thiel's funding Hulk Hogan's successful lawsuit against *Gawker*: If a billionaire had supported Sherrod's lawsuit against Breitbart and by winning shut them down, would you be upset?

and college students are adults—were flipping out and acting like babies, a sixteen-year-old girl in Canada simply did some research. She found some utterly indefensible comments Milo had made about pedophilia and leaked them to a conservative group, and within a few days Milo had lost his book deal and his job . . . at *Breitbart*, no less. The irony could not have been sweeter for some.

If you can put aside your anger, if you can put aside the unfortunate fate that befell Sherrod, you can see what masterful music Breitbart and O'Keefe are able to play on the instruments of online media. When they sit down to publish on their blogs, they are not simply political extremists but ruthless seekers of attention. From this attention comes fame and profit—a platform for bestselling books, lucrative speaking and consulting gigs, donations, and millions of dollars in online advertising revenue.

Their subtle felonies against the truth are deliberate and premeditated. The way to beat them is not by freaking out. It's by beating them at their own game. And sooner is better—because every day we wait there is more collateral damage.

# XV

## SLACKTIVISM IS NOT ACTIVISM

### RESISTING THE TIME AND MIND SUCK OF ONLINE MEDIA

> There is no more Big Lie, only Big Lulz, and getting gamed is no shame. It's the seal on the social contract, a mark of our participation in this new covenant of cozening.
>
> —*WIRED*

YOU SIT DOWN TO YOUR COMPUTER TO WORK. FIVE minutes later you're on your fifth YouTube video of talking babies. What happened? Do you just not have any self-control? Sorry, but self-control has got nothing to do with it. Not when the clip was deliberately made more attractive by subliminally embedded images guaranteed to catch your attention. Not when the length of the video was calibrated to be precisely as long as average viewers are statistically most likely to watch. Not when autoplay starts the next video before you have time to click away.

Would you also be surprised to hear that the content of the video was designed around popular search terms? And that the title went through multiple iterations to see which got the most clicks? And what if the video you watch after this one (and the one after that and after that) had been recommended and optimized by YouTube with the deliberate intention of making online video take up as much time in your life as television does?[1]

No wonder you can't get any work done. They won't let you.

The key, as megawatt liberal blogger Matt Yglesias advised when interviewed for the book *Making It in the Political Blogosphere*, is to keep readers addicted: "The idea is to discourage people from drifting away. If you give them a break, they might find that there's something else that's just as good, and they might go away."

We once naively believed that blogs would be a boon to democracy. Unlike TV, the web wasn't about passive consumption. Blogs were about engagement and citizen activism. Blogs looked like they would free us from a crummy media world of bias, conflict, manipulation, and sensationalism. But as James Fenimore Cooper presciently observed in the nineteenth century, "If newspapers are useful in overthrowing tyrants, it is only to establish a tyranny of their own."

Tyranny is an understatement for the media today. Those between the ages of eight and eighteen are online roughly eight hours a day, a figure that does not include texting or television. America spends more than fifty billion minutes a day on Facebook, and nearly a quarter of all internet browsing time is spent on social media sites and blogs. In a given month, blogs stream something like 150 million videos to their users. So of course there is mass submission and apathy—everyone is distracted, deliberately so.[2]

The idea that the web is empowering is just a bunch of rattling, chattering talk. Everything you consume online has been "optimized" to make you dependent on it. Content is engineered to be clicked, glanced at, or found—like a trap designed to bait, distract, and capture you. Blogs are out to game you—to steal your time from you and sell it to advertisers—and they do this every day.

## CHEATING IS EVERYWHERE

You see a link to a video in a YouTube search that makes it look like a hot girl is in it, so you click. You watch, but she's nowhere to be found. Welcome to the art of "thumbnail cheating." It's a common tactic YouTube publishers use to make their videos more tantalizing than the competition.

The most common play is to use a girl, preferably one who looks like she might get naked, but it can be anything from a kitten to a photo of someone famous. Anything to give the clip an edge. Some of the biggest accounts on YouTube were built this way. The technique can drive thousands or even tens of thousands of views to a video, helping it chart on "most viewed" lists and allowing it to spread and be recommended.

Online video publishers do this with YouTube's consent. Originally, YouTube chose a video thumbnail from the halfway, one-quarter, or three-quarters points of the video. So smart manipulators simply inserted a single frame of a sexy image at exactly one of those points in order to draw clicks. Members of the YouTube Partner Program—the people who get paid for their contributions to YouTube through ad revenue and make millions for the company—are allowed to use *any* image they choose as their thumbnail, even images that don't ever appear in the video. Sure, YouTube asks that the image be "representative," but if they were actually serious about quashing profitable trickery, why allow the practice at all?

Because this is an endless battle for clicks and attention. Everyone is trying to get an edge.

## FAKE NEWS

I was speaking with my father the other day and he asked me a question about some news story he'd read. What he said was confusing and didn't quite add up. So I looked online and found it. Oops, the story was from the *Onion*. It was satire. Shared on Facebook and glanced at only for its headline, though, it seemed real. No wonder people voted a notorious liar into office—they've gotten used to being lied to!

The *Onion* isn't the only one who exploits this phenomenon, of course. Andy Borowitz, the left-wing satirist, knows that a huge portion of his traffic comes from unthinking clicks by people who confuse satire with real headlines. And the *New Yorker*, who publishes him, benefits from that confusion.

More recently we've seen a rise in publications that specialize in almost outright propaganda—actual fake news. Sites like *Denver Guardian*, *Info-Wars*, *National Report*, *70 News*, *The Political Insider*, and *Ending the Fed*. Headlines like FBI AGENT SUSPECTED IN HILLARY EMAIL LEAKS FOUND DEAD IN APPARENT MURDER-SUICIDE. WIKILEAKS CONFIRMS HILLARY SOLD WEAPONS TO ISIS . . . THEN DROPS ANOTHER BOMBSHELL! BREAK-ING: FOX NEWS EXPOSES TRAITOR MEGYN KELLY, KICKS HER OUT FOR BACKING HILLARY. These are not real publications and the claims in those headlines are not true. But that's precisely the point. *They feel true.* People share and spread them for the same reasons that, deep down, motivate you to share most of the articles you share on Facebook or Twitter, as Ricky Van Veen pointed out in his excellent TEDx talk: They confirm what you want to be true and what you want to reflect your identity.

Even when the sites are reputable, the content might not be. Even reputable outlets seem to be unable to resist the urge to traffic in fake news. For instance, I'm no fan of Ben Carson. When I saw this *USA Today* headline, I just shook my head: BEN CARSON JUST REFERRED TO SLAVES AS "IMMIGRANTS." What an asshole, right? The *New York Times* headline is not much better: BEN CARSON REFERS TO SLAVES AS "IMMIGRANTS" IN

FIRST REMARKS TO HUD STAFF. If the *Times* and *USA Today* say it, it's got to be true. But it was because I had this immediately negative reaction to Ben Carson, because it seemed almost too boneheaded even for him, that I urged myself to check the article out. Turns out, after speaking about immigrants coming to America via Ellis Island, Carson had said:

> *There were other immigrants who came here in the bottom of slave ships, worked even longer, even harder for less. But they too had a dream that one day their sons, daughters, grandsons, granddaughters, great-grandsons, great-granddaughters, might pursue prosperity and happiness in this land.*

Only someone trying to deliberately wrench those remarks out of context would think Carson—who is black, by the way—was referring to slaves as willing immigrants. He clearly said they came here in slave ships and was making a point most people who disagree with his policies would agree with—that African Americans have had to work even harder than immigrants to fulfill even the most basic dreams for their children. Yet all of that was lost because somebody wanted to get more traffic for their article.

I still don't like Ben Carson. But I dislike him for *real* reasons, not because of fake news. I cannot stress enough how important this distinction is. The more an article feels like it is true, the more skeptical you should be about it. If you haven't heard of the website before, it's probably because it's not legitimate. Be discerning. Be cynical. Don't let "close enough" be your standard for truth and opinion. Insist on accuracy and on getting it right.

## SELLING YOU TO THE HIGHEST BIDDER

Ever noticed those little "From Our Partners" or "From Around the Web" thumbnails and links that appear on the pages of basically every major online publisher these days, from the *Huffington Post* to CNN.com to *Slate*? If you didn't know, those sites aren't really "partners." These links are not handpicked stories that the site's editors thought worthy of referral (would anyone ever willingly link to an article from Allstate Insurance?).

No, these links are part of an ad unit. The biggest providers in this space are companies like Taboola and Outbrain. The point is to trick users interested in more content into clicking on scammy ads loosely disguised as content: "People Struggling with Credit Card Debt May Be in for a Big Surprise." "My Wife and I Tried Blue Apron: Here's What Happened." "10 Celebs Who Lost Their Hot Bodies." Even as I write this, the *New York Times* is running their own version of one of these ads at the top of their site: "Why Irish Pubs Are a Metaphor for American Immigration" . . . sponsored by Guinness.

It's probably not a coincidence that a good many of those links have bikini-photo thumbnails, weight-loss "success" stories, or celebrity names in the headline. Sites get paid by the click and users can't unclick, so tactics that encourage that action are all that matter at the end of the day. More important, great content publishers are far less likely to need to buy traffic than crappy publishers or scammy salespeople. It's just people selling credit cards and mindless gossip at high margins' need to chase the idiots who click those things.

If that feels a little gross, it should. When you're on Fusion.net, thinking they care about you, in fact, they've done the calculation and found that it's more profitable to send you away to another site than it is to keep you there reading more of the original content they make themselves.

Of course, not every site makes this bargain. I asked Patrick de Laive, cofounder of TheNextWeb.com, why "From Our Partners" links were conspicuously absent from his site. His reply: "The main reason why we're not doing something like that is that we don't see the value for our readers. It might be an okay revenue stream, but as long as there is no clear value for our readers, we don't want to bother them with it." But the reality is most sites do.

## DRUGGED AND DELUSIONAL: THE RESULT

I remember seeing Jeff Jarvis, the blogger best known for his condescending media pontificating, at a tech conference once. He sat down next to me, ostensibly to watch and listen to the talk. Not once did he look up from his laptop. He tapped away the entire time, first on Twitter, then on Facebook, then moderating comments on his blog, and on and on, completely oblivious to the world. It struck me then that whatever I decided to do with the rest of my life, I did not want to end up like him. Because at the end of the talk, Jarvis got up and spoke during the panel's Q&A, addressing the speakers as well as the audience. In the world of the web, why should not paying attention preclude you from getting your say?

That's what web culture does to you. Psychologists call this the "narcotizing dysfunction," when people come to mistake the busyness of the media with real knowledge, and confuse spending time consuming that with doing something. In 1948, long before the louder, faster, and busier world of Twitter and social media, Paul Lazarsfeld and Robert Merton wrote:

> The interested and informed citizen can congratulate himself on his lofty state of interest and information and neglect to see that he has abstained from decision and action. In short, he takes his secondary contact with the world of political reality, his reading and listening and thinking, as a vicarious performance. . . . He is concerned. He is informed. And he has all sorts of ideas as to what should be done. But, after he has gotten through his dinner and after he has listened to his favored radio programs and after he has read his second newspaper of the day, it is really time for bed.[3]

This is the exact reaction that our current online system produces: apathy without self-awareness. To keep you so caught up and consumed with the bubble that you don't even realize you're in one. The more time kids spend online, studies show, the worse their grades are. According to a Nielsen study, active social networkers are 26 percent *more* likely to give their opinion on politics and current events offline, even though they are exactly the people whose opinions should matter the least.

"Talkativeness is afraid of the silence which reveals its emptiness," Kierkegaard once said. Now you know why sharing, commenting, clicking, and participating are pushed so strongly by blogs and entertainment sites. They don't want silence. No wonder blogs auto-refresh with new material every thirty seconds. Of course they want to send updates to your phone and include you on e-mail alerts. No one is listening to you—they're laughing at you. They're glad you're distracted. They're happy you're posting on social media, because it means you're not showing up at city council meetings, because it means you're not voting. It's time that both sides face up to the incredible manipulation that's happening to both parties (by that I mean people, not political parties). Twitter isn't designed to help you get in and get out with the best information as quickly as possible—it's supposed to suck you into either a contentious world of argument and debate or an echo chamber that reassures you everyone thinks like you do. Facebook is supposedly one of the largest news sources in the world, and days after the election, it denied that the news it shared could have possibly impacted users' behavior in a significant way. With manipulative tactics that range from exploiting the so-called attention gap to giving voice to propagandistic campaign surrogates to addictive UX features to editors warping coverage around their own "narrative," we're all drowning in a sea of unreality.

If the users stop for even a second, they may see what is really going on. And then the business model would fall apart.

## HOW TO MAKE AMERICA GREAT AGAIN

My son was born on November 9, 2016. The surprise of the election results had sent my wife into labor. The previous few months had been particularly unhappy ones for me. Not because there was anything wrong in my life; on the contrary, in my life things were going quite well. The source of my misery? I was caught up in the news cycle.

I told myself it was partly my job. But the reality was, I was doing less of my job. How could it have been otherwise? I'd become consumed by a divisive, contentious, scandal-driven news loop. Twitter. Google News. Apple News. Facebook. Longreads and hot takes via Instapaper. CNN. E-mail conversations. NPR.

My media diet had gone from abstemious to addicted. As we sat in the recovery room and I caught myself pulling up my Twitter account to read another article from another person who had undoubtedly been wrong about the election (as I myself embarrassingly had), I felt a wave of shame.

What the hell was I doing? Here, in the hospital, in this important moment in my life, I was trying to read the news?

I'd venture to guess that there is someone else who, deep down, can at least relate to that sentiment: fellow (and admitted) news junkie, and now president, Donald Trump.

It's time we all came to terms with our compulsion: How is anyone going to make America or themselves great again, if we're all glued to our devices and television screens? How can anyone maintain their sanity when everything you read, see, and hear is designed to make you stop whatever you're doing and consume because the world is supposedly ending?

To think it is his morning viewing of *Fox & Friends*, his evening tune-in to *Hannity*, and his regular checking of silly conspiracy-ridden Twitter accounts that have been responsible for some of his administration's most boneheaded and unnecessary scandals.

In the 1990s political scientists began to speak about what they called the CNN effect. The basic premise was that a world of twenty-four-hour media coverage would have considerable impact on foreign and domestic policy. When world leaders, generals, and politicians watch their actions—and the actions of their counterparts—dissected, analyzed, and speculated about in real time, the argument goes, it changes what they do and how they do it . . . much for the worse.

When they came up with this theory, CNN was mostly a niche channel. The idea that it would soon be only a part of a vast attention-sucking ecosystem that went far beyond broadcasting twenty-four hours a day was inconceivable. Today the news machine includes not only dozens of cable channels but also millions of blogs and hundreds of millions of social media accounts—all of which operate in real time, creating billions of bits of content a second.

How can anyone make tough decisions while trying to keep abreast of this? How do they know what is real chatter and what is fake? The answer is they can't. They just get whipped around and are as confused as everyone else.

I marked the day after the election by doing the following: I deleted Twitter from my phone. I deleted Facebook from my phone. I deleted the Google News app from my phone. I figured out how to remove Apple

News from Siri. I removed CNN from my nightly scan of the television channels.

I wasn't interested in being jerked around anymore. I didn't need to follow every meaningless update or fall for every outrageous headline. It was preventing me from seeing the bigger pictures. Now, if only politicians and leaders could do the same. The world would be a better place.

# XVI

## JUST PASSING THIS ALONG

### WHEN NO ONE OWNS WHAT THEY SAY

> Our readers collectively know far more than we will ever know, and by responding to our posts, they quickly make our coverage more nuanced and accurate.
>
> **—HENRY BLODGET, EDITOR AND CEO OF *BUSINESS INSIDER***

> Truths are more likely to have been discovered by one man than by a nation.
>
> **—DESCARTES**

HENRY BLODGET, IN A REVEALING ONSTAGE INTER-
view with reporter Andrew Sorkin, explained the increasingly common
cycle like this: "There are stories that will appear on Gawker Media—huge
conversations in the blogosphere—everything else. It's passed all over.
Everyone knows about it. Everybody's clicking on it. Then, finally, an approved source speaks to the *New York Times* or somebody else, and the
*New York Times* will suddenly say, 'Okay now we can report that.' "

On Twitter you'll see a common phrase in people's bios: "Retweets ≠
endorsements," meaning that just because they share something doesn't
mean they agree with it or know if it's true or not. The venture capitalist
Marc Andreessen often jokingly tweets alongside breaking news, "Huge,
if true . . ." (in reality, news is meaningless unless true). In White House
press briefings and now from politicians themselves we see a version of
this attitude: Statements are prefaced with "It's being reported that" or
presented as "alternative facts." Errors are being defended with "Lots of
people were saying it." Just imagine you're the guy whose job it is to apologize to the British ambassador because the president stupidly accused
British spies of helping Barack Obama wiretap him. Just imagine actually
having to say, as a White House official later told reporters, "Mr. Spicer
and General McMaster both explained that [Trump] was simply pointing
to public reports and not endorsing any specific story."* I almost pitied
Sean Spicer: "All we're doing is literally reading off what other stations
and people have reported. We're not casting judgment on that."

Apparently we live in a world where at even the highest and most sensitive level information is passed on without being vetted, where the final
judgment of truth or falsity does not fall on the outlet reporting it or the

---

* Even more absurd, the "public report" was actually just a comment by an on-air contributor
to Fox News with no foreign policy background, who was later pulled because of it.

**TRUST ME, I'M LYING**

person spreading it but on the readers themselves. As a *TechCrunch* editor described it, "With social media, there are no editors. There is no waiting for confirmation. When you tweet or re-tweet, you are not checking the facts or even so much concerned if you are spreading a lie. . . . But this is how process journalism now works. It's journalism as beta."

Is it any wonder, then, that we are drowning in inaccuracies and mistakes? I don't think so.

Nearly everyone involved in media and politics is shirking their duty—and that makes them ripe for exploitation (or in the case of American Apparel and CNN, a missile that can strike your company at any time). And yet most of the social media elite want this for our future.

## THE DELEGATION OF TRUST

Reporters can hardly be everywhere at once. For most of recent history, media outlets all used the same self-imposed editorial guidelines, so relying on one another's work was natural. When a fact appeared in the *Chicago Tribune*, it was pretty safe for the *San Francisco Chronicle* to repeat that same fact, since both publications have high verification standards.

These were the old rules:

1. If the outlet is legitimate, the stories it breaks are.
2. If the story is legitimate, the facts inside it are.
3. It can be assumed that if the subject of the story is legitimate, then what people are saying about it probably is too.

These rules allow one journalist to use the facts brought forth by another, hopefully with attribution. This assumption makes researching much easier for reporters, since they can build on the work of those who came before them, instead of starting from the beginning of a story. It's a process known as the "delegation of trust."[1]

The web has its own innovation on the delegation of trust, known as "link economy." Basically it refers to the exchange of traffic and information between blogs and websites. Say the *Los Angeles Times* reported that Brad Pitt and Angelina Jolie were splitting up. Perez Hilton would link to this report on his blog and add his own thoughts. Then other blogs would link to Perez's account and maybe the original *Times* source as well. This is an outgrowth from the early days of blogging, when blogs lacked the resources to do much original reporting. They relied on other outlets to break stories, which they then linked to and provided commentary on. From this came what is called the link economy, one that encouraged sites to regularly and consistently link to each other. I send you a link now, you send me a link later—we trade off doing the job of reporting.

The phrase "link economy" was popularized by Jeff Jarvis, whom you met here earlier. His credentials as a blogger, journalism professor at the City University of New York's Graduate School of Journalism, and author of books such as *What Would Google Do?* made him an early influential voice in new media. Unfortunately, he's also an idiot, and the link economy concept he advocated has unquestionably made the media a less reliable resource than it once was.

The link economy encourages blogs to point their readers to other bloggers who are saying crazy things, to borrow from each other without verification, and to take more or less completed stories from other sites, add a layer of commentary, and turn them into something they call their own. To borrow a term from computer science, the link economy is recursive—blogs pull from the blogs that came before them to create new content. Think of how a mash-up video relies on other clips to make something new, or how Twitter users retweet messages from other members and add to them.

But as the trading-up-the-chain scam makes clear, the media is no longer governed by a set of universal editorial and ethics standards. Even within publications, the burden of proof for the print version of a newspaper might differ drastically from what reporters need to go live with a blog post. As media outlets grapple with tighter deadlines and smaller staffs, many of the old standards for verification, confirmation, and fact-checking are becoming impossible to maintain. Every blog has its own editorial policy, but few disclose it to readers. The material one site pulls from another can hardly be trusted when it's just as likely to have been written with low standards as with high ones.

The conditions on which the delegation of trust and the link economy need to operate properly no longer exist. But the habits remain and have been mixed into a potent combination. The result is often embarrassing and contagious misinformation.

A few years back a young Irish student posted a fake quotation on the *Wikipedia* page of composer Maurice Jarre shortly after the man died. (The obituary-friendly quote said in part, "When I die there will be a final waltz playing in my head that only I can hear.") At the time, I'm not sure the student understood the convergence of the link economy and the delegation of trust. That changed in an instant, when his fabricated quote began to appear in obituaries for the composer around the world.

It's difficult to pinpoint where it started, but at some point, a reporter or a blogger saw that quotation and used it in an article. Eventually the quote found its way to the *Guardian*, and from there it may as well have been real. The quote so perfectly expressed what writers wished to say about Jarre, and the fact that it was in the *Guardian*, a reputable and prominent newspaper, made it the source of many links. And so it went along the chain, its origins obscured, and the more times it was repeated, the more real it felt.

This is where the link economy fails in practice. *Wikipedia* editors may have caught and quickly removed the student's edit, but that didn't automatically update the obituaries that had incorporated it. *Wikipedia* administrators are not able to edit stories on other people's websites, so the quote remained in the *Guardian* until they caught and corrected it too. The link economy is designed to confirm and support, not to question or correct. In fact, the stunt was only discovered after the student admitted what he'd done.

"I am 100 percent convinced that if I hadn't come forward, that quote would have gone down in history as something Maurice Jarre said, instead of something I made up," he said. "It would have become another example where, once anything is printed enough times in the media without challenge, it becomes fact."[2]

The proponents of the link economy brush aside these examples. The posts can be updated, they say; that's the beauty of the internet. But as far as I know there is no technology that issues alerts to each trackback or every reader who has read a corrupted article, and there never will be.

Senator Eugene McCarthy once compared the journalists covering his 1968 presidential campaign to birds on a telephone wire. When one got up to fly to a different wire, they'd all follow. When another flew back, the rest would too. Today this metaphor needs an update. The birds still follow one another's leads just as eagerly—but the wire need not always exist. They can be and often are perched on illusions, just as blogs were when they repeated Maurice Jarre's manufactured remarks.

## THE LINK ILLUSION

In the link economy, the blue stamp of an html link *seems* like it will support weight. (As had the links to the *Guardian* story containing the false quote.) If I write in an article that "Thomas Jefferson, by his own remarks, admitted to committing acts considered felonious in the State of Virginia," you'd want to see some evidence before you were convinced. Now imagine that I added a link to the words "acts considered felonious." This link could go to anything—it could go to a dictionary definition of "felonious acts," or it could go to a pdf of the entire penal code for the state of Virginia, or it could just go to a gif that when you click it says, "Ha! You shouldn't have trusted me!" But by linking to something, I have vaguely complied with the standards of the link economy. I have rested my authority on a source and linked to it, and now the burden is on the reader to disprove the validity of that link. Bloggers know this and abuse it.

Blogs have long traded on the principle that links imply credibility. Even Google exploits this perception. The search engine, founded by Larry Page and Sergey Brin when they were Stanford students, copies a standard practice from academia in which the number of citations a scientific paper gets is an indicator of how influential or important it is. But academic papers are reviewed by peers and editorial boards—shaky citations are hard to get away with.

Online links look like citations but rarely are. Through flimsy attribution, blogs are able to assert wildly fantastic claims that will spread well and drive comments. Some might be afraid to make something up outright, so the justification of "I wasn't the first person to say this" is very appealing. It's a way of putting the burden all on the other guy, or on the reader.

People consume content online by scanning and skimming. To use the bird metaphor again, they are what William Zinsser called "impatient bird[s], perched on the thin edge of distraction." Only 44 percent of users on Google News click through to read the actual article. Meaning: *Nobody clicks links*, even interesting ones. Or if they do, they're not exactly rigorous in poring over the article to make sure it proves the point in the *last* article they read.

There was a great April Fool's prank a few years ago where NPR created an article headlined, WHY DOESN'T AMERICA READ ANYMORE? The article looked like it would be a complaint about the decline in reading and critical thinking skills, and so it immediately went viral—shared on Facebook thousands of times. Except if you actually clicked the article, you'd find that what it actually said was:

> *We sometimes get the sense that some people are commenting on NPR stories that they haven't actually read. If you are reading this, please like this post and do not comment on it. Then let's see what people have to say about this "story."*

Countless people fell for that—because they don't actually click links. They just assume they know what's behind them, and often they assume the links confirm whatever they want them to confirm.

If readers give sites just seconds for their headlines, how much effort will they expend weighing whether a blog post meets the burden of proof? The number of posts we read conscientiously, like some amateur copy editor and fact-checker rolled into one, are far outpaced by the number of articles we just assume are reliable. And the material from one site quickly makes its way to others. Scandalous statements get traction wider and faster—and their dubious nature is more likely to be obscured by the link economy when it's moving at viral speed. Who knows how many times you and I have passed over spurious assertions made to look legitimate through a bright little link?

# THE BREAKING NEWS EXCUSE

One of the ways that journalists justify their laziness today is by claiming that breaking news deserves special exemptions from their normal obligations to, you know, actually be right and pass along correct information. That during a mass shooting, a fast-moving election night, some unexpected controversy, there isn't time to do real reporting and so it's better to just pass along the information they have to readers and viewers as it comes in. There are a lot of words they use to describe this technique: iterative journalism, process journalism, beta journalism. Whatever name you use, it's stupid and dangerous.* It calls for bloggers to publish first and then verify what they wrote *after* they've posted it. Publishers actually believe that their writers need to do every part of the news-making process, from discovery to fact-checking to writing and editing in *real time*. It should be obvious to anyone who thinks about it for two seconds why that is a bad thing—but they buy the lie that iterative journalism improves the news.

Erik Wemple, a blogger for the *Washington Post*, writes: "The imperative is to pounce on news when it happens and, in this case, before it happens. To wait for another source is to set the table for someone who's going to steal your search traffic."[3] So by the time I've woken up in the morning, too much misinformation has been spread around the web to possibly be cleaned up. The "incentives are lined up this way," Tommy Craggs would say while he was at *Deadspin*, and we just needed to get used to it.

*Seeking Alpha* practiced it perfectly on one recent story: "If the newspaper is correct, and I have no way of verifying it, then this stock is in big trouble." Really? Can't verify it? *No way at all?* At its best, iterative journalism is what *TechCrunch* does: rile up the crowd by repeating sensational allegations and then pretend that they are waiting for the facts to come in. They see no absurdity in publishing a post with the headline PAYPAL SHREDS OSTENSIBLY RARE VIOLIN BECAUSE IT CARES and then

---

*See Evgeny Morozov's *The Net Delusion* for a discussion of blogs' premature and overblown coverage of the 2009–10 Iranian protests and the subsequent crackdown on activists and social media in Iran.

opening the article with "Now a lot of this story isn't out yet and I have a line in to Paypal [sic] about this, so before we get out the pitchforks lets [sic] discuss what happened."[4]

Arthur Schopenhauer called newspapers "the second hand of history" but added that the hand was made of inferior metal and rarely working properly. He said that journalists were like little dogs: Something moves and they start barking. The problem is that what they're often barking at is "no more than a shadow play on the fall."

Iterative journalists, whether writing for a newspaper a few centuries ago or a blog today, follow blindly wherever the wisps of the speculation may take them, do the absolute minimum amount of research or corroboration, and then post this suspect information immediately, as it is known, in a continuous stream. As Jeff Jarvis put it: "Online, we often publish first and edit later. Newspaper people see their articles as finished products of their work. Bloggers see their posts as part of the process of learning." Or as *Gawker*'s former "media reporter" said: "*Gawker* believes that publicly airing rumors out is usually the quickest way to get to the truth. . . . Let's acknowledge that we can't vouch for the veracity or truth of the rumors we'll be sharing here—but maybe you can." Jesus Christ.

This "learning process" is not some epistemological quest. Dropping the ruse, Michael Arrington, founder of *TechCrunch*, put it more bluntly: "Getting it right is expensive, getting it first is cheap."* And by extension, since it doesn't cost him anything to be wrong, he presumably doesn't bother trying to avoid it. It's not just less costly; it makes more money, because every time a blog has to correct itself, it gets another post out of it—more pageviews.†

The iterative approach sells itself as flexible and informative, but much more realistically, it manifests in the forms of rumors, half-truths, shoddy reporting, overwhelming amounts of needless information, and endless predictions and projections. Instead of using slow-to-respond official sources or documents, it leans on rumors, buzz, and questions.

---

*I'm sure he appreciated the irony of this in 2013 when many blogs, including *Gawker*, wrote posts accusing him of sexual assault. Oh wait, Arrington denied the charges and threatened to sue.

†From an *SB Nation* post about the NFL lockout: "There are 382 more updates to this story. Read most recent updates."

Events are "liveblogged" instead of filtered. Bloggers post constantly, depending on others to point out errors or send in updates, or for sources to contact them.

Iterative journalism is defined by its jumpiness. It is as jumpy as reporters can get without outright making things up. Only the slightest twitch is needed for a journalist to get a story live. As a result, stories claiming massive implications, like takeover talks, lawsuits, potential legislation, pending announcements, and criminal allegations, are often posted despite having minuscule origins. A tweet, a comment on a blog, or an e-mail tip might be enough to do the trick. Bloggers don't fabricate news, but they do suspend their disbelief, common sense, and responsibility in order to get to big stories first. The pressure to "get something up" is inherently at odds with the desire to "get things right."

A blog practicing iterative journalism would report they are hearing that Google is planning to buy Twitter or Yelp, or break the news of reports that the president has been assassinated (all falsely reported online many times now). The blog would publish the story as it investigates these facts—that is, publish the rumor first while they see if there is anything more to the story. Hypothetically, a media manipulator for Yelp would be behind the leak, knowing that getting the rumors of the acquisition out there could help them jack up the price in negotiations. I personally wouldn't kick off reports about the president's death, because I wouldn't get anything from it, but plenty of pranksters would.

If a blog is lucky, the gamble it took on a sketchy iterative tip will be confirmed later by events. If it's unlucky—and this is the real insidious part—the site simply continues to report on the *reaction* to the news, as though they had nothing to do with creating it. This is what happened to *Business Insider* when they wrongly made the shocking claim that New York governor David Paterson would resign. The end of the headline was simply updated: "NYT's Big David Paterson Bombshell Will Break Monday, Governor's Resignation to Follow" became "NYT's Big David Paterson Bombshell Will Break Monday, *Governor's Office Denies Resignation in Works*" [emphasis mine].[5]

They should have learned their lesson months earlier, after falling for a similar hoax. A prankster posted on CNN's online iReport platform that a "source" had told them that Steve Jobs had had a severe heart attack.* It was the user's first and only post. It was posted at 4:00 A.M. It was obviously a hoax. Even the site MacRumors.com, which *writes about nothing but rumors,* knew this post was bogus and didn't write about it. Nonetheless, following its iterative instincts, *Business Insider's* sister blog, *Silicon Alley Insider,* rushed to advance the story as a full-fledged post. Apple's stock price plummeted. Twenty-five minutes later, the story in tatters—the fake tip deleted by iReport, the rumor denied by Apple— *Business Insider* rewrote the lead with a new angle: " 'Citizen journalism' . . . just failed its first significant test."[6] Yeah, that's who failed here. You know who didn't? Those who were shorting Apple stock.

And what are the consequences for blowing it this poorly? There are none. "All that can happen," the famous (and reckless) gossip columnist Walter Winchell once said about one of his breaking scoops, "if it is wrong is that I *goof* again." But hey, at least he was willing to own even that.

Today, as a way of avoiding ever being embarrassingly off base, blogs couch their claims in qualifiers: "We're hearing . . ."; "I wonder . . ."; "Possibly . . ."; "Lots of buzz that . . ."; "Chatter indicates that . . ."; "Sites are reporting . . ."; "Might . . ."; "Maybe . . ."; "Could . . . , Would . . . , Should . . ."; and so on. In other words, they toss the news narrative into the stream without taking full ownership and pretend to be an impartial observer of a process they began.

For example, these are the first two sentences of *New York* magazine's *Daily Intel* blog post about David Paterson, the former governor of New York:

> *After weeks of **escalating buzz** about a New York Times piece that **would** reveal a "bombshell" scandal about New York Governor David Paterson, Business Insider **is reporting** that the story will **likely** come out tomorrow and will be followed by the governor's resignation (!!).*

---

*I imagine these repeated and exhausting rumors of Jobs's death made it all the more painful for his family when they were eventually placed in the position, three years later, of announcing that he had actually passed away. No family should have to worry: *Are people going to believe us?* or *Will he get less than his proper due because the public's patience has been wasted through so many premature reports?*

> *Though the nature of the revelation is **still a mystery, reports are** that this story is "much worse" than Paterson's publicly acknowledged affair with a state employee [emphases mine].*[7]

Welcome to Covering Your Ass 101. Nearly every claim is tempered by what *might* happen or attributed to someone else. Nearly every claim attributed to someone else links to some other site. But what does the writer actually think? What are they willing to own based on their personal reporting and knowledge? Not much. They want to say all they can and nothing at the same time—the height of disingenuous hedging. Which worked out great for *Daily Intel*, since the story turned out to be totally wrong. Not that anyone learned from the mistake—the posts were just updated with more speculation and guessing. One mistake is replaced by more mistakes.

"There is nothing more shocking than to see assertion and approval dashing ahead of cognition and perception," Cicero said a long time ago (or maybe I just made it up—are you going to check?). But that's how it works online . . . on purpose. As they say, it's not a bug—it's a feature.

## A BROKEN PHILOSOPHY

*May* becomes *is* becomes *has*, I tell my clients. That is, on the first site the fact that you "may" be doing something becomes the fact that you "are" doing something by the time it has made the rounds. The next time they mention your name, they look back and add the past tense to their last assertion, whether or not it actually happened. This is recursion at work, officially sanctioned and very possible under the rules of the link economy.

Under these circumstances it is far too easy for mistakes to pile on top of mistakes or for real reporting to be built on lies and manipulations—for analysis to be built on a foundation of weak support. It becomes so easy, as one reporter has put it, for things to become an amalgam of an amalgam.

The link economy encourages bloggers to repeat what "other people are saying" and link to it instead of doing their own reporting and standing behind it. This changes the news from what has happened into what someone said the news is. Needless to say, these are not close to the same thing.

One of my favorite books is Kathryn Schulz's *Being Wrong: Adventures in the Margin of Error.* Though media mistakes are not the subject of the book, Schulz does do a good job of explaining why the media so regularly gets it wrong. Scientists, she says, replicate each other's experiments in order to prove or disprove their findings. Conversely, journalists replicate one another's conclusions and build on them—often when they are not correct.

The news has always been riddled with errors, because it is self-referential instead of self-critical. Mistakes don't occur as isolated incidents but ripple through the news, sometimes with painful consequences. Because blogs and the media have become so interdependent and linked, a lapse of judgment or poor analysis in one place affects many places.

Science essentially pits the scientists against each other, each looking to disprove the work of others. This process strips out falsehoods, mistakes, and errors. Journalism has no such culture. Reporters look to one-up each other on the same subjects, often adding new scoops to existing stories.

Meanwhile, people like Jeff Jarvis explicitly advise online newspapers and aspiring blogs not to waste their time trying "to replicate the work of other reporters." In the age of the link, he says, "this is clearly inefficient and unnecessary." Don't waste "now-precious resources matching competitors' stories" or checking and verifying them like a scientist would. Instead, pick up where they left off and see where the story takes you. Don't be a perfectionist, he's saying; join the link economy and delegate trust.

When I hear people preach about interconnectedness and interdependence—like one reporter who suggested he and his colleagues begin using the tag NR (neutral retweet) to preface the retweets on Twitter that they were posting but not endorsing—I can't help but think of the subprime mortgage crisis. I think about one bank that hands off subprime loans to another, which in turn packages them and hands them to another still. *Why are you retweeting things you don't believe in?!* I think about the rating agencies whose job was to monitor the subprime transactions but were simply too busy, too overwhelmed, and too conflicted to bother doing it. I think of falling dominoes. I wonder why we would do that to ourselves again—multiplied many times over in digital.

Of course replication is expensive. But it is a known cost, one that should be paid up front by the people who intend to profit from the news. It is a protection and a deterrent all at once. The unknown cost comes from failure—of banks or of trust or of sources—and it is borne by everyone, not just the businesses themselves.

When Jarvis and others breathlessly advocate for new concepts they do not understand, it is both comical and dangerous. The web gurus try to tell us that this distributed, crowdsourced version of fact-checking and research is more accurate, because it involves more people. But I side with Descartes and have more faith in a scientific approach, in which every man is responsible for his own work—in which everyone is questioning the work of everyone else, and this motivates them to be extra careful and honest.

The old media system was a long way from perfect, but their costly business model at least tried to find independent confirmation where possible. It advocated editorial independence instead of risky interdependence. It was expensive, sure, and definitely unsexy, but it was a step above the pseudo-science of the link economy. It was certainly better than what we have online, where blogs do nothing but report what "[some other blog] is reporting," where blogs pass along unverified information using the excuse "but I linked to where I stole it from."

To simply know where something came from, or just the fact that it came from somewhere else, does not alleviate the problems of the delegation of trust. In fact, this is the insidious part of the link economy. It creates the appearance of a solution without solving anything. Some other blog talked to a source (don't believe them? here's the link) *so now they don't have to.* That isn't enough for me. We deserve better.

# XVII

## CYBERWARFARE

### BATTLING IT OUT ONLINE

Companies should expect a full-scale, organized attack from critics. One that will simultaneously overrun blog comments, Facebook fan pages, and an onslaught of blogs, resulting in mainstream press appeal. Start by developing a social media crises plan and developing internal fire drills to anticipate what would happen.

**—JEREMIAH OWYANG, ALTIMETER GROUP, WEB-STRATEGIST.COM**

Never forget, the press is the enemy, the press is the enemy. . . . Write that on a blackboard one hundred times.

**—RICHARD NIXON**

IN BYGONE DAYS A COMPANY MIGHT HIRE A PR MAN TO make sure people talked about their company. Today, even a company with little interest in self-promotion must hire one, simply to make sure people *don't* say untrue things about their company. If it was once about spreading the word, now it's as much about stopping the spread of inaccurate and damaging words.

When the entire system is designed to quickly repeat and sensationalize whatever random information it can find, it makes sense that companies would need someone on call 24/7 to put out fires before they start. That person is often someone like me.

One of my first big contracts was a ten-thousand-dollar gig to handle a group of trolls who had been vandalizing a client's *Wikipedia* page and filling it with lies and rumors. These "facts" were then showing up in major newspapers and on blogs that were eager for any gossip they could find about the company. "How do we just make it stop?" the company pleaded. "We just want to be left alone."*

It's the same predicament Google found itself in when Facebook hired a high-profile PR agency to execute an anonymous whisper campaign against them through manufactured warnings about privacy. Bloggers of all stripes had been pitched, with the idea of building enough buzz for the grand finale: editorials in the *Washington Post*, *Politico*, *USA Today*, and the *Huffington Post*. Like my client, Google was stunned by the plot. Imagine a $200 billion company saying, "Make it stop. We just want to be left alone." But they were effectively reduced to that. "We're not going to comment further," Google told reporters during the firestorm of controversy. "Our focus is delighting people with great products."

---

*I heard an even more anguished version of this cry from the family of a celebrity who contacted me after their son's death. They wanted help with *Wikipedia* users who were inserting speculative and untrue information about his tragic accident.

Sure, go ahead and focus on that, Google, but it doesn't matter. Once this arms race has begun, things can't just go back to normal. It escalates: A company sees how easy it is to plant stories online and hires a firm to attack its competitor. Blindsided by the bad publicity, the rival hires a firm to protect itself—and then to strike back. Thus begins an endless loop of online manipulation that can cost hundreds of thousands of dollars. And that's the easiest of the PR battles a company may have to face.

Consider what happened to the French yogurt giant Danone, which was approached by Fernando Motolese, a video producer in Brazil, with two hypothetical videos.

One, he said, was a fun spoof of their yogurt, which was designed to improve digestive health and, um, other bodily functions. The other, he said, was a disgusting version of the first video, with all the indelible scatological images implied by such a spoof. He might be more inclined to release the first version, he said, if Danone was willing to pay him a fee each time it was seen.

"It felt sort of like blackmail," said Renato Fischer, the Danone representative who fielded the inquiry, to the *MIT Technology Review*.[1] Well, that's because it *was* blackmail. It was extortion via viral video.

Nor is a profit motive the only thing that might make someone utilize these tactics. The hacking of the DNC in 2016—potentially by Russian operatives—and the hacking of Sony Pictures—potentially by North Korea—were both attempts to intimidate and influence through this kind of media shakedown.

## THE IMPLICIT SHAKEDOWN

Motolese's hustle is one of many styles of a shakedown that happens across the web countless times a day. Its only distinguishing feature was its brazenness. It's usually couched in slightly more opaque terms.

Take Michael Arrington's *TechCrunch* post entitled "Why We Often Blindside Companies." What begins as an apparent discussion of the site's news policy I see as a veiled threat to the Silicon Valley tech scene. After a start-up founder had, for the "second time," publicly announced news about her own life before Arrington's site had a chance to write about it

(*TechCrunch* told her they were writing a story about her, so she broke the news herself), Arrington decided to make an example out of her. First he told his readers that he had nasty personal information on the founder that he had been reluctant to publish. This was a not-so-subtle reminder that he had dirt on everyone and that his personal whim decided whether it got out or not. Then Arrington took his stand, saying the founder would no longer be "getting any calls from [him] in the future to give her a heads up that [*TechCrunch* is] breaking news about her start up." As though the journalist's job to speak to sources they are writing about were a courtesy. He concluded on a friendlier note: "Treat us with respect and you'll get it back. That's all we ask."' He may have ended his post nicely, but his message sounds no less extortionary to me than Motolese's.[2]

Afghan warlords have a name for this strategy: *ghabban*, which means to demand protection from a threat that you create. Many blogs employ it subtly, extorting through a combination of a sense of entitlement and laziness. A mostly positive 2010 *Financial Times* article about the rising influence of blogs covering the luxury watch market featured a small complaint from a watch manufacturer about a blogger who often got important details and product specifications wrong, in addition to having typos and bad grammar. In response, the editor of another watch-industry blog, *TheWatchLounge*, leaped to the site's defense: "What is the luxury watch industry doing to help him become a better writer?" he demanded to know. "And for that matter what is the industry doing to help any of these bloggers become better writers?"[3]

I would ask the same question of him that I once posed to a blogger who kept getting a story about American Apparel wrong. "When you find a mistake," he'd said, "e-mail me and point it out." I had to ask: Hey, man, why is it *my* job to do *your* job?

A while back, a plane of a major airline experienced potentially catastrophic trouble in the air. Despite a flaming engine and poor odds, the pilot managed to land it safely, saving the lives of four-hundred-plus passengers. Yet, as events transpired, Twitter users went berserk and reported

---

*Before he ran for president, then-senator Barack Obama advised his fellow politicians about the burgeoning political blogosphere: "If you take these blogs seriously, they'll take you seriously." As long as we can all admit that we have to assuage bloggers' egos in order to be treated fairly. . . .

that the plane had tragically crashed. In reality, not only had the plane landed safely, but the pilot acted like a gentleman from another generation, offering the passengers his personal telephone number if they had more questions or wanted someone to talk to. He exuded humble and quiet heroism that should have been recognized.

Only nobody knew about it, because the story online was so different. The *Harvard Business Review* criticized the airline for not responding quickly enough with marketing spin and for not magically stopping the rampant online speculation. They wrote: "What a pity that social media users, in their well-known enthusiasm for being first to share breaking news to their followers, would unwittingly *conspire* to obscure the big story of a pilot's life-saving landing" [emphasis mine].

Yes, *a pity*. A word a neighborhood thug might use in the hypothetical "It'd be *a pity* if something ever happened to this nice little shop of yours," and then try to collect monthly protection. These *are* the economics of extortion. The threat is less overt than "pay us or else," but it's a demand nonetheless. You must provide more fuel to the story and get out in front of it (even when there are more important things going on, like, you know, not letting the jet crash), or your reputation will be ruined. To not do this is to risk a vivid misperception that is impossible to correct with the truth, or anything else.

## A CULTURE OF FEAR

Most social media experts have accepted this paradigm and teach it to their clients without questioning it: Give blogs special treatment or they'll attack you. At any time, a hole could be dug by blogs, Twitter, or YouTube that the company must pay to fill in. And depending on the intentions of the person who dug it, they may also ask to be paid to not dig any more.

The Russian tactic of *kompromat*—releasing controversial information about public figures—is real and only more dangerous in an era where blogs publish first and verify second (if at all). When the public has been primed to jump on and share salacious gossip on social media, even upstanding citizens are vulnerable. In fact, it's the good people who are most vulnerable since it's more interesting to gawk at sordid revelations when they are least expected than it is to, say, hear about the one millionth instance of corruption or dishonesty emanating from the Trump family. The essence of *kompromat* is that it doesn't matter if the information is true or not, or whatever disturbing means it was acquired, it just matters that it can intimidate and embarrass. And the media enables this tactic—they thrive on it.

Being right is more important to the person being written about than to the person writing. So who do you think blinks first? Who has to spend thousands of dollars advertising online to counteract undeserved bad press? Who ultimately hires a spinmaster like me to start filling the discussions with good things just to drown out the bullshit? It's certainly not the media who is beefing up their fact-checking department to make sure innocent people aren't hurt.

Today there are dozens of firms that offer reputation-management services to companies and individuals. Though they dress up their offerings with jargon about performance metrics and customer feedback, their real service is to handle the disturbing, nasty, and corrupt dealings I've talked about in this book, so you don't have to. Navigating this terrain has become a critical part of brand management. The constant threat of being blindsided by a false controversy, or crucified unfairly for some misconstrued remark, hovers over everyone in the public sphere. Employees, good, bad, or disgruntled and desperate for money, know that they have the means to massively embarrass their employers with well-placed accusations of mistreatment or harassment. People know that going to a blog like *Consumerist* is the fastest way to get revenge for any perceived customer-service slight.

That there are a million eyes watching, each incentivized to demagogue their way to a traffic payday, dominates discussions in corporate boardrooms, design departments, and political strategy sessions. What effect does it have? Aside from making them rightly cynical, it forces them to act in two ways—deliberately provocative or conservatively fake. In a word: unreal.

Blogs criticize companies, politicians, and personalities for being artificial but mock them ruthlessly for engaging in media stunts and blame them for even the slightest mistake. Nuance is a weakness. As a result, politicians must stick even more closely to their prepared remarks. Companies bury their essence in even more convoluted marketing-speak. Public figures cannot answer a question with anything but "No comment." Everyone limits their exposure to risk by being fake.*

It's now common for indie bands to avoid or turn down as much online press as possible, with some even going as far as obscuring their likenesses or withholding their names. Why? They are petrified of the backlash that has sunk so many promising "blog-buzz" bands that came before them. With the hype comes the threat of hate, and I don't think this is limited to music blogs.

Overstock.com was compelled to address this unpredictable and aggressive web culture in a 10-K filing with the SEC. It is a precautionary measure many companies will have to take in the future—to let investors know how blogs could impact their financials with little warning and little recourse. Designating it as one of three major risk factors to the company, Overstock.com wrote,

> Use of social media may adversely impact our reputation. There has been a marked increase in use of social media platforms and similar devices, including weblogs (blogs), social media websites, and other forms of internet-based communications which allow individuals access to a broad audience of consumers and other interested persons. Consumers value readily available information concerning retailers, manufacturers, and their goods and services and often act on such information without further investigation, authentication and without regard to its accuracy. The availability of information on social media platforms and devices is virtually immediate as is its impact. Social media platforms and devices immediately publish the content their subscribers and participants post, often without filters or checks on accuracy of the content posted. The opportunity for [the] dissemination of information, including inaccurate information, is seemingly limitless and readily available. Information concerning the Company may be posted on such platforms and devices at any time. Information posted may be adverse to our interests, it may be inaccurate, and

---

*In his book *The Psychopath Test*, Jon Ronson, a journalist, suggests that the real way to get away with "wielding true, malevolent power" is to be boring. Why? Journalists love writing about eccentrics and hate writing about dull or boring people—because it's boring.

*may harm our performance, prospects or business. The harm may be immediate, without affording us an opportunity for redress or correction. Such platforms also could be used for dissemination of trade secret information, compromise of valuable company assets all of which could harm our business, prospects, financial condition and [the] results of operations.*

Alarmist? Maybe. But I have seen hundreds of millions of dollars of market cap evaporate on the news of some bogus blog post. When the blog *Engadget* posted a fake e-mail announcing a supposed delay in the release of a new iPhone and Apple operating system, it knocked more than $4 *billion* off Apple's stock price.

Maybe you're not sympathetic to big corporations. What about when *Eater LA** published a report from an anonymous reader stating that a popular Los Angeles wine bar not only had egregious health code violations, but also was advertising gourmet items on its menu while really serving generic substitutes?

*Besides not adhering to simple food saftey [sic] standards, such as soap, sanitizing, and throwing out chicken salad that's 2 weeks old, 90% of all "fresh" menu items are cooked days beforehand and sit in the fridge.*

Like so many online reports, this one turned out to be wrong. *Completely wrong.* So *Eater* added an update that said the proprietors disputed the story. Yet the post—the disgusting hygiene allegations and the headline—remained the same. The post stayed up for people to read and comment on. Only after a second update—prompted by the threat of a lawsuit—did *Eater* begin to admit any wrongdoing. It said, in part:

*We ran this tip without contacting the owners of the restaurant, who have since refuted the tip in its entirety. We apologize to the owners of the restaurant, and our readers, for not investigating our source's*

---

*\*Eater* is now owned by Vox Media.

*claims before airing them on the site. The resulting post didn't rise to
our standards, and we shouldn't have published it.*

Imagine if the restaurant had been a larger, publicly traded company.
Stocks move on news—any news—and rumors passed on by high-profile
blogs are no exception. It does not matter if they are updated or corrected
or part of a learning curve; blogs are read by real people who form opinions and make decisions as they read.

I was once invited to a lunch at Spago with the then-CEO of the *Huffington Post*, Eric Hippeau. Some of the site's editors attended for a bit of a
roundtable discussion about the media during lunch. It was 2010, and the
internet and national media were in a frenzy over reports of accelerator
malfunctions causing unintended accelerations in Toyota cars. While we
were eating, Eric asked the group a question: How could Toyota have better responded to the wildly out of control PR crisis?

Given that this was a room full of internet folks, as soon as the answers
started, the pontification became overwhelming: "I think transparency is
critical." "These companies need to be proactive." "They needed to get out
in front of this thing." "The key is reaching out to bloggers." Blah, blah,
blah.

It was a conversation I'd heard a thousand times and seen online almost every day. Finally I interrupted. "None of you know what you're
talking about," I said. "None of you have been in a PR crisis. You've never
seen how quickly they get out of hand. None of you have come to terms
with the fact that sites like yours, the *Huffington Post*, pass along rumors
as fact and rehash posts from other blogs without checking them. It's
impossible to fight back against that. The internet is the problem here, not
the solution."

In subsequent months I would be vindicated more than I could have
anticipated at the time. First, the *Huffington Post* was hit with a PR crisis
and failed miserably at responding by the standards they laid out at lunch.
When sued by a cadre of former and current writers for their unpaid
contributions, the *Huffington Post* was anything but "transparent." They
clammed up, likely on the advice of their lawyers, and didn't cover the
lawsuit on their own site. It was not until a few days later that Arianna

Huffington posted her first—and the only—statement about it on the *Huffington Post*. Hardly "being proactive" or "getting out in front of it." What else could she have done? The lawsuit was probably a money grab, but the *Huffington Post* had to mostly stand there and take a public beating, watching powerlessly as other blogs gleefully dissected and discussed the lawsuit without a shred of empathy.

Second, and most important, Toyota was largely exonerated after a full investigation by NASA, no less. Many of the cases of computer issues supposedly causing unintended acceleration were disproved entirely, and most were found to be caused by driver error. Drivers had been hammering the accelerator instead of the brakes! And then blaming the car! In other words, the scandal that Toyota was so heavily criticized for not handling right had been baseless. Toyota hadn't been reckless; the media had. It was sites like the *Huffington Post*, so quick to judge, that had disregarded their duties to their customers and to the truth. As journalist Ed Wallace wrote for *Businessweek* in an apology to Toyota, "[A]ll the reasons why the public doesn't trust the media crystallized in the Toyota fiasco."

But of course none of that really matters because there is still that residual stain. Even in telling this story I am unintentionally hurting Toyota. I am repeating those unforgettable words in the same sentence: Toyota. Accelerator malfunction. Scandal. Which leaves Toyota asking the same question that wrongly disgraced former U.S. secretary of labor Ray Donovan asked the court when he was acquitted of false charges that ruined his career: "Which office do I go to to get my reputation back?"

## WHERE THERE IS SMOKE THERE IS FIRE

The real trick in this game is to repeat something enough times that it begins to sound true. One of the things I noticed during the 2016 election was anytime I said something negative about Trump, I would suddenly get hit with tweets from accounts with no followers. By that I mean *literally* zero followers. How hard is it to get one friend?

Hard when you're a fake account. Increasingly, smart media manipulators have realized that one way to make things seem real is by straight up gaslighting. Political campaigns, CEOs, and foreign governments can pay to create accounts that bombard influencers like journalists with information. Say something negative about Trump, and you'll hear from what look like legitimate Trump supporters who try to intimidate you. Write something about a company, and watch as the comments section fills up with barely literate praise.

Russia is a well-known user of this tactic as well. They call it *dezinformatsiya*—essentially disinformation via trolling. In the United States we call it "astroturfing"—using fake accounts or supporters to create what appear to be shows of real opinion around the internet. Another word for this is "shitposting"—whenever you see an online conversation suddenly interrupted by what seems like an unhinged person ranting about this issue or that issue. You might dismiss them, but they still managed to catch your attention for a second.

This manages to fool even seemingly skeptical readers. Professor Kate Starbird at the University of Washington explained to the *Seattle Times*, "Your brain tells you 'Hey, I got this from three different sources,'" she says. "But you don't realize it all traces back to the same place, and might have even reached you via bots posing as real people. If we think of this as a virus, I wouldn't know how to vaccinate for it."

You can see why these strategies would work if done on a large scale. If you were a reporter and saw that a petition had sixty thousand signatures, would you bother to investigate where those signatures came from? If you were an editor and you suddenly got fifteen e-mails pointing you to the same link, might you pass it along to a writer to cover? If you were a public figure and you kept getting tweets about something, maybe you'd reply and ask, "Has anyone heard about this?" and even in questioning it you've helped push that fake idea along.

This isn't a conspiracy theory. During the election, it was found that both candidates had large numbers of fake followers on Twitter. It was also revealed that one of the very wealthy founders of Oculus Rift had put money behind a group dedicated to shitposting anti-Hillary memes. When caught, he would tell the *Daily Beast*, "You can't fight the American elite without serious firepower. They will outspend you and destroy you by any and all means."

# WEAPONIZING INFORMATION

Let me tell you about another unbelievable media event that happened over a meal. I wasn't at this one but apparently Ben Smith, the editor of *BuzzFeed*, was. It was hosted by Uber at the Waverly Inn in New York City. At the dinner, Uber executive Emil Michael spoke candidly about the company's plans to deal with the unfair and biased media coverage it believed it was receiving. Smith, a guest at the event, recounted what he heard the next day:

> Over dinner, he outlined the notion of spending "a million dollars" to hire four top opposition researchers and four journalists. That team could, he said, help Uber fight back against the press—they'd look into "your personal lives, your families," and give the media a taste of its own medicine.

He even named specific journalists and editors he would want to go after. This was alarming to many in the media because of how closely it came on the heels of a leaked internal report from Uber about its plans to "weaponize facts" in its fight against the taxi industry.

Not only can the media be a tool to attack others, but it can also itself attack people and be attacked in turn.

We are starting to see this in politics—little events here or there that the conspiratorially minded might suspect had deeper backing than it appeared. The 2008 election was nearly derailed when the same "citizen reporter," on separate occasions, tricked both Obama and a campaigning Bill Clinton into saying something vulnerable and honest by misrepresenting herself. The sixty-one-year-old woman later admitted that the two figures had "had no idea [she] was a journalist," nor that she was recording them with a hidden device. Then, angered by the lack of compensation from the *Huffington Post* for her "scoops," she resigned by publishing private e-mails between herself and Arianna Huffington—just to get one last blast of attention at someone else's expense. *Anyone* can write for the *Huffington Post*, which means anyone could potentially have the same impact. One blog, one recorder, and bam.

Even Trump himself was badly damaged when a clip of him recorded without his knowledge a decade earlier was leaked to the media. It's also interesting to see how hard he was hit by the so-called Trump dossier, which made all sorts of sensational allegations about Trump's dealings in Russia, purportedly based on high-level intelligence sources and research.

Who was originally responsible for funding and creating this report? The answer is almost too good to be true. The report was funded first by Republicans who sought to keep Trump from getting the party's nomination and then by Clinton's supporters trying to beat him in the general election. In other words, it was partisan-funded opposition research. And who ran it, despite admitting they were unable to verify its content? *BuzzFeed*! That's right—the very same site who scored headlines by revealing exactly how malicious organizations might undermine and attack their enemies by doing opposition research and weaponizing it.

Without irony, Ben Smith defended the decision to run the report by saying, "The instinct to suppress news of this significance is precisely the wrong one for journalism in 2017." But here's the thing—it's only significant news if it is true! How can any person prepare for or defend themselves against scandal or innuendo when the media have utterly abdicated their role in vetting the information they publish?

Whether the United States and its elections were interfered with by the Russians I cannot say—but it is pretty obvious how they could have been. The media has admitted they're open for business and will take even the most suspect information. Apparently the only validation needed—as *BuzzFeed* showed with their publication of the Trump dossier—is that there is already significant chatter about something online. (And we know how easy that is to fake.)

I'll give you one last example of how information can be weaponized, and it's one from personal experience. A few years ago, a friend was screwed over by a famous talent agent (with a legendarily bad temper and a reputation for screwing people over). His chances of actually beating such an opponent in court were slim—he didn't have the resources. So we worked through how he could have a lawyer draft a letter announcing his *intention* to file a lawsuit, which he could then leak to gossip blogs after sending it to the agent. He didn't need to file an actual lawsuit, mind you; in such a small industry, simply the public airing of the claims—that someone had stolen someone else's work project like that—through an intention letter and the subsequent media coverage (on *TMZ*, *ESPN*, and a host of other blogs) was its own form of leverage.

I ran into the friend later and learned the outcome of the tactic: The agency paid him $500,000 and admitted defeat. I think about this often. That agent might have screwed my friend over, but how easily could this tactic used in response be abused, used against an innocent party? What strikes me is not that it was some elaborate, orchestrated con—I don't feel like I discovered some criminal instinct inside myself either—it's that the tools were so accessible and easy to use, it was almost difficult not to do so. In fact, it came so effortlessly that I didn't even remember doing it until he reminded me.

The way someone can be exploited through both the legal and political systems (anyone can be sued for anything and anyone can be accused of anything) and the media, when they cover it (claiming libel of a public figure generally requires malicious intent or reckless disregard of the truth) reminds me of the gruesome accident in *Meet Joe Black* in which Brad Pitt's character is hit by a car, tossed up in the air, and hit by another car going in the other direction.

To not be petrified of a shakedown, a malicious lie, or an unscrupulous rival planting stories is to be unimportant. You only have nothing to fear if you're a nobody. And even then, well, who knows?

# XVIII

## THE MYTH OF CORRECTIONS

> Our web folks will ask, "Can't we post it and say we're checking it?" The feeling nowadays is, "We don't make mistakes, we just make updates."
>
> **—ROXANNE ROBERTS, *WASHINGTON POST* RELIABLE SOURCES COLUMNIST**

> You end up chasing Tweets that spread faster than you can keep up; it's like putting toothpaste back in the tube, except the toothpaste is alive and didn't like it in the tube and is dreaming of Broadway.
>
> **—TOM PHILLIPS, INTERNATIONAL EDITOR OF MSN, CREATOR OF *IS TWITTER WRONG?***

> Is it not obvious that society cannot continue indefinitely to get its news by this wasteful method? One large section of the community organized to circulate lies, and another large section of the community organized to refute the lies! We might as well send a million men out into the desert to dig holes, and then send another million to fill up the holes.
>
> **—UPTON SINCLAIR, *THE BRASS CHECK***

ITERATIVE JOURNALISM IS POSSIBLE BECAUSE OF A BE-
lief in the web's ability to make corrections and updates to news stories.
While fans of iterative journalism acknowledge that increased speed may
lead to mistakes, they say it's okay because the errors can be fixed easily.
They say that iterative journalism is individually weak but collectively
strong, since the bloggers and readers are working together to improve
each story—iteratively.

As someone who has both been written about as a developing story and
worked with people who are written about this way all the time, I can assure you that this is bullshit. *Corrections online are a joke.* All of the jus-
tifications for iterative journalism are not only false—they are literally the
opposite of how it works in practice.

Bloggers are no more eager to seek out feedback that shows they were
wrong than anyone else is. And they are understandably reluctant to admit their mistakes publicly, as bloggers must do. The bigger the fuckup,
the less likely people are to want to cop to it. It's called "cognitive disso-
nance." We've known about it for a while.

Seeing something you know to be untrue presented in the news as true
is exasperating. I don't know what it feels like to be a public figure (I realize it's hard to be sympathetic to their feelings), but I have had untruths
spread about me online, and I know that it sucks. I know that as a press
agent, having seen that many of these mistakes bloggers make are easily
preventable, it is extra infuriating. And they feel absolutely no guilt about
making them.

If you want to get a blogger to correct something—which sensitive clients painfully insist upon—be prepared to have to be an obsequious
douche. You've got to flatter bloggers into thinking that somehow the
mistake wasn't their fault. Or be prepared to be an asshole. Sometimes the
resistance is so strong, and the entitlement so baked in, that you have to

risk your friendly-to-each-other's-face relationship by calling the blogger out to their publisher boss.

Sometimes it has to get even more serious than that. One of my all-time favorite blogger correction stories involves Matt Drudge, the political blogger sainted in the history of blogging for breaking the Monica Lewinsky story. But few people remember the big political "scandal" Drudge broke before that one. Based on an unnamed source, Drudge accused prominent journalist and Clinton adviser Sidney Blumenthal of a shocking history of spousal abuse—and one covered up by the White House, no less.

Except none of it was true. Turns out there was no evidence that Blumenthal had ever struck his wife, nor was there a White House cover-up. The story quickly fell apart after it became clear an anonymous Republican source had whispered into Drudge's ear to settle a political score against Blumenthal. Drudge eventually admitted it to the *Washington Post*: "[S]omeone was using me to try to go after [him]. . . . I think I've been had."

Yet Drudge's posted correction on the story said only, "I am issuing a retraction of my information regarding Sidney Blumenthal that appeared in the *Drudge Report* on August 11, 1997." He refused to apologize for the pain caused by his recklessness, even in the face of a $30 million libel suit. And four years later, when the ordeal finally ended, Drudge *still* defended iterative journalism: "The great thing about this medium I'm working in is that you can fix things fast."[1]

There's only one word for someone like that: dickhead.

And at the end of the day, will it even make a difference? The original story almost always spreads faster than the correction. Even if it didn't, the very fact that you are trying to get a correction shows that the incorrect version already has a big head start. There's an old saying: "A lie makes its way across lots, while the truth has to go around by the dirt road." It's true: Sensational mistakes have an advantage over sober, meticulous, or disappointing facts. It'd just be nice if the people whose job it is to be right for a living (reporters) would anticipate and adjust for it. (Unless that isn't their job???)

# CORRECTING PEOPLE WHO ARE WRONG FOR A LIVING

I once gave the show *The Price Is Right* a five-hundred-dollar American Apparel gift card to use as a prize. We thought it'd be funny, since the show is television's longest-running guilty pleasure. (Honestly, I was just excited as a fan.) The episode aired in September and was quickly posted by one of my employees on the company's YouTube account. Everyone loved it and got the irony—a cool brand slumming it on a show only old people care about. Well, everyone got it except the popular advertising blog *Brand Channel*, which posted a nonironic piece titled "American Apparel Taps Drew Carey for Image Turnaround."[2] With excruciating obliviousness they proceeded to discuss the merits of my "surprising choice" to film a "back-to-school commercial, featuring a mock version of classic US game show *The Price Is Right* hosted by an all-American TV personality Drew Carey."

How does one begin to correct that? This idiot didn't even bother to look up who the host of *The Price Is Right* was and figured it was easier to assume the whole thing was an elaborate hoax than to, you know, e-mail and ask why we'd appeared on the show. And what am I as the publicist supposed to do? If I had even known how to communicate to that idiot that Drew Carey was, in fact, the actual host of *The Price Is Right*, and that the video the blogger watched was a clip from an actual episode and not a commercial, I still would have to convince the writer to retract the *entire thing*, because an update couldn't have fixed how wrong it was. Since I no longer foolishly hope for miracles, I didn't even try to correct it, even as other blogs repeated the claims. I just had to sit there and watch as people believed something so stupid was true; the writer was wrong to the point of it actually working to their advantage.

If I'd wanted to try to get a correction, however, it would not have made much of a difference. Getting a correction posted takes time, often hours or days, occasionally weeks, because bloggers deliberately drag their feet. Posts do most of their traffic shortly after going live and being linked to. By the time your correction or update happens, there is hardly much of an audience. I recall sending e-mails to *Gawker* and *Jezebel* on several occasions over matters of factual errors and not receiving a response. Only after e-mailing again (from the same device) was I told, "Oh, I never got your e-mail." Sure, guys, whatever you say. My anonymous tips seem to arrive in their inboxes just fine—it's the signed corrections that run into issues.

My experience is not uncommon. A friend, a car blogger earnestly passionate about his job, once e-mailed the writer of a less-than-reputable car site after they published a rumor that turned out to be false.

> Him: Why keep the headline up, since we now know it's not
>     true?
> Blogger: You guys are so funny.

Bloggers often stick their updates way down at the bottom, because they are vain, just like the rest of us—they'd rather not shout their mistakes loudly for all to hear, or have them be the first thing the reader sees. In other cases, blogs will just paste your e-mail at the bottom of the post, as though it's "your opinion" that they're wrong. Of course, it isn't just an opinion or they wouldn't have been forced to post it. But they get to keep the article up by framing it as a two-sided issue. The last thing they want to do is rewrite or get rid of their post and throw away the few minutes of work they put into it. "He lies like a newspaper" was a common midnineteenth-century expression about people you couldn't trust. Or as Lincoln once joked to a friend about the "reliability" of newspapers, "They lie and then they re-lie." One could swap out "newspaper" for "blog" in those quotes, and they'd be just as accurate now as 150 years ago.

## BEING WRONG

Factual errors are only one type of error—perhaps the least important kind. A story is made of facts, and it is the concrescence of those facts that creates a news story. Corrections remove those facts from the story—but the story and its thrust remain. Even writers who are averse to acknowledging errors but have nevertheless done so will only under the rarest of circumstances follow the logic fully: The challenged fact requires a reexamination of the premises built on top of it. In other words: We don't need an update; we need a *rewrite*.

It's a real golden age for journalists when they not only get traffic by posting jaw-dropping rumors, but then also get traffic the next day by shooting down the same rumors they created. I once heard Megan Mc-Carthy (*Gawker*, Techmeme, *CNET*) speak at a SXSW panel about how false stories, such as fake celebrity death reports, spread online. During the Q&A I got up and asked, "This is all well and good, but what about mistakes of a less black-and-white variety? You know, something a little more complex than whether someone is actually dead or not. What about subtle untruths or slight mischaracterizations? How does one go about getting those corrected?" She laughed. "I love *your* idea that there can be nuance on the internet."

It's too hard to get complicated things right, so why bother?

## THE PSYCHOLOGY OF ERROR

If it were simply a matter of breaking through the endemic arrogance of bloggers and publishers, iterative journalism might be fixable. But the reality is that learning iteratively doesn't work for readers either—not even a little.

Think of *Wikipedia*, which provides a good example of the iterative process. By 2010 the article on the Iraq war had accumulated more than twelve thousand edits, enough to fill twelve volumes and seven thousand printed pages (someone actually did the math on this for an artistic book project). Impressive, no doubt. But that number obscures the fact that though the twelve thousand changes collectively result in a coherent, mostly accurate depiction, it is not what most people who looked at the *Wikipedia* entry in the last half decade saw. Most of them did not consume it as a final product. No, it was read, and relied upon, piecemeal— while it was under construction. Thousands of other *Wikipedia* pages link to it; thousands more blogs used it as a reference; hundreds of thousands of people read these links and formed opinions accordingly. Each corrected mistake, each change or addition, in this light is not a triumph but a failure. Because for a time the article was wrongly presented as being correct or complete—even though it was in a constant state of flux. Think about it: Do you make a habit of checking back on *Wikipedia* pages just to make sure nothing has changed?

The reality is that while the internet allows content to be written iteratively, the audience does not read or consume it iteratively. Each member usually sees what he or she sees a single time—a snapshot of the process— and draws his or her conclusions from that.

An iterative approach fails because, as a form of knowledge, the news exists in what psychologists refer to as the "specious present." As sociologist Robert E. Park wrote, "News remains news only until it has reached the persons for whom it has 'news interest.' Once published and its significance recognized, what was news becomes history." Journalism can never truly be iterative, because as soon as it is read it becomes fact—in this case, poor and often inaccurate fact.

Iterative journalism advocates try to extend the expiration date of the news's specious present by asking readers to withhold judgment, check back for updates, and be responsible for their own fact-checking.* Bloggers ask for this suspended state of incredulity from readers while the news is being hashed out in front of them. But like a student taking a test and trying to slow down time so they can get to the last few questions, it's just not possible.

Suppressing one's instinct to interpret and speculate, until the totality of evidence arrives, is a skill that detectives and doctors train for years to develop. This is not something we regular humans are good at; in fact, we're wired to do the opposite. The human mind "first believes, then evaluates," as one psychologist put it. To that I'd add, "as long as it doesn't get distracted first." How can we expect people to transcend their biology while they read celebrity gossip and news about sports?

The science shows that not only are we bad at remaining skeptical, we're also bad at correcting our beliefs when they're proven wrong. In a University of Michigan study called "When Corrections Fail," political scholars Brendan Nyhan and Jason Reifler coined a phrase for it: the "backfire effect."[3] After being shown a fake news article, half of the participants were provided with a correction at the bottom discrediting a

---

*Conveniently, this reading style would generate the most pageviews for the blog.

central claim in the article—just like one you might see at the bottom of a blog post. All of the subjects were then asked to rate their beliefs about the claims in the article.

Those who saw the correction were, in fact, *more likely* to believe the initial claim than those who did not. And they held this belief *more confidently* than their peers. In other words, corrections not only don't fix the error—they backfire and make misperception worse.

What happens is that the correction actually reintroduces the claim into the reader's mind and forces them to run it back through their mental processes. Instead of prompting them to discard the old thought, as intended, corrections appear to tighten their mind's grip on the now disputed fact.

In this light, I have always found it ironic that the name for the *Wall Street Journal* corrections section is "Corrections & Amplifications."* If only they knew that corrections actually are amplifications. But seriously, there can't really be that many cases where a newspaper would ever need to "amplify" one of its initial claims, could there? What are they going to do? Issue an update saying that they didn't sound haughty and pretentious enough the first go-round?

Bloggers brandish the correction as though it is some magical balm that heals all wounds. Here's the reality: Making a point is exciting; correcting one is not. An accusation is much likelier to spread quickly than a quiet admission of error days or months later. Upton Sinclair used the metaphor of water—the sensational stuff flows rapidly through an open channel, while the administrative details like corrections hit the concrete wall of a closed dam.

Once the mind has accepted a plausible explanation for something, it becomes a framework for all the information that is perceived afterward. We're drawn, subconsciously, to fit and contort all the subsequent knowledge we receive into our framework, whether it fits or not. Psychologists call this cognitive rigidity. The facts that built an original premise are gone, but the conclusion remains—the general feeling of our opinion floats over the collapsed foundation that established it.

---

*By contrast, the wire service Reuters puts their updates and new facts at the top of their articles and often reissues them over the wire to replace the older ones.

Information overload, "busyness," speed, and emotion all exacerbate this phenomenon. They make it even harder to update our beliefs or remain open-minded. When readers repeat, comment on, react to, and hear rumors—all actions blogs are designed to provoke—it becomes harder for them to see real truth when it is finally presented or corrected.

In another study researchers examined the effect of exposure to wholly fictional, unbelievable news headlines. Rather than cultivate detached skepticism, as proponents of iterative journalism would like, it turns out that the more unbelievable headlines and articles readers are exposed to, the more it warps their compass—making the real seem fake and the fake seem real. The more extreme a headline, the longer participants spend processing it, and the more likely they are to believe it. The more times an unbelievable claim is seen, the more likely they are to believe it.[4]

It is true that the iterative model can eventually get the story right, just like in theory *Wikipedia* perpetually moves toward higher-quality pages. The distributed efforts of hundreds or thousands of blogs can aggregate a final product that may even be superior to what one dedicated newsroom could ever make. When they do, I'll gladly congratulate them—they can throw themselves a tweeter-tape parade for all I care—but I'll have to remind them when it's all over that it didn't make a difference. More people were misled than helped.

The ceaseless, instant world of iterative journalism is antithetical to how the human brain works. Studies have shown that the brain experiences reading and listening in profoundly different ways; they activate different hemispheres for the exact same content. We place an inordinate amount of trust in things that have been written down. This comes from centuries of knowing that writing was expensive—that it was safe to assume that someone would rarely waste the resources to commit to paper something untrue. The written word and the use of it conjures up deep associations with authority and credence that are thousands of years old.

Iterative journalism puts companies and people in an impossible position: Speaking out only validates the original story—however incorrect it is—while staying silent and leaving the story as it was written means that the news isn't actually iterative. But acknowledging this paradox would undermine the premise of this very profitable and gratifying practice. I can't decide if it is more ironic or sad that the justification for iterative journalism needs its own correction. If only Jeff Jarvis would post on his blog: "Oops, turns out errors are a lot more difficult to correct than we thought . . . and trying to do so only makes things worse. I guess we shouldn't have pushed this whole ridiculous enterprise on everyone so hard."

That would be the day.

Instead, the philosophy behind iterative journalism is like a lot of the examples of bad stories I have mentioned. The facts supporting the conclusions collapse under scrutiny, and only the hubris of a faulty conclusion remains.

# XIX

---

# THE TWENTY-FIRST-CENTURY DEGRADATION CEREMONY

---

## BLOGS AS MACHINES OF MOCKERY, SHAME, AND PUNISHMENT

> It is taking one's conjectures rather seriously to roast someone alive for them.
>
> **—MICHEL DE MONTAIGNE**
>
> We grow tired of everything but turning others into ridicule, and congratulating ourselves on their defects.
>
> **—WILLIAM HAZLITT, "ON THE PLEASURE OF HATING" (1826)**

SOCIOLOGIST GERALD CROMER ONCE NOTED THAT
the decline of public executions coincided almost exactly with the rise
of the mass newspaper. Oscar Wilde said it best: "In the old days men had
the rack. Now they have the Press."

If only they had known what was coming next: Online lynch mobs.
Social media shaming Smear campaigns. Snark. Cyberbullying. Distrib-
uted denial of service attempts. Internet meltdowns. Anonymous tipsters.
Blog wars. Trolls. Trial by comments section.

It is clear to me that the online media cycle is a process not for developing truth but for performing a kind of cultural catharsis. Blogs, I understand from Wilde and Cromer, serve the hidden function of
dispensing public punishments. Think of the Salem witch trials: They
weren't court proceedings but ceremonies. In that light, the events three
hundred years ago suddenly feel very real and current: They were doing
with trumped-up evidence and the gallows what we do with speculation
and sensationalism. Ours is just a more civilized way to tear someone to
pieces.

My experience with digital lynch mobs is unique. I get frantic calls
from sensitive millionaires and billionaires who want me to fend these
mobs off. Occasionally they ask that I discreetly direct this mob toward
one of their enemies. I am not afraid to say I have done both. I feel I can
honestly look myself in the mirror and say the people I protected deserved
my efforts—and so did the people I set my sights on. But it is a power I
don't relish using, because once I start, I don't stop.

Ask the blogger we went after during Tucker's movie campaign. The ad
I ran, which the blog *MediaElites* later called "one of the most despicable
personal attacks" they'd ever seen, read in part: "Tucker Max Facts #47:
Domestic violence is not funny. Unless *Gawker* editor Richard Blakeley

gets arrested for it."* The *New York Post* once caught wind of a campaign of mine against an enemy after my e-mail account was hacked. They were so appalled that they ran a full-page article about it in their Sunday edition: "Charney [really, me] Wages Bizarre Cyber Battle." This article, along with the press I'd bagged to embarrass our target, hangs on my wall like a hunting trophy. It is interesting to me that when I pointed the attention back toward the media (in the domestic assault case involving the editor), it was a "despicable personal attack," but when the media does it to other people it's called journalism.

## THE DEGRADATION CEREMONY

These acts of ritualized destruction are known by anthropologists as "degradation ceremonies." Their purpose is to allow the public to single out and denounce one of its members. To lower their status or expel them from the group. To collectively take out its anger at them by stripping them of their dignity. It is a we-versus-you scenario with deep biological roots. By the end of it, the disgraced person's status is cemented as "not one of us." Everything about them is torn down and rewritten.

The burning passion behind such ceremonies, William Hazlitt wrote in his classic essay "On the Pleasure of Hating," "carries us back to the feuds, the heart-burnings, the havoc, the dismay, the wrongs, and the revenge of a barbarous age and people." You can nudge blogs toward those dangerous instincts. They love the excitement of hunting and the rush of the kill without any of the danger. In the throes of such hatred, he writes, "the wild beast resumes its sway within us."

What happens when that happens?

Ask Justine Sacco, who tweeted a misunderstood joke about AIDS, became a trending topic on Twitter, and lost her job. Ask news anchor Brian Williams, who saw decades of goodwill evaporate because he exaggerated a story in a way that every normal person has a hundred times.

---

*Blakeley *had* been arrested recently for a domestic dispute, and the story had been covered up by his colleagues. I wanted people to know. He later pled guilty, but only to harassment.

Ask Monica Lewinsky, who dared have consensual sex with a married man twenty years ago and is still paying for it. Ask Jonah Lehrer, the author and speaker who got caught making up quotes and recycling some of his old material in articles online and became a favorite punching bag of journalists.*

I think about Jonah because I relate to him. We've never met, but I share an editor and a speaking agent with him. I certainly can't afford a $2.25 million historic home in Laurel Canyon like he apparently once did, but from my books and career as a similarly young though less accomplished author, I might be able to buy a condo nearby.

When the story first broke about him, I hated him. I cheered on the people who were attacking him. *Serves him right,* I thought. It was only in reading Jon Ronson's absolutely spectacular book *So You've Been Publicly Shamed,* perhaps the best book on online culture of the last decade, that I got the proper perspective on the infamous plagiarist and fabulist.

That perspective is this: *There but for the grace of God go I. There but for the grace of God goes any of the rest of us.*

In one of the book's more remarkable passages, Ronson writes:

> We all have ticking away within us something we fear will badly harm our reputation if it got out—some "I'm glad I'm not that" at the end of "I'm glad I'm not me." . . . Maybe our secret is actually nothing horrendous. Maybe nobody would even consider it a big deal if it was exposed. But we can't take that risk. So we keep it buried.

What is your shame? Can you even bring yourself to mouth it silently to yourself? Or does even that seem like tempting fate? Imagine what would happen if someone found out about it; imagine what they could do to you with it. Personally, I think my work and my behavior are aboveboard. I believe my passwords and accounts to be secure. But I wouldn't bet my life on it. Would you?

Yet increasingly those are the stakes required for the gamble of daily

---

*By the way, many passages in this book are adapted from writing I have done online as well. I'm not embarrassed about it. It's my writing. I can do what I want with it. So can Jonah.

life. Our online culture is both fueled by and ruled by this bitterness and anger that pretend that other people aren't human beings.

Justine Sacco makes a dumb joke. Celebrities take private nude photos that get hacked. Brian Williams embellishes a story or has a generous memory. Amy Pascal says something offensive in an e-mail. Jonah Lehrer self-plagiarizes.

The fact that many of us have done the same and gotten away with it, or in fact sit on far darker secrets, is pushed aside. After all, there are page-views to get. Social share bonuses to collect. Pain to sublimate. Right, bloggers?

None of this is to say that these people—or other people who raise our ire—did nothing wrong. They usually did. In fact, almost all the people who have been publicly shamed have done "something abhorrent." But even if it is something shameful, that doesn't mean you should be *shamed for it*. We got rid of public shaming as a form of criminal punishment because it is cruel. We definitely shouldn't be doing it to people without a trial. Lincoln lived long before the internet, but in one of his early speeches he made a warning that echoes to this day: "There is no grievance that is a fit object of redress by mob law." Especially something dumb somebody said or did when they were a kid!*

Most of what I'm saying here was said much more eloquently and per-suasively in Monica Lewinsky's TED talk, "The Price of Shame." But ini-tially I didn't even watch it. Why would I? *She's a joke*, I thought. Even when I saw it shared widely on Facebook by my friends, my first mental justification for watching it was thinking I might be able to make fun of it and TED in an article. In fact, it's very good, and wise, and important. And I feel like a heel for having dismissed it out of hand.

As she says in the talk, her scandal was the first to be amplified and distributed through the internet. It was the initial glimpse of what human nature + digital tools does to the crowd. It is not a pretty sight—and surely was a horrific experience. The person who felt the consequences most painfully was the one who had done the least amount wrong, was the least culpable, and could least afford the cost. And today, from the seeds of that

---

*Dear Critics: Please remember this sentence if you ever try to use old or deleted passages from this book against me in the future.

scandal, we now live in a world where, as she aptly summarizes, "public humiliation is a commodity and shame is an industry."

It's a wringer we've gone on to put so many people through, from Lehrer to Sacco to Amy Pascal to people whose names should have never been made public in the first place. Whatever their actual wrongdoings, we treated them like they weren't human beings. We deliberately pretended that we weren't human beings with our flaws too.

This is not how we solve things. It's not how the world is improved.

It just feels good for a fleeting moment. And it makes a select handful of media and technology entrepreneurs wealthy while their goons feel important.

This is the shame of our public shamings.

## DISAGREE WITH SOMETHING? JUST MAKE FUN OF IT

*New Yorker* critic David Denby came closest to properly defining snark in his book *Snark: It's Mean, It's Personal, and It's Ruining Our Conversation.* He didn't succeed entirely, but "[s]nark attempts to steal someone's mojo, erase her cool, annihilate her effectiveness [with] the nasty, insidious, rug-pulling, teasing insult, which makes reference to some generally understood shared prejudice or distaste" will do.

My test is a little simpler: You know you're dealing with snark when you attempt to respond to a comment and realize that there is nothing you can say.* The remark doesn't mean anything—though it still hurts—and the person saying it doesn't care enough about what they said—or anything else, for that matter—that you can criticize them back. If I called you a douche, how would you defend yourself without making it worse? You couldn't.

Snark is an incredibly effective weapon in enforcing norms and dismissing ideas you don't like. Just make fun of someone until they can't be taken seriously anymore. That's the ethos of much of today's media.

---

*I also like Goethe's couple-hundred-year-old statement: "In recent times Germans have assumed that freedom of the press is nothing more than being free to cast scorn on one another in public."

Yet a snark victim's first instinct is to appeal to reason—to tell the crowd, "Hey, that's not true! They're making this up!" Or appeal to the humanity of the writer by contacting them personally to ask, "Why are you doing this to me?" I try to stop clients from doing this. I tell them, "I know this must hurt, but there's nothing you can do. It's like jujitsu: The energy you'd exert in your defense will be used against you to make the embarrassment worse."

Snark is profitable and easy for blogs because they don't care about anyone on the other side of it. It's the perfect device for people who have nothing to say but who *have* to talk (blog) for a living. Snark is the grease of the wheels of the web. Discussing issues fairly would take time and cognitive bandwidth that blogs just don't have. Snark is the style of choice because it's click-friendly, cheap, and fast.

Bloggers love to hide snark in adjectives, to cut an entire person down with just a few words. You find it in nonsensical mock superlatives: Obama is the "compromiser in chief." So-and-so is a perv. Jennifer Love Hewitt gains a few pounds and becomes Jennifer Love Chewitt. So-and-so is rapey. So-and-so is basic or an asshat or a goon or, as someone once wrote about me, they have a "punchable face." What does any of this even mean? Why do bloggers say things like these? Lines such as these are intended not so much to wound as to prick. Not to humiliate but to befuddle. Not to make people laugh but to make them smirk or chuckle. To annihilate without effort.

You can see snark (and its problems) embodied in Nikki Finke, the notorious Hollywood blogger, and her annual tradition of "live-snarking" Hollywood award shows on the blog *Deadline Hollywood*. One year Finke's live-snarking of the Academy Awards was filled with constant criticism that the show was "gay" because it had too much singing and dancing. Funny, right? The height of incisive comedy, to be sure. After repeatedly calling it the "gayest Oscars ever," Finke turned around and railed against the Academy's choice to recognize comedian Jerry Lewis with a humanitarian award because of his "antigay slurs"—jokes he'd told during his telethon that raised *more than $60 million* for muscular dystrophy. "Humanitarian my ass," she wrote. Good one, Nikki.

The same goes for the *Deadspin* piece "What Does Mike Pence Think Happens at Restaurants?" which makes fun of the vice president's decision to never dine alone with a woman other than his wife. I'll admit I thought it was weird when I heard Pence refused to eat with a member of the opposite sex (I mean, who cares?), and I thought the headline was a funny take on it. Then I read the article, which includes this remarkable admission: "Full disclosure: I am making fun of myself here, too. My wife and I have been married for nine years, and in those nine years I have not shared a one-on-one meal with any other women except maybe my mother or sister." So to get that straight, the writer is guilty of the same thing he's mocking the vice president for!

This is snark in its purest form: just preposterously, self-righteously full of shit. In Finke's case she had made her own gay jokes, but somehow she's not only *not* a hypocrite, she's superior to Lewis, even though the man actually gets off his ass and helps people. In the *Deadspin* piece, the writer claims his reasons were different—that he has never eaten alone with a woman other than his wife because (and I quote) he is an "asocial hermit," but that's sort of the whole point, even though his reason is actually *weirder* this doesn't stop him from making fun of someone else. Bloggers love snark because it isn't undermined by pathetic hypocrisy.* Snark is magical that way.

Think about how often people are labeled douchebags (or, more recently "bros"):

## Your Daily Douchebag: John Mayer Edition (PerezHilton.com)

## Meanwhile . . . McCain Locks Up the Notorious Douchebag Demographic (*Huffington Post*)

## Are MGMT Douchebags? Does It Matter? (*Huffington Post*)

---

*It's like the line from Walter Winchell: "Democracy is where everybody can kick everybody else's ass. But you can't kick mine."

## Bud Selig Is Bad for Baseball, a Douchebag
### (*SB Nation*)

## Internet "Douchebag" Allthis Responds to Controversy (*VentureBeat*)

To be called a douche or a bro or any such label is to be branded with all the characteristics of what society has decided to hate but can't define. It's a way to dismiss someone entirely without doing any of the work or providing any of the reasons. It says, "You are a fool, and everyone thinks so." It is the ultimate insult, because it deprives the recipient of the credentials of being taken seriously.

I'm not saying dueling was a good thing but at least there used to be a remedy if your honor was insulted or your dignity threatened. What are you supposed to do today? Just take it. Just let people slander and mock you—in front of millions of people!

The always controversial and often mocked Scott Adams, creator of *Dilbert*, once said in an interview: "Ideas are society's fuel. I drill a lot of wells; most of them are dry. Sometimes they produce. Sometimes the well catches on fire." We have to be able to handle that—as adults—and forgive and forget the occasional stupid remark. We can't turn everyone into a laughingstock, or pretty soon the only type of person left will be Donald Trump.*

Because you know who doesn't mind snark or mockery? Who likes it? The answer is obvious: People with nothing to lose. People who need to be talked about, like attention-hungry reality stars. There is nothing that you could say that would hurt the cast of *Jersey Shore* or DJ Khaled or the Cash Me Outside girl. They need you to talk about them, to insult them, and to make fun of them or turn them into memes is to do that. They have no reputation to ruin, only notoriety to gain.

---

*In fact, I would argue the endless hounding and marginalization of someone like Scott Adams by certain controversy-loving websites is what turned him into a Trump supporter. I think there are a lot of people who got accused of being racist, sexist or any number of other things (when they were really just being dumb or intellectually lazy) who have ended up *embracing* that side of themselves now that they've been branded by it.

So the people who thrive under snark are exactly those who we wish would go away, and the people we value most as cultural contributors lurk in the back of the room, hoping not to get noticed and hurt. Everything in between may as well not exist. Snark encourages the fakeness and stupidity it is supposedly trying to rail against. In fact, I don't think it's controversial to say that Trump thrives in our new media world in part because he, like some superbug that has become immune to antibiotics, transcends snark and criticism. His rise might be due less to his media manipulation skills than to his unadulterated shamelessness. And so I want you to think about that the next time you lazily dismiss someone with a joke. It might work on them—but think about whom it *doesn't* work on and whether the alternative is better.

## THE COSTS OF SCANDAL HYSTERIA

A few years ago I was part of a high-profile multimillion-dollar lawsuit involving Dov Charney and Woody Allen. After being accused early on in a series of sexual harassment lawsuits, Dov and American Apparel ran two large billboards in New York City and Los Angeles featuring a satirical image of Woody Allen dressed as a Hasidic Jew with the words "The Highest Rabbi" in Yiddish. Allen sued the company for $10 million for wrongfully using his likeness.

You may remember hearing about it. But you probably didn't know that the billboards—which ran for only a few weeks—were intended to be a statement against the kind of hysterical media-driven destruction talked about here. They were designed to reference the public crucifixion Allen had endured during a personal scandal years earlier. Ironically, this was totally lost because blogs and newspapers were too focused on the lawsuit's big-name celebrity drama to discuss the intended message.

In response, I helped Dov write a long statement that was eventually turned into an editorial in the *Guardian*. It said, in part:

> My intention was to call upon people to see beyond media and lawsuit-inspired scandal, and to consider people for their true value and for their contribution to society.

*I feel that the comments of a former friend of Woody Allen, Harvard professor and famous civil rights lawyer Alan Dershowitz, apply to this particular phenomenon: "Well, let's remember, we have had presidents . . . from Jefferson, to Roosevelt, to Kennedy, to Clinton, who have been great presidents. . . . I think we risk losing some of the best people who can run for public office by our obsessive focus on the private lives of public figures."*

*I agree that the increasingly obsessive scrutinization of people's personal lives and their perceived social improprieties has tragically overshadowed the great work of too many artists, scientists, entertainers, entrepreneurs, athletes, and politicians, including Woody Allen.[1]*

Dov was no angel but I think he deserved better, at least when it came to the media coverage. The lawsuits against him were complicated and little intelligent reporting was ever done on them—reporting beyond the sensational claims in the legal documents (I don't recall many articles following up when claims were dropped or recanted).*

In any case, blogs are our representatives in these degradation ceremonies. They level the accusations on behalf of the "outraged public." Even if we are not angels in our lives, we ask: How dare you hold yourself up in front of us as a human being? If you don't feel shame, then we will make you feel shame—or perhaps, *you will feel shame so we don't have to.* The onlookers delight in the destruction and pain. Blogs lock onto targets for whatever frivolous reason, which makes sense, since they often have played a role in creating the victim's celebrity in the first place, usually under equally frivolous pretenses.

It used to be that someone had to be a national hero before you got the privilege of the media and the public turning on you. You had to be a president or a millionaire or an artist. Now we tear people down just as we've begun to build them up. We do this to our fameballs. Our viral video stars. Our favorite new companies. Even random citizens who pop into the news because they did something interesting, unusual, or stupid.

---

*Stranger still, now that Dov is starting over with a new company, the same outlets that once criticized him are publishing overblown puff pieces that mostly ignore the many horrible things they previously accused him of. Because that would get in the way of their new clickworthy narrative.

First we celebrate them; then we turn to snark, and then, finally, to merciless decimation. No wonder only morons and narcissists enter the public sphere.

It feels good to be a part of something—to tear down and berate. It's not surprising to me that the media would want to assume this role. Consider how the ceaseless, staged, and artificial online news chase makes today's generation of reporters feel. They attended an expensive grad school and live in New York City or San Francisco or Washington, D.C. The wondrous $200,000-a-year journalism job is not some myth to them; it was an opportunity dangled in front of them—and then taken away. Their life is nothing like that myth. Bloggers must write and film and publish an insurmountable amount of material per day, and only if they're lucky will any of it be rewarded with a bonus or health insurance. Yet the people they cover are often rich and successful or, worse, idiotic and talentless reality television stars. It's enough to make anyone bitter and angry. And indeed they are. They grind with the "rage of the creative underclass," as *New York* magazine called it.

Philosopher Alain de Botton once pointed out that Greek tragedies, though popular entertainment in their day, had a purpose. Despite being gossipy, sometimes salacious, and often violent, they taught the audience to think about how easily an unfortunate situation could befall them, and to be humbled by the flaws of another person. Tragedies could be learned from. But the news of the twenty-first century, he writes, "with its lexicon of perverts and weirdos, failures and losers, lies at one end of the spectrum," and "tragedy lies at the other."

There is no intent to instruct in what we see on blogs. Just *gawking*. That is their true function. Their degradation is mere spectacle that blogs use to sublimate the general anxieties of their readers. To make us feel better by hurting others. To stress that the people we're reading about are freaks, while we are normal.

And if we're not getting anything out of it, and nobody learns anything from it, then I don't see how you can call blogs anything other than a digital blood sport.

# WELCOME TO
# UNREALITY

The quack, the charlatan, the jingo, and the terrorist
can flourish only where the public is deprived of
independent access to information. But where all
news comes at second-hand, where all testimony is
uncertain, men cease to respond to truths and
respond simply to opinions. The environment in
which they act is not realities themselves but the
pseudo-environment of reports, rumors, and
guesses. The whole reference of thought comes to
be what somebody asserts and not what actually is.

—WALTER LIPPMANN,
*LIBERTY AND THE NEWS*

IN THIS BOOK I HAVE ILLUSTRATED THE WAYS IN WHICH bloggers, as they sit down at their computers, are prompted to speculate, rush, exaggerate, distort, and mislead—and how people like me encourage these impulses.

Blogs are assailed on all sides by the crushing economics of their business, dishonest sources, inhuman deadlines, pageview quotas, inaccurate information, greedy publishers, poor training, the demands of the audience, and so much more. These incentives are *real*, whether you're the *Huffington Post* or some tiny blog. Taken individually, the resulting output is obvious: bad stories, incomplete stories, wrong stories, unimportant stories.

To me, many of these individual failings were my opportunities. I was able to get coverage for my clients out of it; I was able to advance ideas that I thought were worthwhile. But when I started to see what this process amounted to *collectively*—the cumulative effect of tens of thousands of such posts, written and uploaded day in and day out—my pride turned to fear. This is always a good question: What if everyone did what you were doing? What would that world look like? I started not to like the answer.

What is the result of millions of blogs fighting to be heard over millions of other blogs—each hoping for a share of an increasingly shrinking attention span? What happens when people figure out that Reddit or Twitter can be used to get CNN to cover you? What happens when the incentives ripple through every part of the media system? What happens when the "truth" no longer really matters—not to readers or reporters?

These results are unreality. A netherworld between the fake and the real where each builds on the other and they cannot be told apart. This is what happens when the dominant cultural medium—the medium that feeds our other mediums—is so easily corrupted by people like me.

When the news is decided not by what is important but by what readers are clicking; when the cycle is so fast that the news cannot be anything else but consistently and regularly incomplete; when dubious scandals pressure politicians to resign and scuttle election bids or knock millions from the market caps of publicly traded companies; when the news frequently covers itself in stories about "how the story unfolded"—unreality is the only word for it. It is, as Daniel Boorstin, author of 1962's *The Image: A Guide to Pseudo-Events in America*, put it, a "thicket . . . which stands between us and the facts of life."

## A SLOW CREEP

Let's start with a basic principle: Only the unexpected makes the news. This insight comes from Robert E. Park, the first sociologist to ever study newspapers. "For the news is always finally," he wrote, "what Charles A. Dana described it to be, 'something that will make people talk.'" Nick Denton told his writers the same thing nearly one hundred years later: "The job of journalism is to provide surprise."* News is only *news* if it departs from the routine of daily life.

But what if most of what happens is expected? Most things do not depart from the routine. Most things are not worth talking about. But the news *must* be. And so the normal parts of life are omitted from the news by virtue of being normal. I don't mean to say that the constant search for newness or the unexpected is what distorts the news. That would be unfair, because *almost everything* blogs do distorts the news. But this one basic need—fundamental to the very business of blogging—inherently puts our newsmakers at odds with reality. It can only show us a version of reality that serves their needs.

What's known as news is not a summary of everything that has happened recently. It's not even a summary of the most important things that have happened recently. The news, whether it's found online or in print, is just the content that successfully navigated the media's filters. Possibly with my help. Since the news informs our understanding of what is occurring around us, these filters create a constructed reality.

---

*Remember Bennett as well, trying "not to instruct, but to startle."

Picture a funnel. At the top we have everything that happens, then everything that happens that comes to be known by the media, then everything that is considered newsworthy, then what they ultimately decide to publish, and finally what spreads and is seen by the public.

The news funnel:

# ALL THAT HAPPENS

## ALL THAT'S KNOWN BY THE MEDIA

### ALL THAT IS NEWSWORTHY

#### ALL THAT IS PUBLISHED AS NEWS

#### ALL THAT SPREADS

In other words, the media is in some ways inherently a mechanism for systematically limiting what the public sees.

But we seem to think that the news is informing us! The internet is what technologists call an "experience technology." The more it is used, the more trust users have in it. The longer a user engages with it, the more comfortable they get and the more they believe in the world it creates.

As we become immersed in blogs, our trust in the information we get from them increases. I saw an example of this very clearly in my own education: I watched "internet sources" go from strictly forbidden in school research to the status quo, and the citing of *Wikipedia* articles in papers from unacceptable to "okay, but only for really general background information." Internet culture has done one thing with this trust: utterly abused it.

# EMBRACING THE FAKE

In April 2011, *Business Insider* editor Henry Blodget put out an advisory to the PR world. He was drowning in elaborate story pitches and information about new services. He just couldn't read them all, let alone write about them. So he proposed a solution: The publicists could write about the product launches of their own clients, and Blodget's site would edit and publish them. "In short," he concluded, "please stop sending us e-mails with story ideas and *just contribute directly to Business Insider.* You'll get a lot more ink for yourself and your clients and you'll save yourself a lot of wasted work" [emphasis mine].[1] His post was seen more than ten thousand times, and each and every view, I can only assume, was followed by a marketer cumming all over their pants.

In Blodget's overzealous drive to create traffic for his site, he didn't mind misinforming. He didn't care who wrote it, so long as it got pageviews. He was willing to let PR and marketing professionals and people like me write material about their own clients—which he would then pass off as real news and commentary to his readers.

He was early to this trend but hardly the only one to follow it. Today, with almost every major media outlet opening their platform up to self-interested contributors, when all the protections against conflicts of interest or even basic factual inaccuracies have disappeared, the vast majority of the information we find in the media is biased or manipulated. Worse, every major television channel seems to think that campaign surrogates— that is, naked shills for certain politicians—deserve airtime as a means of being balanced. It's surreal and scary to watch real spin be created in real time, to watch what are supposed to be objective news outlets *paying* campaign operatives to come up with lies on behalf of candidates right in front of you. And part of the reason they allow this? The outraged response online from partisan websites is good for traffic and branding. The reason CNN lets Scottie Nell Hughes say dumb things is because those dumb things get lots of attention. It's the same reason they let men and women embarrass themselves on reality television. But at least nobody thinks reality TV is news. We know that it is trash.

# FROM THE FAKE, THE REAL

The process is simple: Create a pseudo-event, trade it up the chain, elicit real responses and action, and you have altered reality itself. I may understand the consequences of it now, but that doesn't stop a part of me, even as I write this, from seeing this thirst as an opportunity to insert messages into the discussion online. You can't count on people to restrain themselves from taking advantage of an absurd system—not with millions of dollars at stake. Not when the last line of defense—the fourth estate, known as the media—is involved in the cash grab too.

From here we get the defining feature of our world today: a blurred line between what is real and what is fake; what actually happens and what is staged; and, finally, between the important and the trivial.* There is no doubt in my mind that blogs and blogging culture were responsible for this final break. When blogs can openly proclaim that getting it first is better than getting it right; when a deliberately edited (fake) video can reach, and within hours require action by, the president of the United States; when the perception of a major city can be shaped by what photographs spread best in an online slideshow; and when someone like me can generate actual outrage over advertisements that don't actually exist—the unreal becomes impossible to separate from the real.

"The news media is a giant mind, a giant, unquiet, overstimulated mind that won't let itself rest—and won't let the rest of us rest," is how Gavin de Becker put it in *Fear Less*. That's the problem. If fake news simply deceived, or if the glut of information only harmlessly distracted, that would be one thing. The problem with unreality and pseudo-events is not simply that they are unreal; it is that they don't *stay* unreal. While they may themselves exist in some netherworld between real and fake, the domain in which they are consumed and acted on is undoubtedly real. In being reported, these counterfeit events are laundered and passed to the public as clean bills—to buy real things. The anxiety of the media be-

---

*An actual *TechCrunch* headline: RUMORS OF APPLE RUMORS NOW LEADING TO RUMORS OF COUNTER-RUMORS.

comes the anxiety of the world, and it becomes the weakness by which the powerful are able to control and direct us.

The news might be fake, but the decisions we make from it are not. As Walter Lippmann wrote, the news constitutes a sort of pseudo-environment, but our responses to that environment are not pseudo but *actual* behavior. In 1922, Lippmann warned us "about the worldwide spectacle of men"—government officials, bankers, executives, artists, ordinary people, and even other reporters—"acting upon their environment moved by stimuli from their pseudo-environment."

That world is exactly what we have now. It's a world where, in 2002, Vice President Dick Cheney leaked bogus information to an attention-hungry reporter for the *New York Times*, and then mentioned his own leak on *Meet the Press* to help convince us to invade Iraq.[2] "There's a story in the *New York Times* this morning, and I want to attribute the *Times*," Cheney said, citing himself, using something he had planted in the press as proof that untrue information was now "public" and accepted fact. He used his own pseudo-event to create pseudo-news. It's a world where Trump becomes president by getting the media to repeat his dystopian paranoia and negativity enough times that people start to really believe that things are terrible—they substitute objective reality for the narrative they hear online and on TV.

I used unreality to get free publicity. Cheney used his media manipulations to drive the public toward war. Trump used it to stir tensions with our neighbors and to slander entire races and regions. And no one was able to stop it. By the time they did the facts had been established, the fake made real by media chatter, and real wars had been waged. From the pseudo-environment came actual behavior.

Welcome to unreality, my friends. It's fucking scary.

# XXI

## HOW TO READ A BLOG

### AN UPDATE ON ACCOUNT OF ALL THE LIES

> Truth is like a lizard; it leaves its tail in your fingers and runs away knowing full well that it will grow a new one in a twinkling.
>
> —IVAN TURGENEV TO LEO TOLSTOY

WHEN YOU SEE A BLOG BEGIN WITH "ACCORDING TO A tipster . . . ," know that the tipster was someone like me tricking the blogger into writing what I wanted.

When you see "We're hearing reports," know that "reports" could mean anything from random mentions on Twitter to message-board posts, or worse.

When you see "leaked" or "official documents," know that really means someone just e-mailed a blogger, and that the documents are almost certainly not official and are probably fake or fabricated for the purpose of making desired information public.

When you see "BREAKING" or "We'll have more details as the story develops," know that what you're reading reached you too soon. There was no wait-and-see, no attempt at confirmation, no internal debate over whether the importance of the story necessitated abandoning caution. The protocol is going to press early, publishing before the basic facts are confirmed, and not caring whether it causes problems for people.

When you see "Updated" on a story or article, know that no one actually bothered to rework the story in light of the new facts—they just copied and pasted some shit at the bottom of the article.

When you see "Sources tell us . . . ," know that these sources are not vetted, they are rarely corroborated, and they are desperate for attention.

When you see someone call themselves a "bestselling author," know that they probably mean their self-published book was number one in a tiny category on Amazon for five minutes, and the same goes for every "top-ranked" podcast and "award-winning" website.

When you see a story tagged "EXCLUSIVE," know that it means the blog and the source worked out an arrangement that included favorable coverage. Know that in many cases the source gave this exclusive to multiple sites at the same time or that the site is just taking ownership of a story they stole from a lesser-known site.

When you see "said in a press release," know that it probably wasn't even actually a release the company paid to officially put out over the wire. They just spammed a bunch of blogs and journalists via e-mail.

When you see "According to a report by," know that the writer summarizing this report from another outlet has but the most basic ability in reading comprehension, little time to spend doing it, and every incentive to simplify and exaggerate.

When you see "We've reached out to so-and-so for comment," know that the blogger sent an e-mail two minutes before hitting "publish" at 4:00 A.M., long after they'd written the story and closed their mind, making absolutely no effort to get to the truth before passing it off to you as the news.

When you see an attributed quote or a "said so-and-so," know that the blogger didn't actually talk to that person but probably just stole the quote from somewhere else, and per the rules of the link economy, they can claim it as their own so long as there is a tiny link to the original buried in the post somewhere.

When you see "which means" or "meaning that" or "will result in" or any other kind of interpretation or analysis, know that the blogger who did it likely has absolutely zero training or expertise in the field they are opining about. Nor did they have the time or motivation to learn. Nor do they mind being wildly, wildly off the mark, because there aren't any consequences.

When you hear a friend say in conversation "I was reading that . . . ," know that today the sad fact is that they probably just glanced at something on a blog.

## RELYING ON ABANDONED SHELLS

The process for finding, creating, and consuming information has fundamentally changed with the advent of the web and the rise of blogging. However, the standards for what constitutes news are different, the vigor with which such information is vetted is different, the tone with which this news is conveyed is different, and the longevity of its value is different. Yet, almost without exception, the words we use to describe the news and the importance readers place on them remain the same.

In a world of no context and no standard, the connotations of the past retain their power, even if those things are fractions of what they once were. Blogs, to paraphrase Kierkegaard, left everything standing but cunningly emptied them of significance.

Words like "developing," "exclusive," and "sources" are incongruent with our long-held assumptions about what they mean or what's behind them. Bloggers use these "substance words" (like *Wikipedia*'s weasel words) to give status to their flimsy stories. They use the language of Woodward and Bernstein but apply it to a media world that would make even Hearst queasy. They give us what George W. S. Trow called "abandoned shells."

Why does this matter? We've been taught to believe what we read. That where there is smoke there must be fire, and that if someone takes the time to write down and publish something, they believe in what they are saying. The wisdom behind those beliefs is no longer true, yet the public marches on, armed with rules of thumb that make them targets for manipulation rather than protection.

I have taken advantage of that naïveté. And I'm not even the worst of the bunch. I'm no different from everyone else; I too am constantly tricked—by bloggers, by publishers, by politicians, and by marketers. I'm even tricked by my own monstrous creations.

# THE AGE OF NO AUTHORITIES

And so fictions pass as realities. Everyone is selling and conning, and we hardly even know it. Our emotions are being triggered by simulations—unintentional or deliberate misrepresentations—of cues we've been taught were important. We read some story and it feels important, believing that the news is real and the principles of reporting took place, but it's not.

Picture a movie poster for an independent film that wants to be received as artistic and deep. It probably features the laurel leaves icon—for awards like "Best Picture," "Critics' Choice," or "Official Selection." These markers originally symbolized a handful of important film festivals. Then it became important for every city, even neighborhoods inside cities, to have their own film festival. There are also the significant differences in the "winners" and the few dozen or even hundreds of "selections." The use of the festival laurels is to conjure up the implicit value associated with scarcity for the viewer despite the enormous gap between the connotation and the reality.

The laurel leaf illusion is a metaphor for the web. It underpins everything from the link economy—a link looks like a citation, yet it is not—to headlines that bait our clicks. It's why trading up the chain works and it's the reason why you could get your name in the press tomorrow through HARO.

What these people are trying to do is to find some, any, stamp of approval or signal of credibility. Blogs have a few minutes to write their posts, few resources, and little support, but because of the One-Off Problem they need to be heard over thousands of other sites. They desperately need something that says, "This is not like those other things," even though it is. So they make up differentiators and misuse old ones.

"In the age of no-authority," wrote Trow, "these are the authorities."

We live in a media world that desperately needs context and authority but can't find any because we destroyed the old markers and haven't created reliable new ones. As a result, we couch new things in old terms that are really just husks of what they once were. Skepticism will never be enough to combat this. Not even enough to be a starting point.

It is now almost cliché for people to say, "If the news is important, it will find me." This belief itself relies on abandoned shells. It depends on the assumption that the important news will break through the noise while the trivial will be lost. It could not be more wrong. As I discovered in my media manipulations, the information that finds us online—what spreads—is the worst kind. It raised itself above the din not through its value, importance, or accuracy but through the opposite, through slickness, titillation, and polarity.

I made a lot of money and had a great time playing with the words that make up the news. I exploited the laziness behind the news and people's reading habits. But from the abuse of abandoned shells came another one.

Our knowledge and understanding is the final empty, hollow shell. What we think we *know* turns out to be based on nothing, or worse than nothing—misdirection and embellishment. Our facts aren't facts; they are opinions dressed up like facts. Our opinions aren't opinions; they are emotions that feel like opinions. Our information isn't information; it's just hastily assembled symbols.

There is no way that is a good thing, no matter how much I gained from it personally.

# CONCLUSION

## SO . . . WHERE TO FROM HERE?

# CONCLUSION

THE NARRATOR OF ROBERT PENN WARREN'S *ALL THE King's Men*, a brilliant, powerful media manipulator, says that his story

> *is the story of a man who lived in the world and to him the world looked one way for a long time and then it looked another and very different way. The change did not happen all at once. Many things happened and that man did not know when he had any responsibility for them and when he did not.*

In a way that is also my story. I saw the world one way and then I saw it another way and it led to this book, and then years later I see it a slightly different way again. Where does my responsibility begin and end? What guilt do I share? How fair was I to the people I implicated? These are questions that can't be answered but should be asked.

I remember when I was finishing this book for the first time. I felt like I *had* to get it out as soon as possible. I was afraid that the year or so it had taken me to write it had been too long, that if the book didn't get out soon, it would be too late. I'd miss my window and no one would hear me.

It's strange now to have looked at the pages once again and seen that, if anything, I was early. Things were bad then but they were going to get much worse. Things had to get much worse before people would really listen. They might not fully listen now, today, but now ordinary people are primed to understand how bad things are. They've seen the consequences of the current system first hand. They are inclined to believe, finally, that something is very wrong.

If only they could have seen it years ago. For instance, the quote I am about to give you—it feels very current but in fact it's from early 2011.

*Fake news. I don't mean fake news in the Fox News sense. I mean the fake news that clogs up most newspapers and most news websites, for that matter. The new initiative will go nowhere. The new policy isn't new at all. . . . The product isn't revolutionary. And journalists pretend that these official statements and company press releases actually constitute news. . . . Fake news, manufactured, hyped, rehashed, retracted—until at the end of the week you know no more than at the beginning. You really might as well wait for a weekly like the* Economist *to tell you what the net position is at the end of the week.*[1]

The extra irony there is that the person who said it is Nick Denton, the founder of Gawker Media, one of the people I've spent a good portion of this book railing against.

In an interview with the *Atlantic* magazine, Denton claimed he was on a "jihad" inside *Gawker* "against fake news." In the years since, it's something that's become rather common—journalists complaining about fake news. I find that to be a little like Kim Kardashian complaining about how fake reality TV shows are. Not that there is any question about a media jihad. As I have shown in this book, there is one, only it is a war with you, against you. It's me against them, against you. By proxy we fight countless battles for your attention, and we'll go to any length to get it. And yet, even as Denton was saying that and I was writing about it, almost no one knew that another war was going on—a secret war to hold media like *Gawker* legally accountable for its actions.

More than twenty-five years ago, in *Amusing Ourselves to Death*, Neil Postman argued that the needs of television, then our culture's chief mode of communicating ideas, had come to determine the very culture it was supposed to represent. The particular way that television stages the world, he wrote, becomes the model for how the world itself is to be staged.

Entertainment powered television, and so everything that television touched—from war to politics to art—would inevitably be turned into entertainment. TV had to create a fake world to fit its needs, and we, the audience, watched that fake world on TV, imitated it, and it became the new reality in which we lived. The dominant cultural medium, Postman understood, determines culture itself.

Well, television is no longer the main stage of culture. The internet is. Blogs are. YouTube is. Twitter is. And their demands control our culture exactly as television once did. Only the internet worships a different god: traffic. It lives and dies by clicks, because that's what drives ad revenue and influence. The central question for the internet is not, Is this entertaining? but, Will this get attention? Will it spread?

You've seen the economics behind the spread of news online. It's not a pretty picture (although if it were, it'd be a slideshow). Rather than turn the world into entertainment, these forces reduce it to conflict, controversy, and crap. Blogs have no choice but to turn the world against itself for a few more pageviews, turning you against the world so you'll read them. They produce a web of mis-, dis-, and un-information so complete that few people—even the system's purveyors—are able to tell fact from fiction, rumor from reality. This is what makes it possible for manipulators like me to make our living.

I came across a line that put my feelings well: "One cannot feel more helpless than in a place and time when slander settles everything."* So that's how I felt during this book. Helpless.

## HELP & HOPE

In 2012 it didn't look like anyone was going to do anything about it. I deliberately ended this book then without much in the way of solutions—because I didn't think there were any. Apparently I was not as creative or intelligent as the billionaire Peter Thiel (few are), who was at that point quietly funding a legal battle against *Gawker*. In 2007 the site had outed him as gay against his wishes, and after speaking to many other victims of *Gawker*'s publishing philosophy, he decided to put them out of business. The secret war culminated in a $100+ million verdict in 2016 that put Gawker Media into bankruptcy and eventually led to *Gawker* being shuttered (the sister sites were sold off). Their crime? They had published clips from an illegally recorded sex tape of Hulk Hogan. Despite repeated opportunities to remove it, to settle, and to apologize, the site refused. It was their undoing.

---

*Barrows Dunham.

To think, the site whose editor once justified his unfair reporting to one of my clients as just "professional wrestling" was destroyed by a professional wrestler who refused to buy that excuse.

Journalists and First Amendment supporters decried the ruling, arguing that it would have a chilling effect. *We should be so lucky!* is what I say. Journalists should think twice before publishing a sex tape that arrives to their offices in an unmarked envelope. Journalists should do actual research before running stories (*Gawker* would have clearly seen that Hogan had said many times that the tape was recorded without his consent). The public does not have the right to know every single thing people do in their private bedrooms. There is such a thing as "the line" in civilized society.

We used to believe this. We didn't always submit to the rule of an abusive media system, as though those who control it were in charge and not us or our laws. In other countries, libel and defamation laws require a "conspicuous retraction" by the publisher if the claim is proven. A lame update at the bottom of a blog wouldn't cut it there and shouldn't cut it anymore *anywhere*. Colonial newspapers at various points in British history were required to post a security bond in order to enter the publishing business. It was intended to secure payments in the event of a libel action and to ensure some responsibility by the press. It gave the public (and the state) some recourse against publishers who often had few assets to pay for the damage they could potentially inflict. In 1890 future Supreme Court justice Louis Brandeis published an article titled "The Right to Privacy" for the *Harvard Law Review*, which argued that the advent of photography and the proliferation of national and international newspapers required better legal protections for average citizens. It wasn't fair, essentially, that technology allowed lies to damage reputations faster than the truth could fix them. So there is precedent for these types of protections— which blogs show us we desperately need once again. We have simply forgotten about them.

I think we've noticed since the *Gawker* ruling that there has been a kind of chilling effect on the media. Perhaps publishers have learned that actions have consequences—that freedom of speech is not necessarily freedom from responsibility. That there is a difference between aggressive reporting and recklessness and bullying. Hopefully this lawsuit, if only in a small way, has changed the incentives of the media system and proves that an individual can have an impact on how things work.

## OTHER SOLUTIONS

I wish there was an easy solution to all of this. It would help me answer my critics and the defensive bloggers who will invariably whine: "Well, what are we supposed to do about it?" Or, "Okay, wise guy, tell us how to fix it." Well, I don't know the answer. My job was to prove that something was massively, massively wrong and to come clean about my role in it. To prove that we've all been feeding the monster. What exactly to do about it will be the work of those who come after me.

If I saw bright spots or green sprouts, I would have pointed them out. If there were solutions, I would give them to you. But currently I don't see any. In fact, I object to using the word "solution" at all. To seek a solution implies and confirms that this problem needs to even exist. It takes for granted the bad assumptions at the root of blogs—assumptions that are deeply mistaken.

Take the frantic chase for pageviews, for example. This wrongly assumes that the traffic blogs generate is worth anything. It isn't. Sites sell only a fraction of their inventory each month, essentially giving the rest away for fractions of a penny, yet they attempt to grow their traffic above all else. When I wrote the conclusion the first time, the trend was for sites to auto-refresh as a way to generate extra pageviews. More recently the trend has been something called "infinite scroll," which has the same effect. Free pageviews! The advertisers who paid for those impressions were robbed, and the blogs that charged for them are no more than crooks.

Meanwhile, smaller sites that have built core audiences on trust and loyalty sell out their ad space months in advance. They have less total inventory, but they sell all of theirs at higher prices and are more profitable, sustainable businesses. Blogs scramble for a few thousand extra pageviews, and manipulate their readers to do so, because they value the wrong metrics and the wrong revenue stream. They follow short-term and short-sighted incentives.

But incentives can be changed, just as the *New York Times* showed in switching from the one-off to a subscription model under Adolph Ochs. In order to survive as a quality publication, the *New York Times* is redefining its economics once again. The recent implementation of their controversial paywall (which limited readers first to twenty free articles a month and then to ten before requiring them to pay for more access) is a lesson in great incentives. According to economist Tyler Cowen, it means that "the new NYT incentive is to have more than twenty must-read articles each month."[2] The *Wall Street Journal* and other publications have harder paywalls—and guess what? Subscriptions are increasing. How absurd that under the current model—the one that most publishers are sticking with and believe in—there is no imperative to produce these must-read articles, only must-clicks. The *New York Times* recently announced they once again make more total revenue from subscriptions than from advertising. A deep-pocketed donor just agreed to subsidize on $1 million worth of *New York Times* subscriptions for students. This is all very good news. Whether it will be replicated, or whether it *can* be, is another question. Would you pay for most of the crap that is created online? I wouldn't.

As Ed Wallace, the *Businessweek* writer, reminds us: "The first job of the journalist is to ask, 'Is this information true?'" Bloggers refuse to accept this mantle. Instead of getting us the truth, they focus on one thing, and one thing only: getting their publisher pageviews. I don't care that finding the truth can be expensive, that iterative news is faster, or that it's too hard not to play the pageview game. Find another business if you don't like it. Because your profession's *true* purpose is to serve the best interests of your readers—doing anything else is to misread your own long-term interests. Advertisers pay you to get to readers, so screwing the readers is a bad idea.

Readers hold equally exhausting assumptions of their own. The current system of delegated trust and deferred responsibility exists because readers have tacitly accepted the burden that blogs have abdicated. We've assumed it was our duty to sort through the muck and garbage to find the occasional gem, to do their fact-checking for them, to correct their mistakes and call ourselves contributors, when actually we're cogs. We never asked the critical question: If we have to do all the work, what are we paying you guys for?

When intelligent people read, they ask themselves a simple question:

What do I plan to do with this information? Most readers have abandoned even pretending to consider this. I imagine it's because they're afraid of the answer: There isn't a thing we can do with it. There is no practical purpose in our lives for most of what blogs produce other than distraction. When readers decide to start demanding quality over quantity, the economics of internet content will change. Manipulation and marketing will immediately become more difficult. My decision to spend less time online is not a selfish one, though it did make my life better. It's voting with my wallet. If more people do the same, it will have impact.

I also won't deny that marketers—myself foremost among them—are part of the problem too. Nobody forced me to do what I did. I was a bad actor, and I created many of the loopholes I now criticize. Both I and my clients profited greatly from the manipulations I confessed here: Millions of books were sold, celebrity was created, and brands were reinvigorated and built. But we also paid very heavily for those gains with currency like dignity, respect, and trust. Deep down I suspect that the losses may not have been worth the cost. Marketers need to understand this. *American Apparel is no longer in business*. The strategies I talked about in this book were good for notoriety but ultimately mattered very little in the long term.

Don't forget that! Especially the young people reading this book—the type I hear from who come up to me and say it inspired them to get into marketing. I'm flattered and horrified. I want to remind them that if you chase the kind of attention I chased, and use the tactics I have used, there will be blowback. Consider that seriously.

## A NEW AWARENESS

We must rid ourselves of the false beliefs that caused so much of this. Publicity does not come easily, profits do not come easily, and knowledge does not come easily. The delusion that they could was what fed the monster most heartily. It is what propelled us past so many of the warning signs that this was simply not working.

You cannot have your news instantly *and* have it done well. You cannot have your news reduced to 140 characters or less without losing large parts of it. You cannot manipulate the news but not expect it to be manipulated against you. You cannot have your news for free; you can only obscure the costs. If, as a culture, we can learn this lesson, and if we can learn to love the hard work, we will save ourselves much trouble and collateral damage. We must remember: There is no easy way.

To borrow from Budd Schulberg's description of a media manipulator in his classic novel *The Harder They Fall*, too many of us, whether we're in media or marketing or just sharing stories on our social accounts, are indulging "in the illusions that we can deal in filth without becoming the thing we touch."

The current system cannot stand without these faulty assumptions. My contribution was to expose the problem, because once seen for all its contradictions and selfishness, it begins to fall apart. What is known can't jerk us around unwittingly. Before anything can be resolved, the implicit must be made into the explicit.

This may seem simplistic. But I have repeatedly used the metaphor of a feedback loop or arms race in this book—a company hires an online hitman like me, and so their rival does too; a blog tricks their readers with an exaggerated story, and their next post must deceive their skeptical audience more boldly. Opting out of this cycle, choosing not to feed the monster, is not some thankless favor I am asking for. It has massive and immediate implications for the rest of the chain.

Every new invention brings new problems with it. This is true for every medium and every communication method in history. For instance, only in the last thousand years of Latin were spaces inserted between words— a direct result of the spreading of books and scrolls that drowned people in so much text that they couldn't read. Blogs have created their own problems. We too are drowning in information that bleeds together into an endless blur. Someone has to stand up and say the emperor has no clothes—the words have no spaces between them, and goddamn it, that's ridiculous—because only after the problem is identified and the new ideal articulated can creative solutions be found.

Part of writing this book was about a controlled burn of the plays and scams I had created and used along with the best of them. They have become constant dangers to me and the people I care about—to culture itself, in some ways. I not only want to render the tricks useless by exposing how they work, but I want to opt out of doing them myself. I want to force everyone else to opt out as well. Hopefully clearing this ominous pile of debris will make it easier to start fresh.

Of course, I know some of you might ignore that part and use this book as an instruction manual. So be it. You will come to regret that choice, just as I have. But you will also have fun, and it could make you rich.

To those of you whom I have burned in this book, whom I have hurt or taken aim at or criticized or made fun of, I'm sorry. Trust me, I'm lying when I say that. It's just that you deserve better. And the second you stop and walk away, the monster will start to wither, and you will be happy again.

Whether you decide to use this book for good or evil, whether you listen to *all* my advice or just the parts you want to hear? Well, that's on you.

# ACKNOWLEDGMENTS

TO MY MENTORS: I LEARNED THESE LESSONS ON YOUR dime and patience. You taught me a craft and a profession and imbued me with the humility and responsibility not to let it corrupt me or go to my head. Thank you for shaping me into the person I am today—and for showing me what to do . . . and later, what not to do.

Thank you to my literary agent, Stephen Hanselman, whom I called on October 9 with the unsolicited manuscript of this book and by November 15 had more offers on it than I knew what to do with. Thank you to Julia for your tireless work behind the scenes. More important, thank you to Tim Ferriss (so glad we met all these years ago) for introducing us and paving the way.

Thank you to the wonderful staff at Portfolio—my excellent editor Niki Papadopoulos—and to Adrian Zackheim.

Thank you to Erin Tyler for an amazing cover and graphic design. (And to Erich Chen for taking that photo on our journalism trip to St. Louis in college.)

Thank you to my employees, who were often tasked with participating in the escapades detailed in this book. I was training you in the dark arts whether you knew it or not. Use that power responsibly.

Thank you to everyone who has e-mailed me from my site and asked me thought-provoking questions. It was in trying to answer them that I developed many of the ideas described here. Thanks to everyone who read a draft of this book and gave great notes: Nils Parker, Derek Kreindler, Neil Strauss, Andrew McMillen, Amy Holiday, Sep Kamvar, Jeff Waldman, Ian Claudius, Ben Bartley, Drew Curtis, Milt Deherrera, Hristo Vassilev, and Michael Ellsberg. Thanks to those (everyone else I know) who didn't read a draft but endured my many rants about the subject.

Sammy. My rule has always been to keep the crazy at home. You got stuck with the crazy and supported and loved me anyway. I could not have done this—or anything—without you. Thank you. Hi, Hanno (and Bucket, Biscuit, Watermelon, Buddy, Sugar, and Bugar.)

Here's to books.

# APPENDIX

I SAID IN THE INTRODUCTION THAT I WAS NOT THE ONLY media manipulator out there. I'm definitely not—I don't even think I was particularly exceptional. These interviews that I have included in the appendix should provide proof of that. Conducted over the last several years, they are straight-from-the-source explanations from manipulators of all political and business persuasions. I e-mailed them questions and they answered. No editing, no bias. Just their honest and often shocking truth.

# "EXCLUSIVE INTERVIEW: HOW THIS RIGHT-WING 'TROLL' REACHES 100M PEOPLE A MONTH"

## *MIKE CERNOVICH*

*New York Observer, October 2016\**

I SHOULD OPEN THIS PIECE BY SAYING THAT I DON'T agree with Mike Cernovich. I'm not saying that to disavow his views out of political correctness, I'm just saying it because it's true. Politically, we do not agree. We've had words a few times on Twitter and when I went to contact him for this interview, I actually discovered that I'd blocked him and forgotten about it. But deciding to interview him for this column had nothing to do with agreeing with Mike and a lot more to do with curiosity.

How does a self-published author of self-improvement books and former lawyer build a Twitter audience that can do as many as 100 million impressions in a month? How does someone with no direct affiliation with any political party create a hashtag that was used by the Republican nominee for president and the Green Party nominee? Why did the *New Yorker* decide to profile him and why does their headline call him a "Troll for Trump"? Is he actually a troll or has he just figured out the media better than many "professionals" and is now using it for his own agenda?

Instead of speculating about these questions or judging from afar, I prefer just to ask. Why not? You don't get infected when you interact with someone you disagree with—or have at times found obnoxious or offensive. In fact, you can usually learn something. Specifically: what makes them tick and how they do what they do (the latter being the most important).

---

\*http://observer.com/2016/10/exclusive-interview-how-this-right-wing-troll-reaches
-100m-people-a-month/.

With that, I'd like to present my interview with the notorious Mike Cernovich, whose alt-right videos, tweets, blog posts and books have made him a new breed of media figure. He's not an official cable news campaign surrogate, he's not a pundit, but he's more than just a troll. He has a real audience. What he produces can have real impact—not always directly, but when filtered through the media system it reaches people who are totally unaware of the source or the way in which news can spread. Nor is he the only one of his kind—on all sides of the spectrum, there are individuals like Mike, shaping what we read, setting the Overton Window in our political debate, stirring things up and laughing (and profiting) as we freak out about it. Which is why you should study how and why he does what he does.

**Tell us a bit about who you are and how you see yourself. Are you an author? A political operator? An agitator? An activist? A pundit? A troll? A marketer? All of the above? How did your unique position as a media figure and public personality come to be?**

My identity is based around being a writer. I can't not write. It's a compulsion. Every day I write about whatever is on my mind, and that's what complicates the story.

People who read *Gorilla Mindset* can't believe some of the political stuff or edgy Tweets I write. There's no unifying brand about me other than I'm a writer who shares my thoughts. Sometimes my thoughts are designed to help people, and other times my thoughts are designed to change the political system and challenge those who need a good fight.

Before a long road trip in the late 90s, I stopped by Barnes & Noble. At the time I was "depressed" or "lost" in that existential, angsty sort of way. I found *How to Stop Worrying and Start Living* by Dale Carnegie in the audiobook section. That book changed my life. I thought to myself, "I'd always like to write a book that will change someone's life."

Many who have read *Gorilla Mindset* find my Twitter too much. The same is true of my podcast, which is inspirational and aspirational and positive.

What is your story or the story of anyone else? You likely help your friends while also feeling jealous of others. There's resentment, hope, fear, anger, and a desire to make a difference on the world.

None of us are good or evil, and that frustrates us because we want to see others as wearing a white hat or black hat. My hat is grey.

The only difference between me and my critics is that I don't lie to the world about who I am. People are complicated and often seemingly hypocritical. Embrace the diversity of your mind.

**The big knock against the media is that it's controlled by powerful elites, that it is corporatized or fake. How does a single individual like yourself—with no direct affiliation to any organization or outlet— manage to have an impact? Whether people agree with you or not, I think there is interest in knowing how you've managed to create a large platform and have a monthly reach in the nine figures.**

Peter Thiel lays out the applicable first principle in his must-read book *Zero to One*. "If you want to create and capture lasting value, don't build an undifferentiated commodity business."

You work in marketing and publishing. What do you tell writers? You tell them to find their own value proposition through differentiation. How do you stand out? Be different.

Most media is the same. If you read *WaPo*, then you don't need to read the *New York Times*. If you read *BuzzFeed*, you don't need to read *Vox* or *Gawker* or *Vice*. You're going to be served up the same generic slop.

If 90% of mainstream media went away, no one would notice. You'd have fewer sites to visit, but you'd still read the same stories. You'd read the story one time rather than re-worded 100 times by 100 "writers."

Individual writers do not stand out. They have bylines as "prestigious" publications, but no one goes to those websites for the writer. Most writers today are commodities. They are fungible. There's a surplus of 24-year old English majors who all think and write the same.

One of America's only original thinkers is Naval [Ravikant]. He observed, "The internet commoditized the distribution of facts. The 'news' media responded by pivoting wholesale into opinions and entertainment."

He is almost exactly right, with this caveat.

Commentary is a commodity because everyone is following the same script. The left and right each have their own scripts. I follow my own script.

When people come to my Twitter or read my blog, they see a direct challenge to the dominant narrative. I currently have a near-monopoly on "anti-media."

If I went away, people would notice, just as people would notice if Tim Ferriss, you, Scott Adams, or James Altucher quit writing.

If a random guy or girl who writes for *Business Insider* or the *Daily Beast* stopped writing, would anyone notice? Maybe for a day or two, if they happened to be friends.

**One of the things I've written about in the past is this concept of how stories are traded up the chain. They start on Twitter or Reddit or a random blog and then make their way to bigger and bigger outlets until eventually it's a national story or a known fact. Have stories or hashtags you've started followed that trajectory? Can you give us some examples? Is it something you consciously think about or try to do?**

What I do on Twitter could be understood [as] the latest iteration of your groundbreaking work in *Trust Me, I'm Lying.* You created news cycle by feeding stories to bloggers desperate for page views. Your methods differed from mine but the principle is the same.

What is a news cycle and how do we control them? I obsess over that question daily, and one lesson learned is that a trending hashtag is newsworthy in itself.

I learned that lesson from the dishonest left. If five people on Twitter post some hashtag opposing "white male patriarchy," then *BuzzFeed* writes it up as, "The internet Totally Exploded on Evil White Men Today!"

Look at the Tweets cited in that "news" story, and you'll often see the top tweet getting 100 RTs—which is for me an ordinary Tweet.

I thus realized that to create news we had to create hashtags that would trend worldwide on Twitter. Me and my readers and viewers created several. Both Jill Stein and Donald Trump have posted to hashtags we started, including #WheresHillary.

Here are some more examples: http://www.dangerandplay.com/2016/03/28/the-future-of-news-social-media-and-the-new-news-cycle/.

**When you say that "Conflict is attention" and "Attention is influence" what do you mean by that? As a media strategy, what does that look like? That one seeks out ideas that are likely to provoke strong emotions? Does it help to believe those things or does that matter? That one should take a combative approach instead of a measured one? How does pure attention lead to action and influence?**

Allow Dana White to explain: "If you take four street corners, and on one they are playing baseball, on another they are playing basketball and on the other, street hockey. On the fourth corner, a fight breaks out. Where does the crowd go? They all go to the fight."

We all love drama. It's human nature. Sport, politics, reality TV. Those all meet the same human need. You helped write a book with laws about dramas and spectacles.

I create compelling spectacles using conflict.

Right now the media has a 6% approval rating, and journalists have been caught in several hoaxes. Rather than criticize the *New York Times*, a big company, I call out the journalist by name. Some call this "bullying," which is laughable. How can someone with a massive platform at the *New York Times* be a helpless victim? The real victims are people the media lies about, like Justine Sacco.

**I certainly see controversy as an underrated strategy. Most people are afraid of it—brands don't want to get complaints, public figures are afraid of backlash or complicated issues, etc—and so the people that can push through controversy often reap big gains very quickly. Trump has certainly been an example of it—for most of the election, he was anti-fragile. The controversies almost made him stronger. But I'm curious, do you think there are limits to these strategies? Do you worry that there is some vulnerability in your own approach—that at some point**

**it could stop making you stronger and suddenly lead to a reversal (not unlike what happened with the Trump tapes)? Is there stuff that you regret or wouldn't do again?**

I have developed a code of honor. I don't go after "civilians" or nobodies.

You are a soldier. You have a big platform, you write for a living, you are in the game. Heck you even called me an idiot or something on Twitter, an unprovoked attack. I thought it was funny and we went back-and-forth. I didn't feel like you "bullied" me, because you didn't.

However I will not write about nobodies. A recent example is Ken Bone. The media humiliated that poor man by publishing his porn-watching habits. Why? Do they have no decency?

I find it fascinating that people criticize me for being "too mean" to famous people and people with huge platforms. Meanwhile those same people use their platforms to attack people like Ken Bone and Justine Sacco.

The media is full of bullies. Anyone who has a problem with me should search their own Twitter history. They did join the Justine Sacco hate mob? Have they tried getting people fired over a Tweet? Did they link to articles discussing Ken Bone's porn habits? If so, they can keep their mouths shut about me. (Or not, they are of course free to criticize me. But [there] had better be a way they do so not from a high horse—they are right on the battlefield with me.)

*[Ed note: I followed up with Mike about the second part of the question and this was his extended answer]*

"Vulnerability" is an interesting concept with a lot of layers. The glib answer is that I'm an anti-fragile author of *Gorilla Mindset* and *MAGA Mindset,* and thus all negative attention could convert into new readers. That ignores deeper issues.

Social shaming has been used throughout human history because it works. It took me a long time to be able to laugh at the attacks, but I will be honest—It feels pretty crappy when what seems like the entire internet is lying about you. Most people are vulnerable to these attacks, and it takes time to learn how to reframe them as a positive. (For every hater, there are 10 people paying attention who don't comment, just as most of us never write positive letters when we receive a good customer experience. We as people tend to speak up mostly to complain.)

As a lawyer defamation lawsuits concern me. I live in California, however, which has strong anti-SLAPP protections. We need a nationwide anti-SLAPP law to protect free speech, and I will not live in a state lacking an anti-SLAPP law.

My articles are fact-checked due to lawsuit risk, and I've passed on some good stories (which turned out to be true) as I wasn't able to fact-check them.

I am socially vulnerable as well. There have been articles written about people who "like" my Tweets. The media does this to socially isolate me. Most "respectable" people are afraid to associate with me openly, as they don't want to deal with the fallout from having the online hate mobs, unleashed by the bullying media, that results from being my friend.

Right now my reputation and relationship to readers are my main focus. As Warren Buffett said, "It takes 20 years to build a reputation and five minutes to ruin it. If you think about that, you'll do things differently." I don't spread hoaxes. People may not *agree* with what I write, but it's earnest and sincere—and in the case of Hillary Clinton's health, usually on target.

As social media and crowd-funding and self-publishing allows writers to go direct to the readers, it doesn't matter to me what the "media elite" think about me. I don't like them, they don't like me, and besides—media coverage doesn't sell books. Blogs, Twitter, YouTube, and podcasts sell books. I am accountable to my readers.

"The people" love me, despite or perhaps because of hoaxing media attacks on me. The best way to take me out would be to send me a hoax story. Despite the conspiracy theories about me, I fact-check what people send to avoid being hoaxed (or sued).

Also, as my profile has grown, people see my tactics change. A little empathy goes a long way. Because of my reach, I can make someone e-famous for a few minutes or longer. Unless someone seeks me out (in which case I assume they want the attention), I avoid people who may not want attention.

I may seem mean online, but I am mean to people who work in the media—the same people who are mean to others for a living. They simply call themselves "journalists" and dismiss all critics as "trolls." Journalism is trolling, full stop.

Those who give attention to others deserve to have attention brought on them. I will continue doing "journalism on journalists" and have some exciting ventures along those lines planned in 2017.

**You're a big fan of Twitter and of live video on places like Facebook and Periscope. I think most technologists have started to see Twitter as a flawed or stagnant platform, and they maybe think live video is up and coming but not arrived yet. Do you agree? Disagree? What's your take on these platforms?**

Live video is the future of journalism. Soon we will have drones with GoPros on them doing "reality journalism." The RNC and DNC both banned drones or else I'd have done that.

Marc Andreessen has said that being "too soon" is as bad as being "too late." Live media is too soon, which is why Twitter is losing money.

Twitter lacks business focus. Twitter is not a social media platform. It's part talk radio, part live news coverage, part political commentary. Twitter needs to be streamlined with those business focuses in mind.

**What's your media diet look like? Is there anything you've learned making the sausage (so to speak) that has changed what you will and won't eat?**

Most of what the liberal media does is outright hoaxing. We've gone from a world where journalists are biased to a world where journalists fabricate stories, as Sabrina Erdely and *Rolling Stone* did.

Independent voices from both sides appeal to me. If you don't lie about the facts, your views won't offend me. It's America, people disagree, no big deal.

My trip to the RNC and DNC sickened me. We've all seen Twitter pundits like Matt Yglesias and Ross Douthat hold course about what Americans think. They don't leave Twitter.

It's hilarious to me that those who accuse people of being "basement dwelling trolls" never leave their neighborhoods to attend a Trump or Clinton rally. They were nowhere to be found during the many massive protests at the DNC.

I have a lot of respect for Michael Tracey, who is a liberal. He tells the truth (as he sees it) about everyone. He isn't a shill for the establishment.

Jim Hoft of *The Gateway Pundit* does a great job of collecting news from across the web. Stefan Molyneux has a great commentary show where he presents a view that contradicts the dominant narrative.

Traditional media hates on *Breitbart,* but I attended the RNC and DNC. *Breitbart* had reporters in the field providing coverage. Where were the *New York Times* and other "legitimate" publications? They were inside the media tents drinking hot chocolate and sucking up to each other.

It may also come as a surprise to many to learn that I respect Glenn Greenwald, even though he'd likely disavow me or call me odious or something.

There is a shortage of real journalism. Most of [what] the "conservative media" does is churnalism—jabbering about what the "liberal media" wrote.

# "MEET THE JOURNALIST WHO FOOLED MILLIONS ABOUT CHOCOLATE AND WEIGHT LOSS"

## JOHN BOHANNON

*New York Observer, June 2015\**

A MAN TRICKS THE ENTIRE MEDIA ESTABLISHMENT AND millions of people into thinking that something unhealthy is actually good for them with a deliberately misleading study. Worse, they now think it's the secret to being healthy. He's a bad person, right?

But what if it was actually an attempt to illustrate the woeful prevalence of junk science and how easily it can be propagated through culture? If the man was a computer hacker who revealed a back door, we might marvel at his mastery and cleverness. If he was a whistleblower, we'd admire his courage.

Some people might be conflicted at the story of John Bohannon, who recently revealed that he'd helped dupe millions of people into believing that chocolate was healthy. He created a fake organization, orchestrated a study to show that chocolate was correlated with weight loss, published it in an open access journal, put out a fake press release, and traded it up the chain until the news appeared in several major media outlets. Now, finally, he's exposed the inner-workings of this stunt (his piece on *i09* has been read more than 835,000 times).

I think John is a hero. I think he's made the world better (or at least more aware) by what he's done. The only people with anything to be embarrassed about are the ones who got caught sleeping on the job. You see, it's journalists who are supposed to protect us against these types of manipulations. They're supposed to weed out the bad studies from the good.

*http://observer.com/2015/06/behind-the-scenes-with-the-journalist-who-fooled-millions-about-chocolate/.

They're supposed to realize that Ship Your Enemies Glitter stunts are blatant money grabs or when self-interested sources should be excluded or qualified. They should see that someone like Charles C. Johnson is exploiting the political dialog.

Yet instead of learning from something like these, outlets like the *Daily Mail* are rushing to cover their ass. They deny they ever fell for it. And even if they didn't—they can't see how much their business models and the model of almost all journalism today needlessly exposes them to such risks. Because they don't care. They don't want to be better or know the truth. The truth would be bad for business.

As John recently told *The Washington Post*, although there is plenty of blame to go around there's one group who deserves it more than any others. "It's the reporters. The reporters and ultimately the editors . . . People who are on the health science beat need to treat [what they write] like science, and that has to come from the editors. You need to talk to a source who has real scientific expertise."

It's clear that reporters, not only in the health space, but everywhere, have stopped caring. Well, maybe a few readers do care. To help with that, I've reached out to John to get a little more information on how his brilliant stunt worked and what else people should know.

**So tell us how you managed to fool not only hundreds of thousands of people and media outlets, but fooled them with something that is on its face, ridiculous?**

Well, did it really seem ridiculous that chocolate can help you lose weight? Compared to the diet headlines you can read every day, it seemed like a fairly normal claim. And that's the problem! Somehow we've all decided that the science of nutrition doesn't matter.

**What gave you the idea—any inspirations you can tell us about? Did you actually think you could pull it off? Was it exhilarating, scary, did you feel guilty? Tell us your thought process.**

I got a call out of the blue in December from Peter Onneken, a German television reporter. It was all his brilliant idea: Do a really bad but authentic scientific study of chocolate and weight loss, then build a media campaign around it. I was skeptical that any of my journalist colleagues would take the bait. But take it they did.

**Was there one outlet or channel that you feel like did more to propagate the narrative than any others?**

A huge thank you must go out to the *Daily Mail*. They even tried to weasel out of it. One of their PR people sent me and NPR an email implying that they hadn't in fact taken the bait, since we accidentally used a screen shot of the wrong *Daily Mail* story. (It was one of their *other* stories about the miraculous health benefits of eating chocolate, if you can believe it.) They were clearly hoping that we would just quietly remove the screen shot and let them off the hook. To my knowledge, they have printed no retraction, correction, or clarification. Here is their story: http://www.dailymail .co.uk/femail/article-3018945/New-study-reveals-eating-chocolate-doesn-t-affect-Body-Mass-Index-help-LOSE-weight.html.

**Some people might say that what you did was unfair or potentially harmful (this is a criticism I got with my stunts). Have [you] heard that at all? I believe you did everyone a favor by pointing out an obvious flaw in the system—it's up to the reporters responsible to make changes around this information. What do you think?**

It is true that these kinds of investigations pose an ethical dilemma. We must weigh the possible benefits against the possible harms. In this case, it is the risk of making some people eat a chocolate bar and embarrassing some bad journalists versus promoting skepticism about diet claims and showing that scientific studies can get misleading results when they don't understand statistics. I'll leave it to your readers to decide for themselves.

**With that in mind, what do you think the solution is? What do we have to change?**

The next time you read a news story that seems to be giving you clear diet advice to lose weight, you should get angry and write to the editor. We have a better understanding of why stars sometimes blow up than why people become obese. This is hard science, not "lifestyle" fodder.

**You did this with something that I do think is relatively harmless and you did come clean. Do you think that the same tactics or manipulation could be used more nefariously? Is that what's happening?**

I think all of the diet-nutrition-fitness media is corrupt. It's bad science and worse journalism, all driven by companies selling rubbish. Oh sorry, you weren't talking about mainstream media?

**Now that you've come clean and revealed the bogus facts behind the story—do you think the original narrative is going to die or keep going like some sort of zombie? Have you seen the corrections you were hoping for?**

I've seen one and only one real correction.

# "EXCLUSIVE: 'DIGITAL DARTH VADER' CHARLES C. JOHNSON ON MANIPULATING POLITICS AND MEDIA"

## CHARLES C. JOHNSON

### New York Observer, May 2015*

I'M NOT SURE WHEN I FIRST BECAME AWARE OF Charles C. Johnson. It may have been from a few tweets he directed at me. It might have been from one of the numerous controversial profiles of him in the *New York Times*, *Politico*, *Gawker* and other places. I do specifically recall being tagged in a tweet for a $500 bounty he'd put on anyone who could get an advertiser to pull out of Al Sharpton's TV show.

It was exactly the kind of political divisiveness that I have tried to cut out of my life over the last few years, so I mostly ignored it. It's also the kind of stunt that has made Charles wildly popular in some conservative circles. He's aggressive, he's unorthodox, he knows which buttons to press. With the collapse of traditional media, he's figured out how to drive media narratives better than just about anyone. In this way, he is very much the heir to the legacy of Andrew Breitbart and James O'Keefe.

For some people, that's an honor. Others consider it a damning insult. To some, Charles is a toxic troll, abusing the system. To an equal number of people, he's a maverick and a truth teller.

I can see it both ways. It's complicated and here's why: Charles cites my book *Trust Me, I'm Lying* as one of his most significant influences. In other words, I may want [to] disavow what he does, but I cannot avoid admitting that he is partially a reflection of myself. It's an unusual posi-

*http://observer.com/2015/05/exclusive-digital-darth-vader-charles-johnson-on-manipulating-politics-and-media/.

tion for an author to be in—to see his own book used in ways he'd rather not have it be used. In fact, in this instance I'm seeing it used in precisely the ways I warned against. At the same time, it'd be hard to argue that Charles C. Johnson is doing anything that your average publicist, blogger, pundit or strategist doesn't do—the only real difference is degree.

When Charles tweeted about my book last week, I decided to act. Why not email him and talk? Clearly we share some common ground, why not connect? Having already spoken to left-wing activists who manipulate the media and the people behind #GamerGate, why not learn from someone equally controversial? We ended up chatting on the phone for about thirty minutes last week discussing everything from the Overton Window to the towns of central California. It was pleasant, provocative and challenging. I came away impressed in a lot of ways. I followed up over email with the questions below. Some of the views he expressed I strongly disagree with. In other answers, I think he nails it. But that is the nature of a figure like Charles—smart, but undeniably frustrating in the ways he uses it.

I hope that Charles's honest and amoral tactics help reveal even more about the media system (sorry, racket) to you, the public. Only when we know how our news really gets made, can we gauge our appetite for consuming it.

**So we've never met, never really spoken, but it occurred to me that I had rather strong opinions about you. Yet, if I really dig into my own views here, I have to admit those opinions come almost entirely from sources I don't trust or respect much. Do you find that that is fairly common with people who interact with you?**

You'd be surprised at the sorts of people I interact with on a day-to-day basis. I'm friendly with dozens of journalists, multiple billionaires, law enforcement, and thousands of everyday researchers. This is how I like it. In Shakespeare the fool was the one who was allowed to tell the truth. I don't mind it if I'm made fun of or mocked so long as all the right people know that I'm right. I simply don't believe that most of the media has any real power at all and that it's only a matter of time before it all implodes.

There was a concerted effort by various publications and blogs to demonize me in 2014, especially after I exposed the *Rolling Stone* scandal and Jackie *[Ed note: Last name has been deleted]*, the lying girl behind it. These include *BuzzFeed, Gawker, Jezebel, Deadspin*, etc., who just made things up about me. Normally this negative attention would have bothered me but I don't really respect all of these sites so I understood what they were doing. They saw a competitor so they reacted negatively. Andy Warhol once said that he doesn't read criticism but measures it in inches. I'm much the same way.

I think a lot of the dislike for me isn't real but a social signaling thing that's used by reporters to vainly assure themselves that I'm not onto something.

**Tell me, how do you describe what it is that you do? What's your livelihood? How does it work? What place do you see yourself fitting in our current media culture?**

I like to tell people I do research and that I'm building a private intelligence network. I own two companies—one is a news company and the other a research firm. The two operate synergistically. I make money from clients, from speaking gigs, from donors, from traffic, and from a hundred or so other sources. I like to use Twitter because that's where the self-appointed cognoscenti create public opinion, i.e. the media or the political class. Jesse James robbed banks because that's where the money is. I mess with Twitter because that's where the people who need to be messed with are. In so doing I combine celebrity culture, nerd culture, and heavy research. It's essentially #GamerGate applied to everything in the cultural space. I really enjoy having people from all over the world work with me to change the narrative and ultimately to change the world.

**David Carr (who I did respect), wrote in his column about you that your style of journalism "says everything about the corrosive, underreported news era we are living through." I agree we live in a corrosive media era, but I would argue that we're anything but "underreported." What would you say to the idea that we have far too much media and**

**that at some point, it's become this giant beast that needs to be constantly fed?**

I spoke to David for 4 hours and explained to him very politely what I was doing and why it was important and in keeping with the journalistic icons we hold dear. He couldn't write the column that I may actually be brilliant so he had to slime me. He kept insisting that I was like the ghost from *Ghostbusters 2* and then he said I was juvenile or something. It was kind of sad. I wrote about the story.

I think there was something very revealing about the *Times* and our media where great reporters like Ray Hernandez and Nicholas Wade don't get the media attention they deserve and ultimately leave the *Times* while recovering crack addicts like Carr—with no technical chops whatsoever—are lionized as the voice of the internet. It's very strange. I don't agree that there is such a thing as too much information and I'm a tad bit disappointed that there's not even more information available. I suppose the human brain is only capable of so much.

**Is there anything you've published that you regret? I've argued in the past that iterative journalism is a real problem—this reporting live, in real time, as everything happens—but you clearly operate your Twitter feed in a sort of stream of consciousness reporting style. Sometimes you get it right, sometimes you don't.**

I regret publishing the wrong photo of Jackie for an hour *[Ed note: last name deleted]*. Other than that, I don't regret anything I've published. I think there are higher standards for me than there are for massive media conglomerates, which is odd, because I have a millionth [of] their resources. Still, I'm profitable and they are not so maybe it doesn't really matter.

I can't think of anything I've gotten wrong. Sometimes I'll be right years later, like I was with U.S. Senator Menendez. Sometimes I'll be proven right in real time as I was with Sony not being hacked by North Korea or Elizabeth O'Bagy, a Syria analyst, manufacturing her credentials to lie us into war. Of course in the media these days it doesn't much matter if you are right. It matters if you can persuade people you are right.

This is kind of a fascinating feature of our time. You have to become a celebrity before people start to listen. I wish this weren't so but it is.

**Who is the least trustworthy person in journalism?**

Shane Smith of *Vice* is a serial con artist who lied about being a wartime correspondent. The notion that his company is worth a billion-plus dollars is laughable. (I wrote about it at the *Daily Caller*.) Anderson Cooper is a close second. The more you dig in on Cooper the more you'll find out he's made up things in his past, too.

**What is the easiest loophole to exploit in our current system?**

The newsroom can never know as much information as the crowd or private network can. There's a certain necessary occupational arrogance that comes with assuming that a few thousand people can know all the news that's fit to print. I'm a bit more suspicious. There's a huge bias toward breaking news. If you can break new news while everyone else is following your lead you can control the future. People are tired of the right-wing and left-wing ghettos.

**If you wanted to pass a totally false story through the media, how would you do it? If you wanted to take someone down, how would you do it? Can you spot when that is happening or being done by other people?**

Well, *Rolling Stone* and NBC News are the experts on fake stories and I had a hand in exposing both of these organizations. I have only one rule—which is that I don't do anything fake. I start with the unguarded moment. Most people have moments where they aren't "on," where they reveal their true selves. Oftentimes it's in decisions they make or don't make. I focus on the "who" behind the headlines. I look at their finances, at their spouses, I go through the public records, and then begin working the phones. I try to learn about how people actually are. There is often a huge disconnect between the public profile and the private self. This is where much of my work gets its power.

The media typically operates in packs on Twitter. They'll be friends that promote one another's work and advance one another's career. I use Twitter to monitor this group activity. I map out the relationships. I also have spies on various listservs and I pay people for information, whether that's in the form of more information, nice dinners, or cash, I leave up to the seller. Usually you'll notice the attack on someone happens all at once. If you can find the origin point you can map the entire relationship network.

**Traffic to your site is relatively small. You have a sizable number of Twitter followers, though not near other news figures and bloggers. Yet you seem to exert an immense amount of influence over certain news stories—often through the same media outlets that probably wish they didn't have to follow your lead. Is this trading up the chain? How does this work?**

I measure traffic to dollar spent rather than just traffic. In that comparison I'm actually doing very, very well. I've never seen traffic [as] the be all and end all of influence. And everyone knows that people lie about traffic figures all the time. The traffic numbers are designed to get the attention of advertisers but there are ways to make money independent of traffic numbers. On Twitter I'm told that I have one of the most viewed but least followed accounts. This is one of the hidden variables that determines how popular an account is.

I understand how Twitter works a lot more than my critics who don't seem to know what open protocols are. Trading up the chain is important but what's more important is to control the mind of your critics, to live in their heads. I think I've figured out how to do that repeatedly and this is actually a very lucrative trick. I'm not interested in spending my brain cells on how to create an ad that you'll click on to sell you hair products. That's not my comparative advantage. Of course I don't much mind ads because they provide another revenue stream.

**I'll be honest: I just don't get some of the things you seem to have very passionately latched on to. What does it matter if Obama is gay? Do you care? What do the pictures in Michael Brown's instagram account mat-**

ter? To an outsider, it seems that you often focus on issues of race, gender and so forth as a wedge. What would you say to that?

I'm interested in taboos. One of the successes of the Obama years was how he made certain inquiry into his past forbidden. I suspect part of that was the fascination that many people had with the novelty of a black president. In essence, the media gave a monopoly to enterprising journalists. As time [goes] on that monopoly has begun to crack. I'll publish more things when Obama is out of office. He is easily one of the most fascinating cons ever perpetrated on the public. However you feel about his politics—and I'm not a fan—there's a lot that isn't known about him and should be.

First thing Obama did when he went to Occidental is join the gay club on campus. This was in 1979. His mentor at Occidental was Larry Goldyn, a very prominent gay man. He lived with gay men in New York. None of the women he is reported to have dated—and there are only two— describes having had a sexual relationship with Obama. He has told several contradictory stories about how he met his wife. Large chunks of his first book have been discredited. I'm fascinated by all of this Obama past. I don't care if he sleeps with men but I do think it's interesting that in 2015 we can't have a black, gay president. Why not? I suspect we've had other gay presidents in the past and yet Obama seems to be off limits because we want to believe the narrative about his family life even though we know Michelle Obama once tried to divorce him.

The reason I published Michael Brown's Instagram and Twitter feed is that it directly contradicts the media narrative that he was a gentle giant. He was anything but. I helped end that narrative rather quickly. I don't believe in publishing conventional material because that's not where my comparative advantage is. Most people in the media all do the same thing and then wonder why they are paid so little. The answer is that they've made themselves redundant.

Race is the biggest taboo in America because our regime is grounded on the idea that we're all naturally equal and that anyone can achieve the American dream. And yet we observe that blacks, on average, still do poorer than other ethnic groups. At a certain point I stopped believing the cultural argument as serious. Why, for example, do Asian-Americans and Jews consistently out earn whites? I started learning more about the differences that exist in IQ between racial groups and about how genetically we are actually quite different from one another. I learned about the MAO-A gene and its theoretical effects on violence. It's my view that as we become a more information based society and that people reap bigger and bigger gains according to their IQ that this inequality will increase, rather than decrease. This development will have all kinds of interesting effects on our politics and society as time goes on.

People actually find it cathartic to violate certain taboos. I try to give them the truth that explodes those taboos. I suspect this is why they keep coming back. That, and they love solving puzzles and exploring and finding out the truth for themselves.

**In that vein, is there anything that is off limits? Anything that should be off limits? I hate getting asked "where do you draw the line" because the line is often private, and usually varies from case to case. But do you struggle with this?**

I do have limits but I'm not prepared to discuss them at this time. I do struggle with it but not as often as you would think.

**You were upfront with me about your having autism. How does that impact what you do?**

I'm not sure and I'm not sure I'm the best person to say. I have always been told that I have high IQ and low empathy but it's hard to say what effect this has on my work or on me.

**When I wrote *Trust Me, I'm Lying*, it was because I hated where I saw political and cultural discourse going. I basically wanted no part of it. Yet, you seem to have read the book and seen what I've seen, and love it. You take this world like a fish to water, don't you?**

Yes, I think it's a manual for living in the 21st century. I no longer believe in persuading people but in using taboos and playing with them to get issues highlighted that would otherwise be ignored. I think there's nothing wrong with it if it's done for the right reasons.

**What do you wish more people knew about you? What do you wish they knew about what you do?**

I think there's this view about me in certain circles that has more to do with status signaling than it does any real contempt or insight. I wish some people knew how deliberative I am and how I regard this as a chess game. It isn't so personal.

**Finally—why are you even talking to me? I know why I'm talking to you: Because why not? There's no reason that people, especially if they disagree with each other based on *what they've read online*—shouldn't connect and have a conversation together.**

I tend to be friendly to people who approach me and assume good faith on my part. I like to talk to people and I like to learn new things.

# "EXCLUSIVE: HOW THIS LEFT-WING ACTIVIST MANIPULATES THE MEDIA TO SPREAD HIS MESSAGE"

*PETER YOUNG*

*New York Observer, February 2015\**

I FIRST HEARD OF PETER YOUNG WHEN A REPORTER AT the Daily Dot asked me if I was somehow involved in 2013's "Ex-Vegans" stunt in which dozens of former vegans were exposed for having eaten meat. After dominating the media cycle for several days, the surprise left hook of the campaign landed: All the traffic and inbound links were redirected to footage of appalling slaughterhouse conditions. Hundreds of thousands of people were unwittingly exposed to the very unpleasantness that media attempts to shield from them.

I'm not a vegan, and I had nothing to do with the campaign—but I do have a lot of respect for its brilliance and execution and for the fact that it reveals a salient fact about our times. Today's media system is a bit like an emperor with no clothes. Peter Young resembles nothing so much as Mathew Carpenter, the man who recently turned a stunt about shipping glitter to your enemies into $100,000. They both understand intuitively how the media works and have used it repeatedly to advance their interests. While they did what they did for very different reasons, I learned that they'd both read my book, *Trust Me, I'm Lying*, and it had influenced their actions.

I thought I would interview Mr. Young because he recently ran another campaign of media manipulation, in this case intended to reveal and ex-

\*http://observer.com/2015/02/exclusive-how-this-left-wing-activist-manipulates-the-media-to-spread-his-message/

pose problems with the TSA watch list (a system which he is intimately familiar with since he is, in fact, on it). In less than eight hours, his blog—which he had constructed entirely for the purposes of getting attention—was picked up by places like Boing Boing, Techdirt and Forbes. And now he's ready to explain exactly what he does to advance his ideology and how it works in today's online-driven culture. He assures me the answers below and the stories on his site are 100 percent true. I'll leave it to you whether or not you want to trust him.

**So tell us, are you really on the TSA watch list and how did that happen?**

In 1998, I was charged with Animal Enterprise Terrorism for my role in freeing foxes and mink from fur farms. This amounted to cutting fences and opening cages at six farms. Under the weight of an 82-year maximum sentence, I became a fugitive for seven years, lived under several aliases, and was arrested at a Starbucks in 2005. I served two years in prison.

Because of the "terrorist" label, in the years since I've had my house raided by the FBI twice, been named as suspect in several animal liberations, found laptops with dead batteries fully charged when removed from storage a year later (do the math), had my garbage stolen by the authorities, and learned a woman who took me on [a] trip to Moab was working for the FBI.

Of it all, the TSA attention is among the least intrusive.

**Now, how does that differ from what was reported in the media and what you put up on your blog? Is there any part of the record you can clear up for us?**

Before my anonymity as "the jetsetting terrorist" was compromised by Forbes, I described the crime that put me on the TSA's watch list as an "activist-related property crime." Animals are considered property in the eyes of the law, so this was accurate. As for the rest: It wouldn't be possible to untangle all the misinformation reported in the media and elsewhere over the years. I can't complain. I probably planted half of it anyway.

*[Editor Note: From what Mr. Young told me when he originally reached out, he created the blog, uploaded the posts, then backdated them so it seemed older and more organic. And until this article was published, no outlet doubted the intentions/legitimacy of the blog.]*

**Tell us how and why you decided to make this something the media would pounce on? What did you do? How did it work? How much traffic /attention did it get?**

The Jetsetting Terrorist was launched with the stated goal of going mainstream within two weeks. It took about eight hours. The specific end-goal was *The Alex Jones Show*. While culturally considered fringe, he has a larger platform than most websites and TV shows. And he hates the TSA. (Spoiler alert: Alex has yet to call me.)

My blueprint—straight from your *Trust Me, I'm Lying* playbook—was as follows:

- Set up an anonymous burner email account.

- Identify people (leftist/libertarian-leaning celebrities and public figures) with large Twitter followings, get their personal email addresses.

- Email them a link to the site and a two-line email about how this is the best site ever and how "surprised" I am they haven't tweeted it yet. Pretty simple.

- Trade it up the chain until hitting something big.

- Leverage my anonymity to offer Alex Jones the exclusive on my identity reveal, for an interview.

Why Twitter? Better credibility-to-ease-of-penetration ratio. Here's what I mean:

Writing a blog post is a time investment. Bloggers are selective of what they dedicate a post to. A prolific blogger might post once or twice a day. A Tweet is copy, paste, done. A prolific Twitter user might post on Twitter

20-plus times a day. But for the purpose of leveraging mentions to receive larger mentions, they are the same: A single tweet has a unique URL that can be sent to larger platforms needing some social proof before running a story. In short, baiting John Cusack into tweeting a link is lower-effort, higher-yield than coverage on a low-level libertarian blog.

I didn't have to go far. Within a few hours of going live, I (anonymously) sent a link to Sean Bonner. Sean and I had spoken at the same conference once and met afterwards. I was a fan of his email newsletter, and he had a decent Twitter following. More importantly: He was a former contributor to Boing Boing.

As a major driver of virality, Boing Boing was a prized target. Going through a current contributor was like storming the gates. Going through a former contributor was sneaking in the back door. Sean tweeted it within minutes. With the anonymous burner account, I sent a link to the tweet to Cory Doctorow at Boing Boing. A few hours later, it was on Boing Boing.

From there I set up 10 more burner accounts and carpet-bombed the internet with this email:

> This is on the front page of Boing Boing right now but they just did
> a weak copy/paste job. Would like to see ____ cover this properly.
>
> A white hipster writes hilarious stories about TSA encounters,
> and flying while on the terrorist watch list. Too good.
>
> The author is anonymous, but worth a try.

I sent this to exactly 103 journalists. I tweaked it slightly to appeal to specific targets. My approach was not scattershot. The majority of emails were sent to journalists who had previously covered the TSA or other civil liberties issues. If done right, you're adding value to the journalist. It is an equitable exchange.

Immediately thereafter, Forbes contacted me for an interview. In a follow up email, the reporter stated she had done a reverse-lookup of my cell number and determined my real identity. The story—outing me as "the jetsetting terrorist"—ran the following week, bringing attention to both the TSA and the bigger issue of classifying a broad segment of the population as "terrorists."

Creating the site and content took three days. And it was methodically crafted to maximize virality.

The elements were:

**Anonymity**: Mystique is powerful.

**It's never been done:** With so much talk about the TSA, no one had gone quite as public with their experiences on the TSA's terrorist watch list.

**Awesome content:** There's no shortcut here. I have a background as a writer, and while I wrote with haste, I put care into maximizing the impact of the prose. A collection of generic and poorly written TSA stories would have gone nowhere.

**Riding the wave of an ongoing conversation:** Controversy over the TSA was a regular part of the public debate. There was a pent up demand for a new angle on an increasingly stale subject.

**Solid tagline:** "I'm a convicted terrorist. I travel a lot. And the TSA won't leave me alone. This is my diary of traveling as a marked man." I spent a lot of time crafting that.

**Going hipster:** The original "about me" sidebar read "How a jetsetting hipster became a jetsetting hipster terrorist." While subtle, portraying myself as a "hipster" was in all likelihood the determining factor in making this viral. When you get "terrorist," "jetsetter," and "hipster" in one place, it's too absurd to not spread. You're clicking that link. (This was, by the way, the only part I changed when my identity was revealed. Calling myself a "hipster" just isn't accurate. And no one uses that word self-referentially.)

**A powerful narrative:** There are 1,000 ways to tell the same story. I put effort into maximizing chances of this getting picked up by utilizing timeless literary narratives, accentuating the underdog effect, the reluctant hero, and (subtle) revenge themes.

**Niching down:** The original plan was "The Hipster Terrorist"— anonymous (and 100 percent true) stories from a convicted "terrorist" documenting the humorous side-effects of life under the "terrorist" label. From stories about awkward dinner-table conversation when meeting a girlfriend's parents, to the baristas at the Starbucks I frequent googling my name (hilarity ensues). While this would be a great blog (and a book

I'll probably write soon), it lacked any timely discussion to piggyback on. Niching down to the TSA was clearly the right move.

### Hipster jetsetting terrorist
To clover.hope
Clover

This was on the front page of Boing Boing over the weekend, but they just did a weak copy/paste job. Would like to see Jezebel cover this properly. He's getting tons of internet love right now, but no one is highlighting what an entitled, pompous douchebag this guy is.

A white hipster writing stories about verbally abusing the TSA (including women) because he's on the "terrorist watch list".

**Before this, you manipulated the media with a stunt to drive attention to conditions in slaughterhouses and factory farms. Why do you feel justified in essentially tricking or circumventing the news process in order to get your message across? Is this something you think more advocates should do?**

The game plan for The Vegan Sellout List was this:

- Launch a site that allowed people to anonymously submit the names and photos of former vegans, and the story behind their rise and fall from veganism.

- Pre-populate the list with 100 former vegans who have a platform (from celebrities to ex-vegans with high-traffic blogs).

- Email all 100 with a link to their entry on the site, and bait them into mentioning it in a blog post or Tweet.

- Concurrently, generate buzz in the vegan blogosphere.

- Parlay all of this to successively bigger blogs, until it hit a huge site that generated serious traffic.

- Pull a bait-and-switch, forcing visitors to watch a video of slaughterhouse footage before entering.

"The Vegan Sellout List" was what the internet craved: Offensive, provocative, shameless, and impossible not to have an opinion on. From launch the goal was *Gawker*. We would consider it a success if we hit *Gawker*. (We spent a considerable amount of time trying to identify writers at *Gawker* who were former vegans to provoke coverage by making it personal, without success. *Gawker* ran the story in under three weeks anyway.)

Our plan worked a little too well. We'd given ourselves a two-month window to build a buzz before getting it mainstream. It hit top-tier outlets like Fox News in under three weeks. When the traffic explosion hit, we weren't prepared. It came so fast and at such volume, it crashed the server. The aborted plan was to utilize a plugin to compel a video view before entering, and with a crashed server the only remaining option was a URL redirect. We sent hundreds of thousands of people to a third-party site that autoplayed a graphic video titled "Meet Your Meat."

In the end, the results were massive: At least 200,000 people baited into getting their first glimpse inside a slaughterhouse. The Vegan Sellout List was vindicated by the results it achieved.

I have friends working for nonprofits who travel in vans to college campuses all year asking people to watch two minutes of slaughterhouse footage. On a good day, they reach 200 people. This is important and noble work. But consider that the Vegan Sellout List may have sent over 1,000 times as many people to the same footage for three days work. Even if only 10 percent of visitors watched the video, this is an incredible return on my time investment.

Everyone doing advocacy work owes it to their message to get acquainted with the concept of leverage, and ways to increase the impact of each unit of effort exponentially. As I asserted in my original statement on this stunt: Before this stunt, most vegans believed the temperature in Hell would have to hit 32 degrees before FoxNews.com would ever send tens (or hundreds) of thousands of their readers directly to graphic slaughterhouse footage. Regarding why these methods are justified: While the lines are increasingly blurred, I apply two different ethical equations to bloggers vs. journalists.

Bloggers: On the internet, being vocally "offended" is the new "look at me I'm cool." It's like being 12 and putting a playing card in your bike spokes. I've met many of the bigger bloggers in the vegan space. Most of them are awesome people. A few of the more drama-centric ones are clearly acting out their own demons. Like, they couldn't get a date in high school (or now), and it's payback time. (To be fair, this is my take on a large swath of the internet, and is not vegan-specific.) This is exactly the type of person The Vegan Sellout List was designed to agitate for traffic. If you've built a career around creating—or spreading—fake drama, then you're fair game.

Regarding larger online media, it's a more delicate equation. However in this instance it was simple: If they consider a list of former vegans to be "news," they've forfeited all journalistic integrity and have left themselves wide, wide open. They're for-profit businesses. I have a message. We're both dealing in the traffic economy. In this instance, I just happen to beat them at their own game.

**What have you learned about the media and its inner-workings from your campaign?**

The unspoken conspiracy that you speak of, that exists between journalists and those seeking publicity is very real. If you have a story that provokes—real or not—they have the time. Give them the promise of traffic and a little plausible denial and you're in. I've received tremendous insights from *Trust Me, I'm Lying* and your Creative Live course. I got to work on The Jetsetting Terrorist the day after finishing the latter. Your point that there is a harmony of interests between journalists and those who wish to hack the media is very powerful, and has proven true.

I've also learned that a big part of your playbook (i.e. manufacturing controversy to generate publicity) is given a nitro boost when executed in the activist realm.

I have to be careful here because it's clear whose side I'm usually on, but there's a small segment who are attracted to social movements because . . . let's just say they have an emotional agenda. To use your term, they're "rage profiteers," reveling in the drama economy. And I've been the hidden hand instigating them for a greater good more times than I would admit. The best case study in this (which I had nothing to do with) was the recent "controversy" around a vegan cookbook titled *Thug Kitchen*. If you ever do a *Trust Me, I'm Lying* update, you have to get this in there. Thug Kitchen was an anonymous vegan blog, where vegan recipes were written in cartoonish "thug" language. It was funny, the blog became popular, and the (anonymous) authors got a book deal.

Weeks before the book's release, the authors revealed their identity. Surprise: They were two attractive white people from Los Angeles. Within days, several small anarchist blogs were buzzing in outrage accusing the authors of "cultural appropriation" and "digital blackface" and calling for a boycott. They announced (and eventually delivered) protests at book signings. This went up the chain like wildfire, and hit Vice just before the book's release. That was four months ago. It's been the best-selling vegan cookbook on Amazon ever since.

I have no knowledge of whether this controversy was real or manufactured. But if the latter, it followed a recipe that couldn't fail:

- Take a target appetizing to leftist and politically radical bloggers (attractive, white, sporty vegans).

- Assign to them some perceived misconduct that fits into one of the top three categories of internet scandal (in this instance: racism).

- Seed excitable elements of the blogosphere with the fake scandal.

If I were the invisible puppet master orchestrating this, I would know that only 0.02 percent of people will be genuinely offended by the *Thug Kitchen* authors being white. But another 60 percent will feign outrage to look cool. And just about everyone else will quietly nod their heads in agreement for fear of being labeled racists themselves.

And what do the authors care? They get six-figures in free publicity. The anarchists get their flavor-of-the-week drama. Win-win.

**Why should we believe you? This is a question I get a lot myself—to which my answer is: Why should I lie? Lying was keeping it a secret— but I am curious to hear your thoughts. Obviously some people would say you undermine the credibility of the cause with these tactics.**

My response is: What's in it for me? I don't have clients (cows in slaughterhouses don't pay), and I don't take credit (I was outed in both instances we're discussing. This would be a longer interview if we got into the stunts I haven't been caught for). If anyone has a point they think defeats the message that animals are exploited (or that the TSA targets people based on their politics), then by all means lay your evidence on the table.

But attacking a message's delivery device and suggesting it undermines the message itself is the work of someone who lacks an argument. Credibility is everything, particularly when you're the bearer of a message people don't want to hear. Much different than artists, whose position I envy. When you're an artist, there is virtually nothing that can harm your reputation.

Most media tends to be good media. With advocacy, it's much more delicate. You have to honor the facts at all costs. The Vegan Sellout List utilized deception of intent, not deception of facts. It was exactly what it purported to be (until the link-redirect): A directory of ex-vegans. The Jetsetting Terrorist was exactly what it claimed: A collection of true stories about a convicted terrorist being harassed by the TSA. I employ Trojan horses, not deception.

**What's next?**

Very little I would admit to.

Despite a compelling interview given by my female co-conspirator, it's looking increasingly unlikely the No. 2 women's magazine will ever run their "How a one-night stand with a radical vegan turned me into an animal rights activist" story. If it does surface, that was all us. While tasteless, a "sex confessional" is just about the only angle to get a message of substance into a publication like that. On the more frivolous front, an anonymous hip-hop project that will make *License To Ill*–era Beastie Boys controversy look amateur. And on the advocacy front, the stakes are too high to reveal my hand. But I will continue to provoke thought into our relationship with animals by any means necessary.

# "EXCLUSIVE: HOW THIS MAN GOT THE MEDIA TO FALL FOR SHIPYOURENEMIESGLITTER STUNT"

## MATHEW CARPENTER

*New York Observer, January 2015\**

LAST WEEK, THE WEB WAS BOTH OUTRAGED AND IN love with a controversial new start-up called ShipYourEnemiesGlitter .com. The premise was both inspired and insane—for $9.99 you could ship a benign glitter bomb to any friend or enemy anywhere in the world. Time.com covered it, and so did *Fast Company*, the *Telegraph*, *Huffington Post*, *TechCrunch* (note: the *Observer* declined to cover it because it seemed suspicious). Then after claiming six figures worth of orders and more than a million pageviews, the founder begged users to stop inundating him with requests and put the whole thing up for auction, where it netted $85,000.

So what the hell was all that? Well, over the weekend, I got a rather unexpected email from Mathew Carpenter, the founder himself. It turns out that he had read my book *Trust Me, I'm Lying* and some of my Beta-beat columns on trading up the chain and media sourcing. This partially inspired his unusual experiment to test his marketing skills, have some fun and see how the media really works. By accident, he revealed two very clear things to us all: how great the demand for weird, funny start-ups actually is and how desperate and derivative the online media is these days. In fact, he told many reporters exactly what he was doing but

---

\*http://observer.com/2015/01/exclusive-how-this-man-got-the-media-to-fall-for -shipyourenemiesglitter-stunt/.

they chose not to print it—for fear it would ruin their story or make them look bad.

In what is now the *Observer*'s second big exclusive on a media stunt that fooled nearly everyone in media, I was able to ask Mathew some questions about what happened, what he saw and what he learned and how this stunt came to be. I hope his answers provide some insight for readers on how the news works these days—but more importantly I hope it chastises increasingly lazy reporters. Oh and I hope everyone gives Mathew some credit, because this whole thing was absolutely brilliant from top to bottom.

**What made you decide to do it and why did you think you could pull this off?**

I run a lot of websites that earn recurring income with very little work. My New Year's resolution was to work on more side projects to keep me occupied whilst improving my marketing & development skills. I read your book about 8 months ago and experimented with a few different ideas before hitting a success with this website.

**It sounds like you traded this up the chain, as I call it, going from one media outlet to the other until it became a major story. Which outlets/ platform did you target first and how did it go from there? Who delivered the most punch/traffic?**

Lately I've found that the media (here in Australia particularly) has become extremely lazy with sourcing. 90% get their stories from aggregation websites which is what I initially targeted. I knew that if the story blew up on websites such as Reddit & Product Hunt that it would be a success. The media attributed the success to being the most upvoted Product of the Day on Product Hunt, however in terms of referral traffic Product Hunt came in 21st.

**Was there any outlet who asked you tough questions or you felt really wanted to see if there was substance to this story? Who was the worst**

in terms of rubber stamping and just repeating whatever they saw elsewhere?

The publication that put in the most effort, in my opinion, was *Fast Company*, who wrote about the website in the most detail and asked the best questions. There were a few outlets that (a) didn't bother asking questions and just referenced already published articles and (b) didn't wait for me to reply to their answers and just went live anyway. I'm looking at you, News Corp.

**A couple of the reporters picked up on your SEO background. You have to tell us, what do you think being linked to and mentioned on essentially every media outlet is going to do for your rankings in search engines?**

For Ship Your Enemies Glitter it's going to mean that no competitor is going to outrank the website for whatever keywords the new owner wants to rank for. It was tempting not to 301 the entire site to my main business website but that would have cost me the $100,000, haha. I was namedropping my other websites hoping for some link juice to them but they were either not mentioned, not linked to, or non-followed links.

**Obviously you were pretty cynical about the media from the beginning, and had explored some of this before, but what did experiencing this make you think? What would you advise people learn from this, either for their own media habits or someone launching a product that they want to get attention for?**

I mean, it really reinforced to me how little fact checking and verification goes into a story. For example, many outlets reported I was a student at a local University which isn't true and I have no idea how they came to that conclusion. It also showed to me the sort of manipulation that some journalists put into a story. Another example was that there was one who asked for proof of the millions of visitors the website received. I provided screenshots of Google Analytics which is about the most accurate traffic tracking software out there, however they refused to accept it and published that I couldn't provide third party proof of the numbers.

**Finally, what's next for you?**

The great thing about this project, no matter how messy my place has gotten from the glitter is that I've met a lot of really smart & creative people from it so hopefully I get to work with them on something cool moving forward.

# "EXCLUSIVE INTERVIEW: MEET MADDOX, OWNER OF THE INTERNET'S 'BEST PAGE IN THE UNIVERSE' "

## MADDOX

*New York Observer, June 2015\**

MADDOX IS THE FIRST WRITER I REMEMBER READING on the web. If you came of age during the first blogging boom, you probably had a similar experience. His writing and his style was influential for a generation of writers, humorists and web entrepreneurs. Since launching in 1997, he's seen hundreds of millions of visitors, developed some of the web's most classic memes, and sold a metric ton of t-shirts. Most of all, he's always been ahead of the curve in terms of online business models and calling out bullshit trends in culture from "extreme" marketing to the swine flu craze.

After a few years of sporadic content, Maddox is back in a big way. More recently, he's built a massively popular podcast, a YouTube channel and regularly taken the media to task for offensive stories on Robin Williams's death, *BuzzFeed*'s nasty habit of stealing content, and media's propensity to pseudo-outrage.

If you had told me as a teenager, when my friends had Maddox stickers on their cars and we all eagerly AIM-chatted each other his pieces, that I'd be interviewing him over a decade later or that he'd occasionally link to my own writing, I probably wouldn't have believed you. But here we are. To continue our series of interviews with influential and insightful voices on the inner-workings of today's new media, I reached out to ask

---

\*http://observer.com/2015/06/exclusive-interview-maddox-talks-buzzfeed-podcasts-and-media-manipulation/.

Maddox his thoughts on media manipulation, some of his least favorite websites, and outrage porn.

**So you were one of the biggest and earliest critics of *BuzzFeed*—not just for the annoying listicles and nostalgia trolling but also for the content they steal from creators like you. A few years and millions of dollars in funding later what do you think of them now?**

They're even worse. I was just reading the gripes of *BuzzFeed* employees I know personally, who were complaining that they weren't given credit for writing, producing or directing any of their videos. Since I wrote my original piece about *BuzzFeed*, many of my friends have found employment at their Los Angeles offices, where they produce much of their video content. Not only does the site take credit for material from other websites, *BuzzFeed* doesn't even credit their own staff for the content they legitimately created. These credits aren't insignificant either, as many of my friends have cobbled together careers based on their credits on small web projects. When *BuzzFeed* publishes content, the creator is, for all intents and purposes, *BuzzFeed* corporation. As a friend very aptly pointed out, The *Onion* doesn't credit individual writers, but they are a satirical news organization whereas *BuzzFeed* is not. The *Onion*'s entire reason for existing is satire with a strong editorial point of view, while *BuzzFeed*'s reason for existing is . . . to generate ad revenue and to trick you into clicking their content. One does it out of necessity to its voice, the other out of ignorance, greed or malice.

**There was the famous screenshot you took last year after Robin Williams's death with ABC running the tasteless footage of his home. Ultimately, you targeted the CEO and they had to apologize and stop. Do you think if you hadn't said anything, would anyone have cared? Of course, a bunch of other outlets also stole your scoop after. I'm guessing you don't think very highly of the whole establishment?**

If I hadn't posted that juxtaposition of real-time helicopter footage on the same page as his family's request for peace during their grief, it's possible that someone else may have noticed the same thing, possibly even from

ABC News. However if it were the latter, there's a tremendous amount of internal pressure not to run problems like this up the corporate ladder. Chiefly, the fact that your boss has an ego and a boss of his or her own; pointing out a mistake like this could embarrass him or her and ultimately cost you your job, or at the very least, a raise or promotion. Would you risk it? Nah, better look the other way. You have bills to pay and mouths to feed. Why rock the boat? Let that asshole Maddox do it.

**You and I talked about some of the sanctimonious coverage of the celeb nude leaks and then the Spider Man/Woman cover. Do you think these people actually care? Or do you think that pretending to be mad—that getting upset and getting other people upset—is a quick way to get traffic?**

There are three reasons at play that, when combined, create a Captain-Planet-esque superhero of shitty motives for outrage: The first reason is that the righteous indignation feels good. We live in an age of relative peace where we don't have a "big devil" like communism or fascism to point to as the source of all our problems. They need a cause that isn't religious since believing in things isn't cool anymore, so finding an enemy that they feel just in hating and blaming makes them feel needed. Second, there is the money motive. It's very lucrative to get those clicks coming to your website. Outrage is big business. And third, as cynical as I am, I can't totally dismiss the possibility that some of these people might actually care. However, their well-intentioned idiocy is often myopic, causing more harm than good.

**Why does the media have to refer to every scandal as a BLANK-gate? What would you rather they do?**

It's a lazy communication device used by journalists as shorthand for "this is a scandal." I'd rather they call it just that: a scandal. Though #GamerScandal doesn't quite have the same ring to it. I think it's irksome because it bothers us as writers to know that some lazy journalist thought they were being clever by using the suffix to get the headline. It's a race to the bottom to see who can coin the word used to describe the scandal of the hour, with no regard for the breadth, scope or context of the issue. For example, the suffix was used to label both "Pardongate," the controversy surrounding Bill Clinton's pardoning of 140 people, and "Nipplegate," when Justin Timberlake exposed Janet Jackson's breast during the Super Bowl halftime show. Though the latter gave rise to the possibly more annoying "wardrobe malfunction."

**Tell us about your media diet. What do you read? Who do you trust? Who should people stay away from? What is the worst outlet in your eyes?**

My favorite news portal is Google News. It shows headlines from a number of different news outlets for popular stories, so you can see at a glance which organizations are trying to spin the narrative. For example, when the GOP-led report on the Benghazi scandal (Benghazi-gate for short) was released, right-wing websites like Fox News wrote headlines like, "GOP lawmakers, Benghazi survivors fume over House report" whereas left-leaning news organizations bristled at the findings, using words like "debunked" to describe the scandal. I take the "truth is usually somewhere in the middle" approach and try to read both left and right-leaning news websites. Though if I'm short on time, I'm partial to BBC or NPR. The dryer and more boring the news, usually the better. Remove the profit motive from the news, be it corporate or outrage-based, and you'll get better news.

**Your stance early on about not taking advertising on your site—because it would change how and what you wrote—was very influential to me. Not just for my own writing, but it helped me to see the subtle but significant warping effect that a business model can have on a medium (which I wrote a lot about in my book). Clearly, history has validated your views there—a huge part of the reason that internet culture is so awful is because of CPM advertising. How has that policy been for you? Clearly, it cost you a lot but are you happy with the choice? What about now with your videos, which are ad-supplemented in some ways?**

The choice to publish in a medium that is funded by advertising, such as YouTube or podcasting, weighed heavily on me. I rationalized the decision by upholding my promise to always keep my written website ad-free to have an outlet to express myself that would always be free of corporate interests and the self-censorship that ensues. Having dipped my toe in ad-funded mediums, I appreciate the freedom I have to say what I want so much more. I'm constantly worried about what I can or can't say when someone is paying the bills. Not having a profit motive to get people to click on my website has allowed me to be more honest as a writer. I don't have to write a listicle to get people to click because I don't make money from that traffic. Frankly, the more traffic that comes to my website, the more I have to pay out of pocket to serve those readers. Success punishes me.

The ad-free model has benefited me in another way: if I praise something, people trust me because they know I don't advertise and have no reason to laud something I didn't truly believe in. It's a very powerful form of trust that money literally can't buy. I feel comfortable with my decision. It's a form of asceticism that has put me in dire straits financially at times, but the sacrifice has led to a greater appreciation for what I do.

**What do you think of podcasting as a medium? It's having a moment here and you've jumped on it in a big way. I remember you tried a radio show with Sirius, what 10 years ago now? Where do you see this going? What opportunities does it afford you?**

Despite the Apple-related etymology of the name, podcasting is an excellent medium and the new home of talk radio. I first started listening to talk when I was 12-years-old, so I was saddened to see the demise of all the talk radio giants. When the last great AM and FM talk stations crumbled, the baton was passed to podcasting, starting with Adam Carolla. He was one of the first to make the successful transition to the new medium and has flourished. My brief stint with Sirius was fun, but didn't last long because there were probably too many cooks in the kitchen.

The cost of entry into podcasting is almost trivial, but the medium is starting to get saturated and the path to success more difficult. That's mostly a good thing, because the podcasts that do succeed are usually the best ones, made by the right people—the type of people who persist and create art, even when nobody is listening, because they love doing it. It has democratized broadcasting, and done it in a way that's free from the specter of advertising. At least in the beginning. The future is bright.

**This is not a media question at all, but I was genuinely surprised to learn when we hung out last year that you ride a bike. I just never saw Maddox on a bike. What else don't we know?**

I actually don't eat a ton of red meat (steak). Though I try to get Korean or American BBQ at least once a month. I'll never give up my bike though. Still the fastest way around town during traffic, guaranteed. I still recommend your episode to people as a "best of" for new listeners. Yours is the only guest-problem to make it to the top-10 list. We still reference your problem all the time. Would love to have you on again. Thanks for these interview questions, that was fun. I wanted to say this up top but didn't want to sound like a circle jerk, but I really appreciate your writing and think that it's insightful and well-written. We think alike on a lot of things, and there are few writers I'd say that about.

# NOTES

## PREFACE

1. Smedley D. Butler, *War Is a Racket*. New York: Round Table Press, 1935.
2. "Editors' Note: July 19," *New York Times*, July 19, 2012, http://www.nytimes.com/2012/07/19/pageoneplus/corrections-july-19.html?_r=0.

## I: BLOGS MAKE THE NEWS

1. Jeremy W. Peters, "Political Blogs Are Ready to Flood Campaign Trail," *New York Times*, January 29, 2011, http://www.nytimes.com/2011/01/30/business/media/30blogs.html.

## II: TRADING UP THE CHAIN: HOW TO TURN NOTHING INTO SOMETHING IN THREE WAY-TOO-EASY STEPS

1. Lindsey Robertson, "The Do's and Don'ts of Online Publicity, for Some Reason," last modified January 12, 2010, http://lindsayrobertson.tumblr.com/post/330892541/the-dos-and-donts-of-online-publicity-for-some.
2. "National Survey Finds Majority of Journalists Now Depend on Social Media for Story Research," January 20, 2010, http://us.cision.com/news_room/press_releases/2010/2010-1-20_gwu_survey.asp.
3. Ibid.
4. NPR staff, "The Music Man Behind 'Entourage' Shares His Secret," last modified November 20, 2011, http://www.npr.org/2011/11/20/142558220/the-music-man-behind-entourage-shares-his-secret.
5. Tina Dupoy, "Tucker Max: America's Douche," last modified September 24, 2009, http://www.mediabistro.com/fishbowlny/tucker-max-americas-douche_b117873; Dakota Smith, "LA Not Particularly Welcoming to Tucker Max," last modified September 24, 2009, http://la.curbed.com/archives/2009/09/la_not_particularly_welcoming_to_tucker_max.php.
6. Mackenzie Schmidt, "16 Angry Women Attempt to Protest the World's Biggest Douche. Or, the Anti–Tucker Max Story, 'I Hope They Serve Subpoenas in Hell,'" last modified October 1, 2009, http://blogs.villagevoice.com/runninscared/2009/10/16_angry_women.php.
7. Dan Shanoff, "Brett Favre on 'Dancing with the Stars?' No. Not Even a Rumor," last modified February 11, 2011, http://www.quickish.com/articles/brett-favre-on-dancing-with-the-stars-no-not-even-a-rumor; Barry Petchesky, "From Bleacher Report to ProFootballTalk: A Brett Favre Non-Rumor Goes National," last modified February 11, 2011, http://deadspin.com/5757958/from-bleacher-report-to-profootballtalk-a-brett-favre-non+rumor-goes-national.
8. Steve Myers, "Florida Quran Burning, Afghanistan Violence Raise Questions About the Power of Media Blackouts," last modified April 7, 2011, http://www.poynter.org/latest-news/making-sense-of-news/126878/florida-quran

-burning-afghanistan-violence-raise-questions-about-the-power-of-media
-blackouts; Jeff Bercovici, "When Journalism 2.0 Kills," last modified April 7,
2011, http://www.forbes.com/sites/jeffbercovici/2011/04/07/when-journalism-2
-0-kills.

### III: THE BLOG CON: HOW PUBLISHERS MAKE MONEY ONLINE

1. TMZ Staff, "TMZ Falls for JFK Photo Hoax," last modified December 28, 2009,
   http://www.thesmokinggun.com/documents/celebrity/tmz-falls-jfk-photo-hoax.

2. Forest Kamer, "Gawker's March Editorial Review Memo: Essentially 'Stop Writing Shitty Headlines.' Also 'MOAR SEX CRIMES PLZKTHX,'" last modified
   April 7, 2010, http://blogs.villagevoice.com/runninscared/2010/04/gawkers
   _march_e.php.

### IV: TACTIC #1: THE ART OF THE BRIBE

1. Ben Parr, "What Do the Big Tech Blogs Such as *Techcrunch* or *Mashable* Look
   For When They Hire Writers?" last modified December 28, 2010, http://www
   .quora.com/What-do-the-big-tech-blogs-such-as-TechCrunch-or-Mashable
   -look-for-when-they-hire-writers.

2. Darren Rowse, "Weblogs Inc. Pays $4 per Post to Bloggers," last modified August
   27, 2005, http://www.problogger.net/archives/2005/08/27/weblogs-inc-pays-4
   -per-post-to-bloggers.

3. David Kaplan, "Updated: *Seeking Alpha* on Track to Pay Its Bloggers $1.2 Million
   This Year," last modified July 5, 2011, http://paidcontent.org/article/419-seeking
   -alpha-on-track-to-pay-its-bloggers-1.2-million-this-year; Joe Pompeo, "*The Awl*
   to Start Paying Its Writers in January," last modified December 14, 2010, http://
   news.yahoo.com/blogs/cutline/awl-start-paying-writers-january-20101214
   -111403-891.html.

4. Henry Blodget, "More Than You Ever Wanted to Know About the Economics
   of the Online News Business—A TWEETIFESTO," last modified March 27,
   2010, http://www.businessinsider.com/henry-blodget-more-than-you-ever
   -wanted-to-know-about-the-economics-of-the-online-news-business-a
   -tweetifesto-2010-3.

5. Jenni Maier, "Tucker Max Proves You Can Pay Celebrities to Tweet Whatever
   You Want," last modified February 9, 2012, www.crushable.com/2012/02/09
   /entertainment/tucker-max-pay-celebrities-to-tweet-213.

6. Nate Silver, "The Economics of Blogging and the *Huffington Post*," last modified
   February 12, 2011, http://fivethirtyeight.blogs.nytimes.com/2011/02/12/the
   -economics-of-blogging-and-the-huffington-post.

7. Victoria Barret, "Is Pure Journalism Unaffordable?" last modified February 17,
   2011, http://www.forbes.com/sites/victoriabarret/2011/02/17/is-pure-journalism
   -unaffordable; Blodget, "More Than You Ever Wanted to Know."

### V: TACTIC #2: TELL THEM WHAT THEY WANT TO HEAR

1. "A Study of the News Ecosystem of One American City," last modified January
   11, 2010, http://www.journalism.org/analysis_report/how_news_happens.

2. Taylor Buley, "Tech's Would-Be Takeover Con Artist," last modified October 27,
   2010, http://www.forbes.com:80/2009/10/27/fraud-stockbrocker-google
   -technology-internet-takeover.html.

3. Sam Biddle, "Malfunctioning Cake Ruins Party and Spews Liquor All Over Oil Tycoons (Updated: Fake)," last updated June 7, 2012, http://gizmodo.com /5916538/malfunctioning-cake-ruins-party-and-spews-liquor-all-over-rich -people.

4. Adrian Chen, "Viral Video of Shell Oil Party Disaster Is Fake, Unfortunately," last updated June 7, 2012, http://gawker.com/5916661/hilarious-video-of-shell -oil-party-disaster-is-fake-unfortunately#13590606485532&{"type":"iframe Updated","height":292}.

## VI: TACTIC #3: GIVE 'EM WHAT SPREADS

1. Nicole Hardesty, "Haunting Images of Detroit's Decline (PHOTOS)," last modified March 23, 2011, http://www.huffingtonpost.com/2011/03/23/detroitdecline_n _813696.html; Stephen McGee, "Detroit's Iconic Ruins," http://www.nytimes.com/ slideshow/2010/03/06/us/0306_STATION_7.html; Andrew Moore, "Slide Show: Detroit, City of Ruins," last modified April 8, 2010, http://www.nybooks.com/ blogs/nyrblog/2010/apr/08/slide-show-detroit-city-of-ruins; *The Observer*, "Detroit in Ruins," last modified January 1, 2011, http://www.guardian.co.uk/artanddesign/ gallery/2011/jan/02/photography-detroit#; Bruce Gilden, "Detroit: The Troubled City," last modified May 6, 2009, http://blog.magnumphotos.com/2009/05/detroit _the_troubled_city.html.

2. Noreen Malone, "The Case Against Economic Disaster Porn," last modified January 22, 2011, http://www.tnr.com/article/metro-policy/81954/Detroit-economic -disaster-porn.

3. Adrianne Jeffries, "Interview with Jonah Peretti, on *BuzzFeed*'s Move into News," last modified January 18, 2012, http://www.betabeat.com/2012/01/18/interview -with-jonah-peretti-on-buzzfeeds-move-into-news.

4. Jonah Berger and Katherine L. Milkman, "What Makes Content Viral?" 2011, Wharton School. http://www.scribd.com/doc/67402512/SSRN-id1528077. I cited an early version of this study (see link) that caused some controversy as the exact wording I quote changed in later drafts published by the study's authors. Nothing they say contradicts their earlier point, but I am including the link to the original for your benefit.

5. Annie Lang, "Negative Video as Structure: Emotion, Attention, Capacity and Memory," *Journal of Broadcasting & Electronic Arts* (Fall 1996): 460.

## VII: TACTIC #4: HELP THEM TRICK THEIR READERS

1. Venkatesh Rao, "The Greasy, Fix-It 'Web of Intent' Vision," last modified August 17, 2010, http://www.ribbonfarm.com/2010/08/17/the-greasy-fix-it-web-of-intent -vision/.

## IX: TACTIC #6: MAKE IT ALL ABOUT THE HEADLINE

1. Kenneth Whyte, *The Uncrowned King: The Sensational Rise of William Randolph Hearst*. Berkeley, CA.: Counterpoint, 2009.

2. Upton Sinclair, *The Brass Check: A Study of American Journalism*. Champaign, IL: University of Illinois Press, 1919.

3. Jenna Sauers, "American Apparel's Rejected Halloween Costume Ideas," last modified October 18, 2010, http://Jezebel.com/5666842/exclusive-american -apparels-rejected-halloween-costume-idea.

4. Eric Schmidt, "How Google Can Help Newspapers," *Wall Street Journal*, December 1, 2009, http://online.wsj.com/article/SB100014240527487041071045745695 70797550520.html.

5. David Carr, "Taylor Momsen Did Not Write This Headline," *New York Times*, May 16, 2010.

6. E. B. Boyd, "Brains and Bots Deep Inside Yahoo's CORE Grab a Billion Clicks," *Fast Company*, August 1, 2011, http://www.fastcompany.com/1770673/how-yahoo -got-to-a-billion-clicks.

## X: TACTIC #7: KILL 'EM WITH PAGEVIEW KINDNESS

1. "Leaked: AOL's Master Plan," *Business Insider*, http://www.businessinsider .com/the-aol-way#-17.

2. http://www.newyorker.com/online/blogs/susanorlean/2.html.

3. Brandon Mendelson, "*Mashable* Continues to Cash In on Death," last modified September 6, 2011, http://ph.news.yahoo.com/mashable-continues-cash-death -173201323.html.

4. Bryan C. Warnock, "Re: RFCs: Two Proposals for Change," last modified August 7, 2000, http://www.nntp.perl.org/group/perl.bootstrap/2000/08/msg1127.html.

5. Nate Silver, "The Economics of Blogging and the *Huffington Post*," last modified February 12, 2011, http://fivethirtyeight.blogs.nytimes.com/2011/02/12/the-eco nomics-of-blogging-and-the-huffington-post.

## XI: TACTIC #8: USE THE TECHNOLOGY AGAINST ITSELF

1. Justin Hall, last modified January 10, 1996, http://links.net/daze/96/01/10.

2. "The *Gawker* Job Interview," last modified January 12, 2008, http://www .nytimes.com/2008/01/12/fashion/13gweb.html.

3. S. Kim, "Content Analysis of Cancer Blog Posts," *Journal of the Medical Library Association* (October 2009) 97: 260–66.

4. Jakob Nielsen, "Long vs. Short Articles as Content Strategy," last modified November 12, 2007, http://www.useit.com/alertbox/content-strategy.html.

5. Jack Fuller, "Public Inauthenticity: A Crisis of Falling Expectations," May 12, 1999, http://newsombudsmen.org/fuller.html.

## XII: TACTIC #9: JUST MAKE STUFF UP (EVERYONE ELSE IS DOING IT)

1. "Seeing Non-existent Things," *Washington Post*, June 18, 1899, accessed July 30, 2011, ProQuest Historical Newspapers.

2. Meranda Watling, "Where to Find Original, Local Story Ideas Online," last modified May 31, 2011, http://www.mediabistro.com/10000words/where-to-find -original-local-story-ideas-online_b4352.

3. M. G. Siegler, "Content Everywhere, but Not a Drop to Drink," February 12, 2012, http://parislemon.com/post/17527312140/content-everywhere-but-not-a -drop-to-drink.

4. Maysa Rawi, "Has American Apparel Gone Too Far with 'Creepy' Controversial New Campaign?" last modified January 11, 2011, http://www.dailymail.co.uk/ fe-mail/article-1346138/Has-American-Apparel-gone-far-creepy-controversial -new-campaign.html.

5. Nate Freeman, "*Gawker* Editor Remy Stern Talks Approach to O'Donnell Story," last modified October 28, 2010, http://www.observer.com/2010/media/gawker

-editor-remy-stern-approach-odonnell-story?utm_medium=partial-text&utm _campaign=media.

### XIII: IRIN CARMON, *THE DAILY SHOW*, AND ME: THE PERFECT STORM OF HOW TOXIC BLOGGING CAN BE

1. Irin Carmon, *"The Daily Show*'s Woman Problem," last modified June 23, 2010, http://Jezebel.com/5570545.
2. Jennifer Mascia, "A Web Site That's Not Afraid to Pick a Fight," *New York Times*, July 11, 2010, http://www.nytimes.com/2010/07/12/business/media/12Jezebel .html.
3. "Women of *The Daily Show* Speak," http://www.thedailyshow.com/message.
4. Dave Itzkoff, "'The Daily Show' Women Say the Staff Isn't Sexist," *New York Times*, July 6, 2010, http://www.nytimes.com/2010/07/07/arts/television/07daily .html.
5. Irin Carmon, "5 Unconvincing Excuses for *Daily Show* Sexism," last modified June 24, 2010, http://Jezebel.com/5571826/5-unconvincing-excuses-for-daily -show-sexism.
6. Irin Carmon, "Female Employees of *The Daily Show* Speak Out," http://Jezebel .com/5580512/female-employees-of-the-daily-show-speak-out.
7. Emily Gould, "Outrage World," last modified July 6, 2010, http://www.slate .com/articles/double_x/doublex/2010/07/outrage_world.html.
8. Irin Carmon, "Judd Apatow Defends His Record on Female Characters," last modified November 10, 2010, http://Jezebel.com/5686517/judd-apatow-defends -his-record-on-female-characters.

### XV: SLACKTIVISM IS NOT ACTIVISM: RESISTING THE TIME AND MIND SUCK OF ONLINE MEDIA

1. Peter Kafka, "YouTube Steps Closer to Your TV with 'Leanback,'" last modified July 7, 2010, http://allthingsd.com/20100707/youtube-steps-closer-to-your-tv -with-leanback.
2. Tamar Lewin, "If Your Kids Are Awake, They're Probably Online," *New York Times*, January 20, 2010, http://www.nytimes.com/2010/01/20/education /20wired.html; "Social Media Report: Q3 2011," http://blog.nielsen.com /nielsenwire/social/.
3. Paul Lazarsfeld and Robert Merton, "Mass Communication, Popular Taste, and Organized Social Action," *The Communication of Ideas* (1948).

### XVI: JUST PASSING THIS ALONG: WHEN NO ONE OWNS WHAT THEY SAY

1. Mark Schneider, "Delegating Trust: An Argument for an 'Ingredients Label' for News Products," October 2005, http://journalismethics.info/online _journalism_ethics/index.htm.
2. Shawn Pogatchnik, "Student Hoaxes World's Media on Wikipedia," last updated May 12, 2009, http://www.msnbc.msn.com/id/30699302/ns/technology_and _science-tech_and_gadgets/t/student-hoaxes-worlds-media-wikipedia/#. Tz7D1iOHeYc.
3. Erik Wemple, "Joe Paterno Dies on Sunday, Not Saturday," last modified January 22, 2012, www.washingtonpost.com/blogs/erik-wemple/post/joe-paterno-dies -on-sunday-not-saturday/2012/01/22/gIQATznwIQ_blog.html.

4.  David Sternman, "American Apparel: In Deep Trouble," last modified January 12, 2012, http://seekingalpha.com/article/319135-american-apparel-in-deep -trouble; John Biggs, "Paypal Shreds Ostensibly Rare Violin Because It Cares," last modified January 4, 2012, http://techcrunch.com/2012/01/04/paypal-shreds -ostensibly-rare-violin-because-it-cares.

5.  Joe Weisenthal, "NYT's Big David Paterson Bombshell Will Break Monday, Governor's Resignation to Follow," last modified February 7, 2010, www.business insider.com/source-nyts-david-paterson-bombshell-to-break-tomorrow -governors-resignation-to-follow-2010-2; Joe Weisenthal, "SOURCE: The NYT's Big David Paterson Bombshell Will Break Soon, Governor's Office Denies Resignation in Works," last modified February 7, 2010, www.businessinsider.com /source-nyts-david-paterson-bombshell-to-break-tomorrow-governors -resignation-to-follow-2010-2.

6.  Henry Blodget, "Apple Denies Steve Jobs Heart Attack Report: 'It Is Not True,'" last modified October 3, 2008, http://www.businessinsider.com/2008/10/apple-s -steve-jobs-rushed-to-er-after-heart-attack-says-cnn-citizen-journalist.

7.  Josh Duboff, "Paterson Reportedly to Resign Monday Following *Times* Story," last modified February 7, 2010, http://nymag.com/daily/intel/2010/02/paterson _reportedly_to_resign.html.

### XVII: CYBERWARFARE: BATTLING IT OUT ONLINE

1.  Antonio Regalado, "Guerrilla Webfare," *MIT Technology Review* (2010), http:// www.technologyreview.com/business/26281.

2.  Michael Arrington, "Why We Often Blindside Companies," last modified June 20, 2011, http://techcrunch.com/2011/06/20/why-we-often-blindside-companies.

3.  Tom Mulraney, "An Open Letter to the Luxury Watch Industry—Help Us, Help You," last modified November 13, 2010, http://thewatchlounge.com/an-open -letter-to-the-luxury-watch-industry-%E2%80%93-help-us-help-you.

### XVIII: THE MYTH OF CORRECTIONS

1.  Howard Kurtz, "Clinton Aide Settles Libel Suit Against Matt Drudge—at a Cost," *Washington Post*, May 2, 2001, www.washingtonpost.com/archive/lifestyle/2001/ 05/02/clinton-aide-settles-libel-suit-against-matt-drudge-at-a-cost/2c79eeaa -4eff-4994-979a-ac310352de5b/?utm_term=.761463b8bc20.

2.  Shirley Brady, "American Apparel Taps Drew Carey for Image Turnaround," last modified September 6, 2010, http://www.brandchannel.com/home/post/2010 /09/06/American-Apparel-Drew-Carey.aspx.

3.  Brendan Nyhan and Jason Reifler, "When Corrections Fail: The Persistence of Political Misperceptions." *Political Behavior* 32: 303–30.

4.  Jeffrey A. Gibbons, Angela F. Lukowski, and W. Richard Walker, "Exposure Increases the Believability of Unbelievable News Headlines via Elaborate Cognitive Processing," *Media Psychology* 7 (2005): 273–300.

### XIX: THE TWENTY-FIRST-CENTURY DEGRADATION CEREMONY: BLOGS AS MACHINES OF MOCKERY, SHAME, AND PUNISHMENT

1.  Dov Charney, "Statement from Dov Charney, Founder and CEO of American Apparel," *The Guardian*, May 18, 2009, http://www.guardian.co.uk/film/2009 /may/18/american-apparel-woody-allen.

## XX: WELCOME TO UNREALITY

1. Henry Blodget, "DEAR PR FOLKS: Please Stop Sending Us 'Experts' and 'Story Ideas'—Here's What to Send Us Instead," last modified April 15, 2011, http://www.businessinsider.com/pr-advice-2011-4.
2. "Conservative Media Silent on Prior Publication of Leaks Favorable to White House," last modified June 30, 2006, www.mediamatters.org/research/2006/06/30/conservative-media-silent-on-prior-publication/136091.

## CONCLUSION: SO . . . WHERE TO FROM HERE?

1. John Hudson, "Nick Denton: What I Read," last modified February 6, 2011, http://www.theatlanticwire.com/entertainment/2011/02/nick-denton-what-i-read/17870.
2. Tyler Cowen, "What's the New Incentive of *The New York Times*?" last modified March 18, 2011, http://marginalrevolution.com/marginalrevolution/2011/03/whats-the-new-incentive-of-the-new-york-times.html.

# WORKS CITED

Alterman, Eric. *Sound and Fury: The Making of the Washington Punditocracy*. New York: Cornell University Press, 2000.

Baker, Jesse. "Gawker Wants to Offer More Than Snark, Gossip," January 3, 2011, http://www.npr.org/2011/01/03/132613645/Gawker-Wants-To-Offer-More-Than-Snark-Vicious-Gossip.

Blodget, Henry. "Post Hate Mail About Our Link to Steve Jobs Heart Attack Report Here," *Business Insider*, October 4, 2008.

Brown, Scott, and Steven Leckart. "*Wired*'s Guide to Hoaxes: How to Give—and Take—a Joke," *Wired*, September 2009.

Butler, Smedley D. *War Is a Racket*. New York: Roundtable Press, 1935.

Campbell, W. Joseph. *Yellow Journalism: Puncturing the Myths, Defining the Legacies*. Westport, CT: Westport Praeger, 2001.

———. *Getting It Wrong: Ten of the Greatest Misreported Stories in American Journalism*. Berkeley: University of California Press, 2010.

Carmon, Irin. "What Went Wrong with Sarah Palin?" *Jezebel*, May 10, 2011.

Carr, David. "Taylor Momsen Did Not Write This Headline," *New York Times*, May 16, 2010.

Chomsky, Noam, and Edward S. Herman. *Manufacturing Consent: The Political Economy of the Mass Media*. New York: Pantheon, 1988.

Crouthamel, James L. *Bennett's New York Herald and the Rise of the Popular Press*. Syracuse, NY: Syracuse University Press, 1989.

Curtis, Drew. *It's Not News, It's Fark: How Mass Media Tries to Pass off Crap as News*. New York: Gotham, 2007.

Del Signore, John. "Choire Sicha, Ex-Gawker Editor," *Gothamist*, December 5, 2007.

Denby, David. *Snark*. New York: Simon & Schuster, 2009.

Epstein, Edward Jay. *News from Nowhere: Television and the News*. New York: Random House, 1973.

———. *Between Fact and Fiction: The Problem of Journalism*. New York: Vintage, 1975.

Farhi, Paul. "Traffic Problems," *American Journalism Review*, September 2010.

Fishman, Mark. *Manufacturing the News*. Austin, TX: University of Texas Press, 1980.

Gawker Media. *The* Gawker *Guide to Conquering All Media*. New York: Atria Books, 2007.

Goldstein, Tom. *The News at Any Cost: How Journalists Compromise Their Ethics to Shape the News*. New York: Simon & Schuster, 1985.

Greene, Robert. *The 48 Laws of Power*. New York: Viking, 1998.

Haas, Tanni. *Making It in the Political Blogosphere: The World's Top Political Bloggers Share the Secrets to Success*. Cambridge, UK: Lutterworth Press, 2011.

Huffington, Arianna. *The Huffington Post Guide to Blogging*. New York: Simon & Schuster, 2008.

Kierkegaard, Søren. *The Present Age*. New York: Harper Perennial, 1962.

Lanier, Jaron. *You Are Not a Gadget: A Manifesto*. New York: Alfred A. Knopf, 2010.

Lippmann, Walter. *Public Opinion*. New York: Free Press, 1965.

Lizza, Ryan. "Don't Look Back," *The New Yorker*, January 24, 2011.

McCarthy, Ryan. "Business Insider, Over-Aggregation, and the Mad Grab for Traffic," Reuters, September 22, 2011.

Morozov, Evgeny. *The Net Delusion: The Dark Side of Internet Freedom*. New York: PublicAffairs, 2011.

Mulkern, Anne C., and Alex Kaplun. "Fake Reporters Part of Climate Pranksters' 'Theater,'" www.enews.net, October 20, 2009.

Munsterberg, Hugo. "The Case of the Reporter," *McClure's*, Volume 28: November 1910–April 1911.

Orlin, Jon. "If It's on the internet, It Must Be True," *TechCrunch*, August 14, 2010.

Owyang, Jeremiah. "Crisis Planning: Prepare Your Company for Social Media Attacks," March 22, 2010, http://www.web-strategist.com/blog/2010/03/22/pre pare-your-company-now-for-social-attacks.

Pariser, Eli. *The Filter Bubble: What the Internet Is Hiding from You*. New York: The Penguin Press, 2011.

Postman, Neil. *Amusing Ourselves to Death: Public Discourse in the Age of Show Business*. New York: Viking, 1985.

———. *Technopoly: The Surrender of Culture to Technology*. New York: Alfred A. Knopf, 1992.

Rosenberg, Scott. *Say Everything: How Blogging Began, What It's Becoming, and Why It Matters*. New York: Crown, 2009.

Rowse, Darren. "'If You Had a Gun Against Your Head to Double Your Readership in Two Weeks, What Would You Do?'—An Interview with Tim Ferriss," *Problogger*, July 25, 2007.

Rutten, Tim. "AOL? HuffPo. The Loser? Journalism," *Los Angeles Times*, February 9, 2011.

Schudson, Michael. *Discovering the News: A Social History of American Newspapers*. New York: Basic Books, 1978.

Silverman, Craig. *Regret the Error: How Media Mistakes Pollute the Press and Imperil Free Speech*. New York: Union Square Press, 2007.

Sinclair, Upton. *The Brass Check: A Study of American Journalism*. Chicago: University of Illinois Press, 2002.

Strauss, Neil. "The Insidious Evils of 'Like' Culture," *Wall Street Journal*, July 2, 2011.

Trow, George W. S. *Within the Context of No Context*. New York: Atlantic Monthly Press, 1997.

Walker, Rob. http://murketing.tumblr.com/post/4670139768.

Wasik, Bill. *And Then There's This: How Stories Live and Die in Viral Culture*. New York: Viking, 2009.

White, Charlie. *Bloggers Boot Camp: Learning How to Build, Write, and Run a Successful Blog*. Waltham, MA: Focal Press, 2011.

# FURTHER READING

I FIRMLY BELIEVE THAT I STILL HAVE MUCH TO LEARN about this subject, and I have not slowed down my research since turning in the manuscript for this book. To continue this journey along with me, and to get monthly recommendations of books (on this topic and all others) sign up for my reading list e-mail. It currently has over eighty thousand subscribers, and it's a great and lively place to discuss books. I would love to hear your recommendations on it as well. Sign up at **ryanholiday .net/reading-newsletter**.

For a list of books that changed my life, check out the Ryan Holiday reading list: **ryanholiday.net/reading-list**.

You can also read my many columns about media from the last several years at **http://observer.com/author/ryan-holiday/**, and for a list of great books about media and marketing to further your study of these topics, just send an e-mail to **TMIL@ryanholiday.net**.

# INDEX

doctored footage, 163
Drudge, Matt, 209
*Drudge Report,* 14, 19, 23, 26, 77, 160n, 161

E!, 152
*Eater LA,* 200–201
Ebner, Mark, 38–39
Edwards, Jim, 140–43
elections, *see* presidential elections
EliteDaily.com, 40
Ellis, Bret Easton, 64
Ellsberg, Daniel, 107
e-mails, 84, 110, 176, 239
    fake, 20, 28–29, 60, 121
    leaked, 55–56
    for sources, 58, 131
emotions, 73–74, 241, 242
    anger, 73, 84; *see also* outrage
    sadness, 73
    valence and, 74–76, 79, 121
*Ending the Fed,* 172
*Engadget,* 44, 122, 128, 200
engagement, 84–85, 97, 170, 232
Entrepreneur.com, 46
Epstein, Edward Jay, 54, 65
errors, 180–81, 187, 190–91, 207, 211–12
    admission of, 200–201, 208
    apologies for, 209
    correction of, *see* corrections
    factual, 211–12
    psychology of, 212–16
    subtle untruths, 212
ethical standards, 122–23, 182
exclusives, 38, 137, 239
experts, xv, 60–62
extortion and blackmail, 195–97

Facebook, xiii, 2, 6, 14, 23, 24, 49, 68, 69, 85, 86, 98, 118, 120, 137, 171, 172, 175, 176, 185

campaign against Google by, 194
    news on, 109, 176
fact-checking and verification, 24, 51, 58, 137, 182, 185, 191, 192, 201, 213, 249
    breaking news and, 186–90, 238
    link economy and, 181–83, 184, 190–92
    sources and, 24, 58, 65–66, 130–31
    standards of, 181
    Twitter and, 180, 181
    *see also* research
facts, 242
    alternative, 180
    errors in, 211–12; *see also* errors
fake:
    accounts, 202–3
    blurred line between real and, 234
    comments, 121
    e-mails, 20, 28–29, 60, 121
    embracing, 233
    events, 100–101, 234–35
    news, xiii, 4, 6, 137, 172–73, 234, 245
    quotations, 183, 184
Fark.com, 25, 136
fashion bloggers, 48
*Fast Company,* 21, 75
FastCompany.com, 106
Favre, Brett, 30–31
fear, culture of, 197–202
Ferriss, Tim, 67
FFFFOUND!, 21
*Financial Times,* 196
finding the angle, 136–37, 142–43
Finke, Nikki, 223, 224
*FishbowlLA,* 27
Fiverr.com, 118
*Fleshbot,* 75
Flipboard, 58
*Forbes,* xv, 32n, 33, 45, 118